Richard Brandt is one of the most influential moral philosophers of the second half of the twentieth century. He is especially important in the field of ethics for his lucid and systematic exposition of utilitarianism.

This new book represents in some ways a summation of his views and includes many useful applications of his theory. The focus of the book is how value judgments and moral belief can be justified. More generally, the book assesses different moral systems and theories of justice, and considers specific problems such as the optimal level of charity and the moral tenability of the criminal law.

D0217495

Facts, values, and morality

Facts, values,
and morality

RICHARD B. BRANDT
University of Michigan

CAMBRIDGE
UNIVERSITY PRESS

Published by the Press Syndicate of the University of Cambridge
The Pitt Building, Trumpington Street, Cambridge CB2 1RP
40 West 20th Street, New York, NY 10011-4211, USA
10 Stamford Road, Oakleigh, Melbourne 3166, Australia

First published 1996

Printed in the United States of America

Library of Congress Cataloging-in-Publication Data
Brandt, Richard B.
Facts, values, and morality / Richard B. Brandt.
p. cm.
Includes index.
ISBN 0-521-57059-X (hardcover). – ISBN 0-521-57827-2 (pbk.)
1. Ethics. I. Title.
BJ1012.B62   1996
170 – dc20   96-3301
                                                                CIP

A catalog record for this book is available from the British Library.

ISBN 0-521-57059-X hardback
ISBN 0-521-57827-2 paperback

Contents

v

Contents

Acknowledgments

A great many philosophers have given me the benefit of advice and suggestions during the years this book was in preparation. Of these I single out a few as especially deserving of thanks.

Of these, the foremost is the late William K. Frankena. I shared lunch will Bill, twice a week, nearly every week during the years I have been associated with the University of Michigan or have lived in Ann Arbor. We discussed the problems of moral philosophy at length. I think he read every word I have written since 1940, and if there are mistakes in what follows, they are matters on which I inadvertently failed to follow his advice. I cherish not only his thoughts about ethics, however, I cherish the years of friendship. Bill was not only a true but a perfect friend. Another close friend with whom I had many philosophical discussions was the late J. Roland Pennock.

I have lived a long time and my debts go back a long way, including conversations with W. P. Alston, John W. Atkinson, Annette Baier, Kurt Baier, Albert Bandura, Lars Bergstrom, Donald Davidson, B. J. Diggs, Karl Duncker, Lars O. Ericsson, A. C. Ewing, Roderick Firth, Allan Gibbard, Alvin Goldman, H. S. Goldman, R. M. Hare, Gilbert Harman, Jonathan Harrison, John Harsanyi, Martin Hoffman, Gregory S. Kavka, Jaegwon Kim, Ralph Linton, David Lyons, Alan Mabe, Mark Overvold, Derek Parfit, E. S. Phelps, John Rawls, Wilfrid Sellars, J. J. C. Smart, N. L. Sturgeon, Patrick Suppes, and J. O. Urmson.

Chapter 1

Introduction

The ultimate motivating goals of traditional ethical theorizing have been substantive: first, to ascertain which states of affairs are desirable in themselves (and how desirable they are); second, to determine which sorts of actions are morally right or wrong, praiseworthy or blameworthy; and third, to ascertain whether a commitment to always doing the morally right thing is desirable from the point of view of the agent's own well-being – and in each case to explain and justify the conclusion.

Not all contemporary writers subscribe to these traditional goals.[1] This book attempts, however, to answer the traditional questions roughly in the following order. As part of the first project, it attempts to adjudicate (or, better, mediate) between hedonist and informed-preference theories of the desirable and to lay the foundations for deciding rationally among various preferences for possible states of affairs. As part of the second project, it attempts to adjudicate between several utilitarian-type and alternative views about which actions are morally right – and then, more specifically and as a consequence, to explain whether

---

[1] For instance, John Rawls, in a recent volume (*Political Liberalism*, New York: Columbia University Press, 1993, p. xviii), writes that the problem of political liberalism "is to work out a conception" of political justice that "the plurality of reasonable doctrines . . . might endorse. The intention is not to replace those comprehensive views, nor to give them a true foundation. Indeed, that intention would be delusional."

1

it is morally required for society to distribute material goods or benefits in a certain way and for individuals to make certain contributions to charity, and for the principles of the criminal law to be formulated and applied along certain lines. I attempt to execute the third project only at the end, in Chapter 10.

How might one go about supporting any proposals on these topics? Is there a reasonable methodology for supporting a theory roughly of the sort we might employ to justify accepting the theories of the empirical sciences? Philosophers have traditionally recommended and relied on rather different methods for justifying their own answers to these questions.

1. Some philosophers have thought that the first two questions may be answered essentially by using the methods of the empirical sciences because of the *meaning* of the traditional value/moral terms in ordinary language. We may call them "old hard-line naturalists." Their first step is to affirm that the actual meaning of evaluative statements in ordinary speech ("is an intrinsically good or desirable thing" or "is the morally right action") is such that evaluative/moral statements are saying the same thing as some properly phrased statement of a type that can manifestly be confirmed by the methods of empirical science. Thus "is morally right" has been construed to mean "will contribute maximally to the happiness of sentient creatures."[2] Alternatively, "is morally wrong" has been construed to mean the same as "would be disapproved of by any person who was factually omniscient, impartial and devoid of emotions toward particular persons but otherwise normal."[3] Another proposal, rather similar to the second of these, put forward by E. Westermarck, is that "It is wrong to do *A*" means the same as "I have an impartial disposition to disapprove of acts like *A*." Such a view hardly leads to a single definite answer to moral questions and has been disfavored by some on that account.[4]

[2] Jeremy Bentham, *An Introduction to the Principles of Morals and Legislation* (Oxford: Clarendon Press, 1876), pp. 3–4.

[3] Roderick Firth, "Ethical absolutism and the ideal observer," *Philosophy and Phenomenological Research* 12 (1952), 317–45.

[4] Edward Westermarck, *The Origin and Development of the Moral Ideas* (New

Such hard-line naturalistic accounts of the *meaning* of moral statements have been rejected by most philosophers today as explanations of the actual meaning of these expressions in the ordinary sense of "meaning," usually because one can assert the value/moral statement but deny or at least be doubtful about the truth of the analyzing statements, or the reverse. So, "that act will maximize human benefit, but is it right?" seems to be a debatable question, about the answer to which one might well be in doubt, not just as a matter of implications of meaning, as it would be if it were like "That man is a bachelor, but has he ever been married?" This argument for rejecting these definitions has been called the "open-question argument" because it is thought that one can affirm the value statement but leave open the question of whether the analyzing statement is true. (Some contemporary philosophers are not convinced that the preceding analyses, especially the second one, are refuted by this argument. There are questions about how to decide when two expressions mean the same thing.) It is sometimes said that if an evaluative statement means the same thing as a statement that can be verified by observation and/or the methods of empirical science, it can be defined in an "empiricist language."

2. A formerly popular view (usually called "nonnaturalism"), like the first one, holds that evaluative/moral statements do assert facts, such as that a certain moral or evaluative property belongs to some action or state of affairs, but differs from hard-line naturalism in holding that this property cannot be explained in an empiricist language, and whether it belongs to a state of affairs cannot be determined by the methods of the empirical sciences or mathematics. (Some advocates think that evaluative/moral terms cannot be defined at all. Philosophers of this persuasion who do define some of these terms employ other normative phrases, such as "it is fitting that" in the definition. Such definitions do not necessarily fall before the open-question argument if the defining terms are themselves normative/moral.)

York: Macmillan, 1906), pp. 1, 17–18, and *Ethical Relativity* (New York: Harcourt, Brace, 1932), pp. 14–15 and 141–2.

If we adopt this theory, we have to explain what all of these terms do mean, how we come to acquire terminology with such meanings – possibly very differently from the usual way in which children learn the meanings of nonmoral words – and how we can be justified in believing such statements to be true. (All theories, of course, have to explain how children come by moral terminology, a job doubtless requiring some speculation but one that presumably may be done with the help of theories of learning and child development in psychology.) The answer of these philosophers to these questions is that we *do* have such concepts, we have somehow acquired them, and we can be justified in believing statements involving them because such statements are, and can be known to be, *self-evident*, at least to intelligent people who have been well brought up – rather like geometry, as it used to be understood and doubtless is still explained in some schools. (Some writers, for instance John Mackie, accept the view that we do have such nonempirical moral/value concepts but think they apply to nothing – that all such statements involving them are false.[5]) But the nonnaturalist–self-evidence view is rather widely rejected today for various reasons. One is a general lack of confidence in the possibility that synthetic propositions are knowable by self-evidence, without appeal to observation and the methods of science. (There are plausible exceptions; see, for instance, C. H. Langford[6] and John Finnis.[7]) Again, it has been noted that conflicting moral propositions appear to be self-evident to different people (perhaps from different societies), so that claims to self-evidence are thought to seem more like a reflection of preferences for a way of life than a report of self-evident, objective truth.

---

[5] John Mackie, *Ethics: Inventing Right and Wrong* (New York: Penguin Books, 1977), pp. 35ff.

[6] C. H. Langford, "A demonstration that a priori synthetic knowledge exists," *Journal of Philosophy* (1946), 20–4. I wrote a critique of the self-evidence view in ethics in 1944: "The significance of differences of ethical opinion for ethical rationalism," *Philosophy and Phenomenological Research* 4, 469–94.

[7] John Finnis, *Natural Law and Natural Rights* (Oxford: Clarendon Press, 1980).

3. A related strategy, close to nonnaturalism, is to rely on intuitions, or at least considered beliefs, about what is good or morally required, which are thought to be reliable insights into the correct answers to *specific* questions of value/moral appraisal (such as "It was wrong to tell that lie"), and a coherent systematization of which will yield correct answers about general principles. On this view, these intuitions are the foundation of normative ethics, roughly comparable to the place of observation in empirical science. Reliance on such intuitions is extremely widespread among philosophers at the present time, often in the belief that there is no other base from which philosophical thinking about values and morality can start. And, of course, these intuitions are phenomena needing careful phenomenological description, but such a description of them need not support an evidential status for them, although many have thought that one can make such a claim for a whole, coherent set of them. We might list, as supporters of such a theory in some form, along with other writers to be discussed in Chapter 6, such philosophers as Thomas Reid, H. A. Pritchard, W. D. Ross, (earlier) John Rawls, and contemporary writers such as Nicholas Sturgeon and W. G. Lycan. I propose to ignore this theory (except in connection with a later discussion of neonaturalism in Chapter 6): No coherent explanation or epistemological account has ever been offered to explain why these intuitions are reliable guides to answering our questions – beyond the "contextualist" view that in all serious thought we must use, as a basis for answering questions in dispute, whatever beliefs are currently not in dispute. I have discussed this view at some length elsewhere[8] and shall discuss it again in Chapter 6.

4. Another view is similar to the foregoing ones in holding that moral/value statements are true or false and evaluatable. Like hard-line naturalism, it affirms that moral/value statements can be appraised by the methods of empirical science, but it differs in holding that its construction of value/moral

---

[8] In *Ethical Theory* (Englewood Cliffs, N.J.: Prentice-Hall, 1959), pp. 190–7, and *A Theory of the Good and the Right* (Oxford: Clarendon Press, 1979), chap. 1.

statements does not even purport to render the *actual* meanings of moral/value statements in ordinary discourse. Call this theory "revisionary naturalism." How then does it construe moral/value statements and why? Writers subscribing to this view may think that it would be good or better, for one reason or another, if people did use ethical language with a certain specified sense, or if their speech was understood in this way, in view of the function of value/moral language in communication and personal reflection. They favor such a change; exactly which change they prefer depends on various considerations, such as clarity, plausibility, and reflection of what we think it reasonable to do in support of evaluations and moralities.

The explanation of this sort that I offer is formulated in Chapter 2 for the intrinsically "desirable" or "good" and in Chapters 4 and 5 for the "morally right." In Chapter 6, we shall see that some quite different proposals are offered by contemporary philosophers.

Who has held such a theory, one I am classifying as a "revisionary" theory? One avowed defender of the view was R. B. Perry, who said that the question for philosophers is not how normative words are used, for they are used confusedly, but how they are best used. He said: "A descriptive definition . . . is an hypothesis. Its crucial test is its bringing to light the systematic structure of some realm of fact. . . . It is an open secret that morality takes conflict of interest as its point of departure and harmony of interest as its goal." So, to say that an act is right is, in effect (if we are clear-headed), to say that no other act would contribute more to "harmonious happiness."[9] I incline to think that Elizabeth Anscombe[10] and Philippa Foot[11] have held versions of revisionary theory, not necessarily naturalistic versions. Another is John Rawls (at one stage), who did not claim

---

[9] *Realms of Value* (Cambridge, Mass.: Harvard University Press, 1954), pp. 2, 13, 87.

[10] Elizabeth Anscombe, "Modern moral philosophy," *Philosophy* 33 (1958), 1–19.

[11] Philippa Foot, *Virtues and Vices* (Berkeley: University of California Press, 1978), especially chap. xi.

that his definition of "just" replicates what ordinary speakers mean by moral terms like "just"; he said he was offering a replacement that serves the same purposes but does not suffer from the problems surrounding such terms in their ordinary senses.[12] I speculate that Kant belongs in the same group. I suggest that he did not think his explanation reflects the ordinary meaning of "duty" (*Pflicht*). Rather, he supposed that morality can command respect only if its principles are binding on all rational beings, and he offered his conception of moral law as law that a purely rational being (not guided by inclinations) would impose on himself as one that would command respect in this way. I suggest that much the same may be true of J. S. Mill. In a passage in Chapter 5 of *Utilitarianism*, in which he made a proposal about what we "imply" by moral terms, he had in mind that a system of social morality would work best, if "wrong" were explained in this way.

I shall not sketch criticisms of revisionary naturalism since the theory I shall support is closely related to it.

5. Still another view, which I discuss in Chapter 6 and call "neonaturalism" (but the proponents of which usually call "moral realism"), usually (but not by all of its recognized adherents) holds that moral *properties* can be known to be *identical* to properties explainable in an empiricist language (like "is morally right" being identical to "maximizes happiness among all courses of action open"), although this identification cannot be derived directly from reflection on the ordinary meaning of evaluative terms, as was held by the old-line naturalists. Rather, the identification is derived (usually but not always) as a consequence of normative ethical theorizing or reflection – essentially making coherent a thinker's evaluative views, or these plus beliefs about scientifically confirmable facts, or beliefs about scientific method. Needless to say, this view has its own puzzles, as we shall see in Chapter 6.

6. There is another theory, which we can call "noncognitivism." Normally, this view is not aimed primarily at finding the

---

[12] John Rawls, *A Theory of Justice* (Cambridge, Mass.: Harvard University Press, 1971), p. 111.

right answers to ethical questions. Its forms provide theories about what is *done* when one makes an ethical statement: Some say that what one does is to express an emotion or attitude; others say that one is prescribing. What is agreed is that ethical statements are not *assertions* of some kind of *fact* and cannot be true or false. (R. M. Hare, however, although holding that ethical statements are prescriptions, has tried very hard to show that some prescriptions are correct, and so aims to give an answer to practical ethical problems; to some extent, this is true of Simon Blackburn.) Most of them – say, writers including A. J. Ayer, C. L. Stevenson, and J. J. C. Smart – aim to give an understanding of ethical discourse, but not primarily to arrive at a correct answer to substantive ethical questions. Their theory, as we shall see, requires amendment and addition, but it contains a great deal of truth. (Indeed, in Chapters 4 to 6, I defend it to some extent.) But this theory is hardly adaptable by itself, in its more traditional forms, to getting the right answers to substantive ethical questions. Its defenders are mainly concerned with what ethical discourse is, not with the prospects for ethical knowledge – not with a methodology for finding ethical truth.

If we want to answer the substantive questions that philosophers have traditionally asked about values and morality, what should we do?

The first step consists in reformulating our questions – in a way, it is hoped, that will be generally acceptable. The terminology of the preceding formulation of the substantive questions, involving "good," "better," "right," and "wrong," is familiar but far from satisfyingly clear. I suggest that essentially the familiar questions about these issues can be put in less puzzling terms. In each case, we can identify a state of mind corresponding to an ethical "belief" or "judgment" – such as, for "good," *desiring* some state of affairs and believing that the desire is not based on some misapprehension of fact and, for "morally wrong," *having an aversion* to *doing* certain sorts of things (and feeling bad if one does them and disapproving of others who do) – and thinking that these attitudes can be appropriately justified. The answers to our normative questions can then be

8

derived from learning exactly which of these states of mind would exist in a person who was factually fully informed – roughly about everything knowledge of which would tend to change that state of mind.

Thus we could say that the first goal of ethical theorizing about what is intrinsically *good* or desirable is to identify which states of affairs would be *wanted*, in a long-range view, for their own sake by a person who was fully factually informed. One possible (but not fully satisfying) answer to this question might be that what is wanted is just happiness. The second question, about what is morally right or wrong, rephrased as the question of which kinds of action a fully informed person would have an aversion to performing (and feel badly if he or she did and disapprove of others who do), can be partly answered by inquiring what kind of social morality, for a society in which a person expected to live, would be wanted by a factually fully informed person who expected (with his or her children) to spend a lifetime there. (There are some complications about actions for which there is an excuse – see below.) One possible answer to this question is that *some* kind of utilitarian morality would be chosen. All this, of course, requires a good deal of explanation.

With these rephrasings in mind, the expectation is that when we have identified (hoped for) general agreement of fully informed persons on mistakes to be avoided, we can go on to identify desires and moralities that avoid these mistakes. It is possible that the eliminative process will not result in the identification of exactly one answer, but instead a range of possibly acceptable answers. (The second possibility may be the best we can hope to get.) When we have found this answer, we can go on to problems of applications: to questions about distributive justice, criminal law, and so on.

A large question is, how can we explain the concept of the "fully factually informed persons," the agreement of whom will identify faults to be avoided and hence indirectly identify correct desires and moralities? We shall develop and defend the preferred conception as we go along.

A statement of this general strategy will explain the title of this book, *Facts, Values, and Morality.* One might wonder how, in principle, any facts of science (including history) might throw light especially on the question of what states of affairs a factually fully informed person would want and what kind of social morality he or she would want. Obviously, if we want to know what desires a fully informed person would have, we must turn to the general theory of motivation, which, it is hoped, will give us an account of the various sources of desires/aversions: some being directly or indirectly native (possibly because of evolutionary adaptation), others being learned, mostly by conditioning but also from the influence of "models" and "identifications." This theory will throw light on the possibility of variations of basic desires among persons/cultures, and if all goes well, it will make clear some possible forms of rational criticism of them, leading to the idea that certain values remain when all possible criticisms have been exhausted.

Somewhat similar reasoning may be used to identify a "correct" morality when we have eliminated all those suffering from defects that adequately factually informed persons would recognize as such. Relevant to this inquiry are facts about how moral norms are learned by individuals, facts about the origins of social moralities or of specific features of a given social morality, and the possible universality of some features of social morality, as well as facts about the variation of moralities around the world. There are also detailed data about the sources of features of various social moralities incompatible with the "absolutism" of some psychologists (who hold that moral norms do not vary when the conception of the action being appraised is the same, at least when the cognitive level of the individual is held constant). The total psychology/sociology of personal morality may make clear possible modes of criticism of moral norms, as well as how a given morality can be recommended to persons. These reflections may lead us to the concept of a fully criticized/supported form of morality – an "optimal" morality – and possibly to a specific proposal about what this form of morality must be – perhaps some type of utilitarian morality. But the fact of variations around the world may lead us to conclude that there is no one *specific* moral code that can claim exclusive validity, as being the morality that every fully informed person would have.

Finally, we shall return to psychological theory and consider what light it may throw on the hoary question of whether a fully factually informed person would subscribe to the optimal morality for his or her society in view of the possible conflict between justified moral requirements and an agent's personal well-being. I think that psychological facts have something to add to this controversy.

All of this must, of course, be spelled out in detail. But it should already be obvious that if the general line of thinking is correct, the world of facts – especially psychological facts – has a great deal of relevance for answering the traditional questions of what is good or desirable and what a justified morality would demand. However, the "facts" on which we shall draw in support of value/moral conclusions will by no means be simply facts from psychological theories: There will also be such facts as the declining marginal utility of money, or the importance of a monetary incentive for productive work, or the impact of therapy on the attitudes of convicted criminals, or the annual rate of abortions in the United States. How reliable these "facts" are and what they prove the reader must judge.

We conclude with a caveat: Contrary to what was suggested earlier, my proposal is not incompatible with some respect for moral intuitions or considered judgments. For there is a social process of pruning that modifies social norms, dropping useless ones and addressing new problems, so it is not unreasonable to adopt a policy of conservatism. For instance, a person might be inclined to think simple utilitarianism the morality most obviously to be recommended but then might defer to an intuition that a student should receive the grade he or she earns, not the one it is utility-maximizing to give. (A "conscience-utilitarian" morality, we shall see, will not face this difficulty.) So we should welcome information about considered opinions, as reasons for more reflection, but without holding that they are decisive for a normative theory.

Chapter 2

What is good in itself and the theory of motivation

In making plans for action, one thing a sensible person seems to do is inquire what things (events, states of affairs) he or she *wants* (or *prefers* to their nonexistence), not as a means to something else (so not like an appendectomy), but just for themselves – provided that the desires/preferences would not be changed if the person knew and represented vividly every fact such that a representation of it would tend to reduce or alter the desires. If the sensible person knows this, at least he or she will get the benefit of unscrambling, to some extent, his or her practical thinking, making it possible to identify and disregard objectives that are neither wanted for themselves nor as means to achieving goals that are wanted for themselves. If someone has found this, we can say he or she has found what is (for him or her) a "good (desirable) thing *in itself*" or "an *intrinsically* good (desirable) thing," although it can be debated whether we should *define* "is intrinsically a good thing [from the person's point of view]" this way. I suggest we should,[1] although I am

---

[1] One cannot claim that this view is uncontentious. Ronald Dworkin, for instance, holds that a human life (a fetus) is "sacred" and an "inviolable intrinsic good," and he thinks many persons' beliefs about art or nature implicitly assume that they too have this status. To have this status is different from being *wanted/preferred* by anyone. A human life is something we "should respect and honor and protect as marvelous in itself." See his *Life's Dominion* (New York: Alfred A. Knopf, 1993), pp. 71–3.

12

not saying that it is an analytic truth that "good" or "desirable" (in ordinary usage) has a meaning of this sort. J. S. Mill has often been criticized for saying that we can determine what is desirable by considering what people actually desire; but it is a different matter to say that something is desirable (for a person) if and only if he or she would desire it if factually fully (and vividly) informed about the objective and everything else that would make a difference if the person knew of it. (Mill has been much less often criticized for saying that to know what is better, we should pay attention to the preferences of experienced persons.) In any case, I am emphasizing that the identification of such events/things would be part of a sensible person's planning for action.

What I want to do, primarily, in this chapter is identify the kinds of events or states of affairs that have the status of being intrinsically desirable for almost everyone. I do not suggest that one and the same answer is true for everyone, much less that all fully informed persons will ideally agree on a given value ordering.

The second thing I want to do in this chapter is to make clear what it is best to *do* (moral considerations put aside for the present). Obviously, we shall not know what it is best to do – what an *ideally* factually informed person in a given situation would want/prefer in his or her *actual* state of information to do unless we know which states of affairs he or she would *want*/prefer for themselves if fully informed.

It is convenient to begin with the second problem: to find a general thesis about what it is best to do given that we already know what things are intrinsically good (for a given person) and how good, relatively, various things are, that is, how strongly, relatively, a given factually informed person would want them.

A view very similar to that stated in the text is proposed by David Lewis in "Dispositional theories of value," substituting "would desire to desire under conditions of fullest imaginative acquaintance" with the object. *Aristotelian Society* 62 (suppl) (1989), 113–38. There is a question of whether "desire to" should be omitted. Lewis allows that on this view it is logically possible that two persons satisfy the criterion but disagree about what they desire to desire.

WANTS AND DECISIONS

Let me begin by roughly sketching how the human motivational system works: what types of states of affairs human beings actually *do* try to bring about and why. Knowing this, we shall be in a position to determine what a fully informed person would choose to do.

Writers on the psychology of motivation have, over the past years, presented a far from uniform front on this topic, so what I say is selective, presenting the view I think most convincing at the present time. This is the view, roughly, that what a person *does* is fixed mostly by his or her relevant desires/preferences – not necessarily conscious ones – *and* beliefs[2] – and, of course, his or her skills and opportunities. (At least this is true of intentional behavior, though perhaps not of biting one's nails or breathing.)

But what is a "desire" (or "preference")? Psychologists generally do not occupy themselves with giving definitions, and we have some options among which to choose. One plausible proposal is that if a person *desires* an outcome *O*, then, if he were informed that he would bring about *O* with some high probability if he were to perform an action *A*, his *tendency* to perform *A* would be increased, how much depending (not wholly) on the strength of his desire. (The "tendency" to do something is partly defined by the thesis that a person always *does* what he has the strongest tendency to do at the time; "relative strength" is identified by how hard he will work or what sacrifices he will make to attain the end.) Alternatively, it has been said that an animal wants something *O* if it persists in behavior (or will vary its behavior) until it sees that *O* has come about. Again, if someone wants something to a significant degree and expects it to occur and it does not, he will be disappointed; or if he expects it will not occur and it does, he will be elated. (Such behavior has been noted in chimpanzees.)[3] Or, again, sometimes it is said that

---

2 We find something like this in Aristotle, *De Anima*, 434, lines 1–10.
3 The first three proposals seem applicable in a study of animal behavior, the fourth less obviously so, and the fifth hardly at all, short of speculations about the inner workings of an animal's mind.

one wants a state of affairs if the conception of it "seems attractive or demanding on behavior."[4] Or we might follow Karl Duncker, who said that desiring that O is (in part) it being the case that, if one imagines the occurrence of O (e.g., the coolness and fluidity of a drink relieving felt dryness), there will be an "empathetical tone of pleasantness" of the imagined event.[5] More generally, we might say that the term "desire" is defined by the totality of psychological law-statements in which it occurs – just as with any theoretical term in the sciences. Alternatively, we might identify a desire as the neurological correlate of such events if only we knew what it is, although, as we shall see, a good deal is already known about the neurology underlying much of this process.

However, it is also generally held that *acts* are not a function *simply* of desires; a person will *tend* to *act* in a certain way depending on her *belief* about the causal route that will lead from where she is to the desired outcome, and also on how probable she believes the desired outcome will be if she takes that route. So, there is a general law about action that partly defines the meaning of "desire": a person will *choose* that course of *action A*, among ones being deliberated as possibilities for her total situation (this may be a very short list!), the total outcomes of which – as she conceives them to be – she most *wants* for themselves (including, as an outcome, the fact that the act itself is of a certain type, say telling a lie or betraying a friend[6]), but with the requirement that the weight, in choosing, of each particular desire is reduced by the degree of (believed) improbability that

---

[4] This view is supported by David McClelland in his *Human Motivation* (Cambridge: Cambridge University Press, 1987). The philosopher Alvin Goldman says that when we want something, the thought of it is "attractive, nice, good, etc., a favorable regarding, viewing or taking." See his *A Theory of Human Action* (Englewood Cliffs, N.J.: Prentice-Hall, 1970), p. 94.

[5] Karl Duncker, "On pleasure, emotion, and striving," *Philosophy and Phenomenological Research* 1 (1941), 391–430.

[6] We shall see that moral commitments involve *aversions* to actions – perfectly good desires – and therefore are included in the scope of the generalization stated in the text. So, recognition of moral considerations is not inconsistent with the general desire/belief theory about action.

the desired outcome will occur if a given course of action is adopted.[7] So, we can say that, roughly, an action is chosen if it will maximize *expectable utility* – "utility" in the sense of getting what is desired by the agent – either immediately or later. "*Expectable* utility of an act" is to be explained as corresponding to the strength of the desire, but *reduced* by the recognized improbability of the outcome's occurring if the act is performed.[8] However, it would be a mistake to assume that actual agents always use all the available or accurate information about probabilities.[9] But actions are a function of desires and beliefs.

There is another complication: When a person is making a decision, he is (normally) not reviewing the whole set of his desires about the future, as an omniscient person might do, or the whole set of different plans for satisfying them (including desires for the welfare or others or of his country). At some points in life, especially if he is thoughtful, a person may undertake a general review of this sort, but hardly a complete one. So, when we say that actions are chosen with a view to maximizing expectable utility, we must bear in mind that ac-

---

[7] I do not mean by "desires" the same as "thinks he wants" or "would avow that he wants." Some psychologists, e.g., David McClelland, hold that we should identify a person's wants by the Thematic Apperception Test, that is, observe the frequency of themes in stories he writes when in a certain want state like hunger. This could be a good way to identify the strength of a person's desires.

[8] For various complications we need to introduce, see Jon Elster, "The nature and scope of rational-choice explanation," in E. LePore and B. McLaughlin (eds.) *Actions and Events* (New York: Basil Blackwell, 1988), pp. 60–72.

[9] Heinz Heckhausen, *Motivation and Action* (Heidelberg: Springer-Verlag, 1991), p. 161. Moreover, an agent's probability estimates are subject to various vagaries. See W. Edwards, "Utility, subjective probability, their interaction," and variance preferences," *Journal of Conflict Resolution* 6 (1962), 42–51; and D. Kahneman and A. Tversky, "Choices, values, and frames," *American Psychologist* 39 (1984), 341–50.

The formula does not, in any case, represent some of the complications noted by economists. See the discussion of Allais's problem in D. M. Hausman's review of John Broome's *Weighing Goods* in *Ethics* 103 (1993), 796ff. Does this problem show that probabilities about outcomes do not have quite the decisive role assigned to them in the text?

tions are not normally chosen with an indefinitely wide view of expectable utility, but rather a much narrower one, chosen with an eye to a particular decision the agent must make. A "prudent" person is one who casts his net rather widely, who brings into his practical thinking a wide set of relevant facts, considered carefully.

Given a superior sum for some action plan, the agent will, depending on some other considerations,[10] form an *intention*: a disposition to begin (at an appropriate time) to follow the initial stage of some plan *A* that, say, is expected to lead to the desired (expected) outcomes (e.g., a satisfying job) at its end stage. After such a plan of action has been instituted, action will be guided by the remainder of the plan and the intended objective, possibly unconsciously.[11] Some philosophers will want more details about this process. For example, it may be said that when the time fixed by the adopted plan as that at which the behavior is to begin is (believed to be) now, the agent will (possibly partly because of the intention, which includes an affectively charged view of the goal state,[12] but also supported by the underlying desire for the expected outcome) begin to execute the plan by trying, or willing, to bring about an initial *basic* bodily action (one she can bring about without its being caused by some other bodily action) – a "willing" sometimes thought of as being the focusing of attention on the prospective basic action or a prescription of it ("Do so and so now!") and perhaps involving an image of the sensations characteristic of the intended movement, any of which will, with

---

[10] See Heckhausen, *Motivation and Action*, chapter 6.

[11] It does not follow that an action thus done is done "intentionally," as this term is used in English. See P. K. Moser and A. R. Mele, "Intentional action," *Nous* 28 (1994), 39–68.

[12] See McClelland, *Human Motivation*, 132. Mook says that every element of a plan "acts to reduce the difference between the existing situation and the sub-goal set for it," as in the case of a singer who aims to match the tone she hears with the imaged intended pitch and corrects for it. D. G. Mook, *Motivation* (New York: W. W. Norton, 1987), p. 313. He says that perceived high utility of a projected action makes it more likely just as real reinforcement of an act makes it more likely in the future (p. 334).

the cooperation of the nervous system, cause the intended action.[13] The intention will, unless there is a change of mind, remain throughout the period necessary to reach the desired outcome, monitoring the sequence of actions in view of the feedback resulting from earlier members of the sequence and other information. This appears to be an analytic reduction of what it is for the self to *act*.[14]

One might wonder what is the basis for accepting the thesis that action is fixed by such a combination – to act so as to maximize expected utility – in view of the agent's *beliefs* and (actual) *desires* at the time of forming an intention.[15] (Of course, the view that a rational choice of action would be selected in this way, to maximize expectable utility, is part of most standard rational choice theory.) Part of the answer is common sense: We know that an intelligent person *will* wager less on a gamble when the prospects of winning are smaller than those of an otherwise identical gamble, so beliefs about probabilities clearly play a role. Moreover, industrial research on choices of occupation has shown that a person's choice is affected both by his wanting the kind of life he expects from a given occupation and by the likelihood of his finding a job in that occupation when prepared for it.[16] Research on achievement motivation has shown that an achievement-oriented person chooses a task depending both on how strongly he wants to achieve (do or be something better, thereby enhancing his pride) and on how strongly he wants not to fail (thereby being ashamed), as well as his judgment about the likelihood of success or failure in that task and his judgment of whether success in that particular

---

[13] For a discussion of William James's theory of ideo-motor action, see my *A Theory of the Good and the Right* (New York: Oxford University Press, 1979), pp. 55–7.

[14] Heckhausen, *Motivation and Action*, pp. 111, 85.

[15] See D. G. Mook, *Motivation: The Organization of Action* (New York: W. W. Norton, 1987), pp. 176–324ff. Another survey of the field, for undergraduates, is J. M. Reeve, *Understanding, Motivation, and Emotion* (New York: Holt, Rinehart and Winston, 1991).

[16] See the summary in V. H. Vroom, *Work and Motivation* (New York: Wiley, 1964).

project shows superior ability to do something.[17] Again, a rat will run faster for a goal box, and start more quickly, depending on how hungry he is (assumed to be a function of the time elapsed since the last feeding), what he believes about the goodies probably in the goal box (his running speed will reflect a recent change[18]), and how frequently he has found them there (= subjective probability).

There is a complication that seems called for: The action tendency seems to be affected by the vividness with which the relevant valued states of affairs are represented.[19] This fact has been noted by various historical philosophers – by Aristotle, who explained preference for a nearer good by saying that belief about a farther good is held only as a man does when he is "asleep, mad, or drunk"; by Hume, who said, "Talk to a man of his condition thirty years hence and he will not regard you"; and by Sidgwick, who said that future "bad effects though fore*seen* are not fore*felt*: the representation of them does not adequately modify the predominant direction of desire as a present fact."[20] The psychologist Kurt Lewin emphasized the fact, and a good deal of research on the related "delay of gratification" effect has been conducted by Walter Mischel and his students.[21] The difficulty of measuring vividness has the effect that the "law" relating desire, belief, and action is not ideally precise, although it is as good as it can be at present.

The general conception just explained, accepted by many psychologists at present, may be called the "expectancy-incentive" theory: that what an agent does depends on her conception of

---

[17] J. W. Atkinson and J. O. Raynor, *Motivation and Achievement* (New York: Wiley, 1974); also Mook, *Motivation*, 487–503.

[18] Heckhausen, *Motivation and Action*, pp. 131, 136.

[19] Brandt, *A Theory of the Good and the Right*, pp. 58–64; Heckhausen, *Motivation and Action*, pp. 169–70.

[20] Aristotle, *Nicomachaean Ethics*, trans. W. D. Ross (Oxford: Oxford University Press, 1954), 1147a, 15–24; David Hume, *Treatise of Human Nature* (Boston: Little, Brown, 1854), Book 2, Part 3; Henry Sidgwick, *Methods of Ethics* (London: Macmillan, 1922), pp. 110–12.

[21] Some of this material is summarized by Brandt, *A Theory of the Good and the Right*, pp. 58–64, and by Heckhausen, *Motivation and Action*, pp. 169–70.

some state of affairs, her wanting it or finding it attractive, and her awareness of a route from here to there, following which is apt to be successful.

It follows from this theory that a person whose motivational system is fully informed will try to *maximize* (his expectable) desire satisfaction, however we conceive what he will want in a given state of information. For the theory tells us that the action a person (or animal) *in fact* performs is (roughly) one of the expected outcomes of which – the ones that come to mind at the time – he most wants at the time (the force of each being reduced by the improbability, in his view, of getting it if the action is performed). Presumably the same "law" holds for a person in a state of full information. Such seems to be the nature of the motivational machinery in creatures ranging from rats to men. If the result of full information is that a person desires for itself only his own enjoyment (or something else, possibly not a state of himself at all), then he will try to maximize that.

Of course, the actual choice situation most people face is that of what to do when they do not know what they would want if fully informed, and know that they hardly have the time or ability to identify what they *now* most want *for itself* or to devise a plan for a course of action that will bring such wanted states of affairs about maximally. People presumably would choose a maximizing form of action if they could readily identify it; but they may obviously prefer to settle for something short of this for the choice they actually have to make in view of the time and effort possibly involved in identifying the best – if indeed that is possible. It has been shown that there are some restricted plans for corrections that normally will be more beneficial than a full-scale review.[22] If it is not clear to a person which is the maximizing-utility kind of action, then how does she in fact decide? This is a matter for empirical psychology.[23] People just do the best they can, perhaps going on a hunch, say about

[22] E.g., see Martha E. Pollack, "Overloading intentions for efficient practical reasoning," *Nous* 25 (1991), 513–36; also David Schimdt, "Rationality within reason," *Journal of Philosophy* 89 (1992), 445–66.
[23] Mook, *Motivation*, chaps. 9 and 10.

whether they might/might not do better if they reflected longer or following the suggestion of a spouse. (Such actions, of course, are ways of maximizing utility in the situation as they see it.) People are idiosyncratic about choices (e.g., in buying a car or a sandwich); by no means do they always weigh the pros and cons of alternative modes of action and when weigh the comparative benefits. But, ideally, the course of action that would be preferred by factually informed people will, I suggest, be the maximization of expected, intrinsically desired states of affairs.

So far, nothing has been said about how *desires* may be affected by information. We shall go into this in much of the remainder of this chapter.

THE SOURCES OF DESIRES AND AVERSIONS

Our next main question is: What types of event would *ideally* factually informed people *want intrinsically* – that is, which desires for events/things in themselves would they aim to satisfy when they are fully informed about facts knowledge of which would tend to change desires? I shall list some types of fact knowledge of which seems to affect the appraisal of desires by informed people. But desires have different types of causal history, and this may affect the impact of knowledge about them. Thus we must go into this genetic matter first in order eventually to identify optimal types of preference/action.

Writers on the theory of motivation have a good deal to say about the sources of desires that derive from bodily needs; they also have a good deal to say about desires that do not.[24] We shall deal with both cases.

Let us begin with desires with a bodily basis – first, thirst and the desire to drink liquids. Dictionaries define "thirst" as un-

[24] See Mook, *Motivation*, pp. 64–96, 471–84, 487–503, 526–35; C. R. Gallistel, *The Organization of Action: A New Synthesis* (Hillsdale, N.J.: Erlbaum, 1980); McClelland, *Human Motivation*; James R. Stellar and Elliot Stellar, *The Neurobiology of Motivation and Reward* (New York: Springer-Verlag, 1985).

pleasant dryness in the mouth and throat caused by the need for liquid. In psychobiology, thirst is an unpleasant state brought about by dehydration of the cells of the body (approximately: Lack of fluid outside the cells is also a factor). The brain is involved in this relation: For instance, there is reason to think that certain cells near the hypothalamus (in the lateral preoptic area) "represent" the intracellular amount of fluid, and this representation partially controls how much is ingested.[25] The onset of thirst first *tends* to produce restlessness. It *may* also potentiate a disposition to approach and drink liquid, possibly as a result of evolutionary selection processes. However that may be, drinking assuages thirst. The unpleasant experience of thirst is reduced by the passage of fluid through the mouth and into the stomach. The reduction of thirst is total when the fluid has reached the cells, hydrating them, and when the extracellular fluid is also at a normal level. (Needless to say, we stop drinking long before that end state is reached, due to messages to the brain during the intervening processes.) After it has been learned by experience that drinking assuages thirst, when one is thirsty the idea of drinking is attractive – this from the "law" that the image of an experience acquires conditioned attractiveness when the experience has been associated with the reduction of an unpleasant need state. But there is a complication in this: The amount of liquid consumed is influenced not only by the magnitude of dehydration but also by the pleasantness of the taste of the fluid.[26] (The prospect of a pleasant taste may induce drinking, e.g., of a Manhattan, even when one is not thirsty at all.) Rats drink more water if it is flavored with saccharin. Wanting to drink something thus has a dual basis: bodily need–based desire and the anticipated pleasantness of drinking some substance. (One may also stop drinking for reasons other than satiation, e.g., a desire to give some of the fluid to one's child.) Drinking behavior can also be sustained by electri-

---

[25] See Mook, *Motivation*, pp. 160ff.
[26] See Carl Pfaffman, "The Pleasure of Sensation," *Psychological Review* 67 (1960), 253–68. We shall discuss the concept of pleasure later. See also McClelland, *Human Motivation*, pp. 83–117.

cal stimulation of relevant centers of the brain during/following drinking. Presumably the mechanism of this causal connection is parallel to that of the natural effect of drinking when thirsty. Consumption of water makes more consumption unpleasant and less attractive, just like injection of a neuroleptic; injection of neuroleptics into the brain prevents drinking behavior even when the animal is physiologically thirsty.

The story is much the same for hunger, another (normally) unpleasant state, caused primarily by a deficiency of glucose in the cells (but of more specific shortages as well, e.g., salt) and the effects mediated by processes in the liver. At least after learning, hunger results in a desire for food. The hungrier we are, the longer is the list of foods that will be attractive and consumed, perhaps from past favorable experience with such behavior or perhaps because of native potentiation of the relevant neurons by the state of depletion. When hungry, eating is normally pleasant. Satiation (which normally makes more eating unpleasant) depends on how much food is passed through the mouth and is eventually filtered into the small intestine and reaches the cells. Certain tissues in the brain largely regulate how much is eaten (mostly from messages from the liver), and damage to them may cause hyperphagia.[27] It also makes a difference how tasty the food is; the pleasantness of the object seems to be a partial regulator of how much is consumed. (Even though one is no longer hungry, one can find the prospect of ice cream with chocolate sauce quite attractive.) There are related processes of interest: the sight of a steak will release insulin, which augments hunger; by contrast, blocking the effects of

---

[27] Activity of the cells in the lateral hypothalamic area during feeding showed an initial sharp increase followed by a sustained decrease. D. McGinty and R. Scymusiak, "Neural unit activity patterns in behaving animals," *Annual Review of Psychology* 39 (1988), 135–68. E. T. Rolls et al. showed that certain neurons in the brain respond to the sight of food, but not to food in the dark or to nonfood objects. Moreover, the response to the sight of food diminished for foods on which the monkeys had been fed to satiety – but not the response to other foods. E. T. Rolls, M. J. Burton, and F. Mora, "Hypothalamic neuronal responses associated with the sight of food," *Brain Research* 111 (1976), 53–66.

dopamine by a neuroleptic apparently reduces the motivation to eat (enjoyment of eating) even when the animal is still in a physiological state of need. Pressing a bar to obtain food pellets, and eating them, is sustained by direct electrical stimulation of the relevant centers of the brain after bar pressing or eating – but much less so if the animal is already sated: It is as if the hedonic effects of the stimulation were muted.[28]

So far, we may view the motivational system of the body as rather like a thermostat. There is an optimal state of the cells necessary for active life. The motivational system *roughly* brings about or stops ingestion of liquid or glucose, depending on what is necessary to maintain the optimal state. As we have just seen, there are complications in all this, allowing for wide variation in individual eating patterns.

I have said nothing of the desire for warmth (not too much), rest, breathing, and avoidance of pain. These reflect bodily needs much as do the desires for food and liquid. The need states and pain are all unpleasant, so that ways of relieving them come to be desired when in the appropriate state.

It is one thing, however, to experience an unpleasant dryness in the throat, and to want to drink something, and another thing to want to drink a particular substance. (But some degree of the desire to drink *something or other*, given what we know about the relation of desires to bodily needs, and the support for a desire by its reduction of an unpleasant bodily need are not things we can doubt.) The aversiveness of thirst is hardwired, but the desire to drink a particular liquid is not. This desire (the *idea* of drinking it being attractive) seems to be produced at least partly by *conditioning* (see footnote 41). And the result is subject to rational criticism. A person thirsty after tennis on a hot afternoon may find the idea of consuming a succession of vodka-and-tonic drinks very attractive because of reflection on such enjoyments in the past; but if she brings to mind vividly what happened the last time she succumbed to such an idea, her *desire* for vodka and tonic may diminish – from asso-

---

[28] See Mook, *Motivation*, pp. 170, 174.

24

ciation with a recalled disaster – but not her thirst. This is not just diminished preference for a *plan* (to drink) but also diminished *desire* for the *experience* of drinking vodka and tonic – the image of the experience no longer being attractive. This fact permits criticism of the desire.

Let us now pause briefly and consider how an agent, who wants to maximize attainment of what he wants, can tell what to do. Of course, in many situations there is no problem. In the case of action that is not deliberated, the want strongest at the time controls the motivational process, except that the effective strength of a desire will be reduced if it is obviously improbable that we shall get the wanted state of affairs if we act in the desiderated way. But sometimes reflection about what we most want is called for. We might have a choice, for instance, about whether to have a fine dinner and no movie, or a movie plus a sandwich, or take time to study for an important examination. How do, or can, we decide which we *want* more (counting the remoter probable consequences)? It seems that what we have to do is *represent* the total consequences of an action (or inaction) as *vividly* as we can (this representation being sufficiently deliberate to make contact with all the relevant desire systems), and then the most wanted event is what we find most attractive (least repellent). In more complex cases we may make pro-and-con lists, strike items from both sides that seem to balance, and then go with the simpler method in responding to the remaining items on the list. (As far as satisfaction in the sense of enjoyment is concerned, we have to rely on memory: whether one state of affairs or the other in the past in comparable circumstances – degree of deprivation or satiation – was more pleasing. I am supposing that we can remember this. Having remembered it, we shall normally find the prospect of it more or less attractive and hence more or less motivating – although, of course, our recollections might be wrong!)

What, then, is the status of the bodily-need-based desires? Must all of them be met in a program for maximizing well-being – a concept not yet explained? We must, of course, recognize an order of priority among them. Perhaps getting oxygen (breathing) comes first,[29] drinking next. But must we say at least most of these desires are necessary for life itself, so that at least most of them must, at least sometimes, take priority over any other desires? It is clear that most of them must rank high. But it is also clear that at least many of them are often subordinate to other desires, such as avoiding loneliness or enhancing self-esteem. A person may obviously prefer being cold (in order to set a record for reaching the North Pole), or eliminate all but the simplest diet and forgo a great deal of rest, in order to assist an ailing mother. It seems as if satisfaction of *bodily* need–based desires alone falls short of maximizing happiness (or of maximizing whatever we have in mind when we speak of personal well-being; see Chapter 10[30]).

There is, however, a whole group of other desires (aversions), the sources of which are different from those of the bodily-need-based desires, which are widespread, although not necessarily universal: affiliative desire (for friends, company), desire for approbation (for esteem and respect from others), aversion to insecurity (of person and property), desire for self-

---

[29] According to Stellar and Stellar in *Neurobiology*, among various mammals maternal protection is the first priority. This, however, is not a matter of bodily need. I come to such cases in a moment.

[30] Trying to identify what makes one happier runs into complications, e.g., since some persons judge their own happiness by their chosen standards for life as a whole, others by summing particular cases of enjoyment. At any rate, investigation seems to show that being employed, satisfactorily married, in love, having frequent social relations, having a satisfactory place of residence, physical attractiveness, leisure time, with a satisfactory standard of living, an income that compares favorably with those of others, and being religious are important for happiness, with the first two being most important. Other factors, which have little or no importance, are age, health, sex, education, level of intelligence, and having children. Income seems to have mixed reports: The wealthier countries report higher levels of happiness, but Japan no more than India and European countries no more than Latin America. See Ed Diener, "Subjective well-being," *Psychological Bulletin* 95 (1984), 542–75. Also, see Angus Campbell, P. E. Converse, and W. L. Rodgers, *The Quality of American Life* (New York: Russell Sage, 1976). See the general review and critique of such surveys by Alvin Goldman, "Ethics and cognitive science," *Ethics* 103 (1993), especially 345–50. The problems seem very complex.

esteem (the ability to view oneself with pride or satisfaction), desire for achievement and for autonomy (freedom to make one's own decisions for one's own reasons), aversion to disorder in one's household/surroundings, desire for knowledge/ understanding of self and world, and desire for novelty (new experiences, new travel, new friends). Satisfaction of these desires is not necessary for life (and so far may not qualify as needs, but if they are universal, they are surely something to be reckoned with).[31] Doubtless there are many other desires in addition to these – for example, my (slight) desire to own a grandfather clock!

Where do these desires come from? And why should there be a satiation effect when something like human company or approbation from others has happened several times, since this is not fixed by bodily chemistry?[32] And why should these desires arise after a period of no satisfaction – after "deprivation time"? (And why should there be similar impacts on preferences among possible targets of bodily based desires, since they seem not to be regulated by homeostatic processes within the organism?)[33]

A natural source of these desires in general is association of the states wanted with states that were satisfying, liked, or pleasant in the past (the opposite for aversions: associations with unpleasant states in the past). Suppose that a certain experience was liked in the past: one imbued with pleasantness, its continuation or repetition being wanted at the time. (Some psychologists think there are just a few native "natural incentives"

[31] See the list by R. B. Cattell, as in McClelland, *Human Motivation*, pp. 46ff. H. A. Murray, *Explorations in Personality* (New York: Oxford University Press, 1938), lists 26 of these.

[32] Some psychologists who recognize this status include R. Eisenberger, "Is there a deprivation-satiation function for social approval?" *Psychological Bulletin* 74 (1970), 255–75; and J. L. Gewirtz and D. M. Baier, "Deprivation and satiation of social reinforcers as drive conditions," *Journal of Abnormal and Social Psychology* 57 (1958), 165–72. On the topic of families, see J. Atkinson and D. Birch, *The Dynamics of Action* (New York: Wiley, 1970), chap. 2, and T. A. Ryan, *Intentional Behavior* (New York: Ronald Press, 1970), pp. 473ff.

[33] See Mook, *Motivation*, chap. 7, especially pp. 244–60.

– variety, having impact, having soft bodily contact with others, pain, bitter tastes and bad smells, lack of consistency with expectation – and that the occurrence of events with these qualities is naturally pleasant or unpleasant and, David McClelland speculates, is associated with the presence of specific hormones.)[34] Then it appears that by the principle of "classical conditioning,"[35] the *image* or *thought* of such an experience or state of affairs will be "imbued with empathetic pleasantness" and the state of affairs imaged become the target of a desire. Why, then, might not these nonbodily desires arise, by classical conditioning, from past *liking* of the experience of having company, being praised, feeling proud of oneself, achieving something, helping someone who needs it, or getting new insight into the world and oneself? And why might aversions not arise from the discomfort due to damage to self or property in the past, from the displeasure of having one's choices directed by others, or from the experience of being disdained by parents or friends? And the same for food preferences.[36] (This, of course,

---

[34] See David McClelland, *Human Motivation*, pp. 125ff., 601. He thinks specific motivations, like the desire to affiliate, "involve affectively toned associative networks built on natural incentives connected with early contact gratifications" (p. 532).

[35] See Mook, *Motivation*, pp. 47, 224ff., 234–5, 238–40, 244–5, 259, 305–7, and 473–76, but see 257–8. See also M. A. van den Hout and H. Merklebach, "Classical conditioning: still going strong," *Behavioral Psychotherapy* 19 (1991), 47–64. For a brief summary of the evidence, see my *A Theory of the Good and the Right*, pp. 91ff. For instance, postcards initially rated as indifferent came to be liked after association with favorable affects; the same held for babies' preference for a red light when it was shown during feeding; and rats came to prefer grape juice to milk when fed the former only when hungry, the latter when sated. It is true that such laboratory-produced preferences are not strong or lasting, but more important preferences may be explained by conditioning when we realize that they are supported by many kinds of rewards, at unpredictable intervals, and during childhood when there is no ability to discriminate among various kinds of contingencies.

[36] See Mook, *Motivation*, pp. 224–46, 473–75. Also see McClelland, *Human Motivation* (1987), pp. 116–65; P. T. Young, *Motivation and Emotion* (New York: Wiley, 1961); David Bindra, "A unified account of classical conditioning and behavior modification," in W. K. Prokasy (ed.), *Classical Conditioning*, Vol. II (New York: Appleton-Century-Crofts, 1972); F. D. Sheffield, "Re-

does not explain the possible phenomena of satiation or deprivation time.)

Some may say this is a mere form of psychological hedonism. And it *is* a *form* of psychological hedonism, "hedonism of the past."[37] This view does not affirm that we desire only pleasure, although pleasant experiences are things we do want. The fact that the occurrence of a past event that we liked controls, to a considerable extent, what we want now does not show that what we want now is just pleasant states of affairs. What we want is an event of a certain sort, which could be getting a piece of knowledge or enhancement of the welfare of our children.

The conditioning account of especially the higher-level desires leaves one fundamental question unanswered: Why do we like (enjoy) certain experiences of ourselves or the world in the first place? If we didn't, there would be no liked experiences, association with which could function to produce desires. Of course, some cases of this may themselves be explained by conditioning. For instance, achievement may be liked because it has been associated with praise and rewards,[38] and much the same may be true for the company of others. But it appears that being in *some* states of affairs, unrelated to bodily needs, may be just pleasant or aversive. Why?

An important possibility is that these states can have an evolutionary explanation: The pleasantness (or aversiveness) of some things enhances survival because when something is pleasant (unpleasant) we seek (want) it (or things like it) or avoid (have an aversion to) it by conditioning, and this may turn out to be a very happy fact for survival (of self or near relatives). For instance, things that taste awful may in the long run be bad for us. Both rats and children acquire a dislike for food the

---

lation between classical conditioning and instrumental learning," in Prokasy (ed.), *Classical Conditioning*. Sheffield suggests that what a conditioned stimulus essentially does is produce some kind of central representation of the unconditioned stimulus (p. 163).

[37] See the theory put forward by L. T. Troland, which he called "hedonism of the past," in *The Fundamentals of Human Motivation* (New York: Hafner, 1967).

[38] B. C. Rosen and Roy D'Andrade, "The psychosocial origins of achievement motivation," *Sociometry* 22 (1959), 185–218.

eating of which is followed by being sick – certainly important for a rat, whose existence depends on scavenging. Phobias concerning snakes, spiders, heights, darkness, and strangers, specific as they are, invite a similar evolutionary explanation – survival of the fit.[39]

How about wanting to help someone who needs it? There is a large literature on this.[40] One possibility (not related to evolutionary theory) is that babies just don't like the sound of other babies crying (perhaps they have developed aversiveness to the sound of a baby's cry by conditioning when their own cry was associated with their own aversive pain/distress), so they are motivated (partly to remove their own distress) to help other children who cry in distress – behavior that appears at a very early age. By further conditioning, they may be disturbed by the sight of another child's blood from a cut. This explanation has some force, but it should be supplemented by an evolutionary explanation – that a native disposition to have sympathetic distress on perceiving the distress of or danger to others, leading to relief by helping behavior, tends, if the others are close relatives (as associates often will be in a primitive society), to continue the (probably) same sympathetic trait in one's relatives and so to be naturally selected. Again, if one helps those who may be expected to reciprocate – from past experience of such reciprocation – such helpful behavior is likely to be beneficial to the individual and the continuation of his relevant

---

[39] See Mook, *Motivation*, pp. 238–42. David M. Buss has emphasized the importance of looking at the adaptiveness of specific desires/traits for groups at an earlier period of time. See his important article "Evolutionary personality psychology," *Annual Review of Psychology* 42 (1991), 459–91. For a general discussion, see J. H. Barkow, L. Cosmides, and J. Tooby, *The Adapted Mind: Evolutionary Psychology* (Oxford: Oxford University Press, 1992).

[40] I have summarized some of this in "The psychology of benevolence and its implications for philosophy," *Journal of Philosophy* 73 (1976), 429–52. For a recent review of the literature on altruism, see Jane A. Piliavin and H. W. Charng, "Altruism: a review of recent theory and research," *Annual Review of Sociology* 16 (1990), 27–65.

genes.[41] So, an unlearned genetic trait is fostered. But we should not overlook the impact of the example of others, whose tenderness toward others, as well as insistence that a child control her own impulses/desires, apparently has a significant influence on empathic behavior.[42]

How about the pleasant pride of achievement or the unpleasant shame of failure? Possibly the pleasure in achievement has survival value. (But possibly this satisfaction is an associative effect of parental congratulations for earlier achievements, just as the pain of failure may be an associative effect of earlier cases of failure when parents were disturbed and others also disdained one.[43]) Others think, however, that both achievement imagery and motivation may come from having been in an environment "relatively rich in achievement cues, in the vocabulary, ideas, and strategies of achievement."[44]

Again, does our satisfaction in attaining a systematic explanatory understanding of ourselves and our world possibly reflect native curiosity – an evolutionary product favoring the survival of those who explore and get information? Note the tendency of animals to explore their environment.[45]

Finally, although it is often suggested that the sexual attractiveness of a possible mate seems to be at least partly a matter of culture – some societies preferring a rounded figure in a female (and we need a theory of changes in such preferences) – this

---

[41] Cf. Donald Campbell, "On the genetics of altruism and the counterhedonic components in human culture," *Journal of Social Issues* 28 (1972), R. L. Trivers, "The evolution of reciprocal altruism," *Quarterly Review of Biology* 46 (1971), Richard Dawkins, *The Selfish Gene* (New York: Oxford University Press, 1976). There is a helpful review of evolutionary-type reasoning in Joseph Shepher, *Incest: A Biosocial View* (New York: Academic Press, 1983).

[42] See the *New York Times*, July 12, 1990. See also Thomas Likona, "Parents as moral educators," in M. Berkowitz and F. Oser, *Moral Education: Theory and Applications* (Hillsdale, N.J.: Erlbaum, 1985), chap. 5.

[43] See Mook, *Motivation*, pp. 487–504.

[44] E. Klinger, "Fantasy and achievement," *Psychological Bulletin* (1966), 303.

[45] See T. S. Pitman and J. F. Heller, "Social motivation," *Annual Review of Psychology* 38 (1987), 461–501.

may not be wholly so; the choice will favor a person who looks young and healthy, which would increase the survival of one's own gene stream.[46]

It seems, then, as if many of our desires and aversions may be explained by a certain pattern: They may arise mostly from a history of pleasant experiences of certain types of object, activity, or situation. These pleasures themselves can be explained either as a result of conditioning by some already liked events, or the disposition to have them is just native, *perhaps* because of evolutionary survival value. None of this, however, so far seems to explain all aesthetic values – why we like colorful sunsets or Mozart's music.[47] And there may be many other types of native liking/disliking that may have no evolutionary explanation; we must just accept them as facts (e.g., being cuddled, the taste of castor oil, a loud noise, or absence of sensory stimulation).

If it is a fact that some things are wanted primarily, in the end, because of "survival of the fittest" processes, they do not, on that account, acquire a superior claim to be good or best in themselves. They have only a claim to be universal features of human nature.

The acquisition of many desires, aversions, likes, and dislikes, however, seems to have sources different from any of those previously discussed. Children tend to imitate the behavior of adults, especially ones they see rewarded for what they do – even imitating Mother in picking up the phone and dialing. More important, the values of someone with whom the child identifies, or whom he respects or is attached to, tend to be adopted by the child. This may occur partly because the child thinks this is a way to be powerful or successful, like the other person, or a way to retain the person's love; or it may be because, in the absence of the admired figure, imitation of him or her may be a partial substitute for the nurturant behavior of the

---

[46] See D. A. Dewsbury, "Comparative psychology, ethology, and animal behavior," *Annual Review of Psychology* 40 (1989), 581–602.

[47] But for preferences for landscapes, see G. H. Orians and J. H. Heerwagen in Barkow et al., *The Adapted Mind*.

other, and so anxiety reducing. Or it may be that the child just wants to be like an admired person – identification.[48] Again, observation of a respected person's being made happy by something may bring about vicarious satisfaction by the same thing in the observer. Doubtless these are more convincing explanations of imitative *behavior* as just a "response." I say more about the mechanisms of acquiring values later in a discussion of how a child acquires a conscience.

THE VARIATION OF VALUES

It should not be surprising if, given this total account – especially that formulated in the preceding paragraph – of the genesis of desires/likings, with impact from differing environments and cultural forms, there is a fair amount of *cultural* (not only individual) disparity about what is wanted or liked. (Nobody, however, likes pain or wants to stop breathing – except in very special circumstances.) And if we trust the reports of ethnographers and are prepared to speculate a bit, then even if we make allowance for the fact that the ethnographers generally visited only one group, so that their reports mostly reflect only what they found striking, we seem to find this expected variation in some desires.

We should note in advance, however, that the generalizations to follow purport to be only averages and are consistent with a great deal of individual variation in a society. In particular, women's desires may differ from men's; other variations may depend on a person's own experiences with illness or death in the family; and so on.

But, to begin, the Netsilik Eskimos (men?) are said to have a passion to excel in strength or in singing. They are also very affectionate toward their children and give them the best food.[49]

---

48 See Ervin Staub, *Positive Social Behavior and Morality*, Vol. 11 (New York: Academic Press, 1979), especially pp. 22–34.

49 Knud Rasmussen, *The Netsilik Eskimos, Report of the Fifth Thule Expedition*, vol. 8, nos. 1 and 2 (Copenhagen: Gyldendal, 1931).

The Hopi Indians have no itch for achievement, power, or prestige, although they desire to be, and to be reputed to be, industrious and sociable. They seem to be very averse to being singled out for praise,[50] although men do take pride in excelling in racing. They are motivated to avoid critical public opinion. They have a strong distaste for violence of any sort. They are concerned about health and death, presumably universal concerns, and about worrying (which they think is a cause of ill health).[51]

The Philippine Ifugao are quite different. They do not seek friendship in the Western sense. Prestige and rank are their chief values, along with wealth – a main reason why they join head-hunting parties. Manifestly, as head hunters, they have no strong aversion to violence.[52] They have affection for their

---

[50] In an experiment, children were sent to the board to do an arithmetic problem, with the instruction to see who could finish first. As a result, no one finished!

[51] W. Dennis, *The Hopi Child* (New York: D. Appleton-Century, 1904); Leo W. Simmons, *Sun Chief* (New Haven, Conn.: Yale University Press, 1942); L. Thompson and A. Joseph, *The Hopi Way* (Chicago: University of Chicago Press, 1944); Laura Thompson, *Culture in Crisis* (New York: Harper and Brothers, 1950), especially chaps. 4 and 5; M. Titiev, *Old Oraibi, Papers of the Peabody Museum of American Archaeology and Ethnology* XXII, no. 1 (1944); R. Brandt, *Hopi Ethics* (Chicago: University of Chicago Press, 1954). Verbal communications are from Solomon Asch.

The writer's data about desires/values are reported, from various informants (four men and two women), in *Hopi Ethics*, pp. 39–52.

There is a question of whether some of these "desires" should not be listed as "moral aversions" (see Chapter 2). If so, the learning of such aversions will presumably be somewhat special (see Chapters 3 and 5). To what extent do social pressures exist to acquire some of the other values, which are apparently standard in some groups? I have no information about this.

[52] They seem a bit like the Yanomamo, who "are one of the most aggressive, unpeaceful groups of people anywhere in the world. Fighting and intimidating others is a constant feature of their existence. The men demand immediate obedience from their women and frequently beat them to ensure it. The men also constantly 'test' each other's 'fierceness.' . . . Moreover, villages frequently wage war against each other, when the men's continual challenges and provocations lead to the ultimate aggressive behavior, the killing of human beings." D. E. Hunter and P. Whitten, *The Study of Anthropology* (New York: Harper and Row, 1976), p. 397.

children but do not object if a child goes to live with a relative. Their desire for autonomy seems low; at least they are willing to sell themselves or their children into slavery, although perhaps only for pressing reasons like payment of debts.[53]

The people of Alor (an island north of Timor in the Dutch West Indies) do not form personal friendships. They seem little motivated to achieve admiration by others or to avoid criticism, although they are sensitive to insults. Men are motivated to get wealth and prestige – indeed, wealth seems almost an obsessive preoccupation. They have affection for children and care about their health, but they allow them to be abused, annoyed, or threatened by others; in one case, prestige was put ahead of one's own child's life. According to the ethnographer, they have little interest in autonomy, order, or knowledge.[54]

So, there seem to be differences in achievement motivation, desire for prestige and power, sensitivity to criticism by others, aversion to violence, and degree of affection for children, doubtless among other things, on a cultural level. Do such (and other) variations imply difference in intrinsic values? Let me leave this question to the speculations of the reader.

We have no clue about how these people came to have the motivations they do. Presumably there is a historical story to be told if we knew more.

TWO THEORIES ABOUT WHAT AN IDEALLY FACTUALLY INFORMED PERSON WANTS INTRINSICALLY: DESIRE SATISFACTION OR ENJOYMENT

I have said that one substantive goal of ethical theorizing is to determine which states of affairs are good in themselves (at least from the perspective of some individual), or, put alter-

---

[53] R. F. Barton, *Ifugao Law, University of California Publications in American Archaeology and Ethnology*, vol. 15, no. 5 (1919).

[54] Cora DuBois, *The People of Alors* (Minneapolis: University of Minnesota Press, 1944). On the importance of wealth, see pp. 132–4, 200; on maltreatment of children, see pp. 51, 62–5, 237–53.

natively, the objects of criticized desires by some persons, for themselves, not just as means to achieve something else. Some philosophers have drawn up a list of things intrinsically good, in this sense, for *everyone*. Thus James Griffin lists (1) personal accomplishment, (2) freedom to decide what to do, by one's own lights, without constraint, (3) having the basic capacities (to move one's limbs, the minimum material conditions required for life, freedom from pain and anxiety), (4) understanding of oneself and the world, (5) enjoyment, and (6) having deep personal relations.[55] (Is Griffin perhaps unduly narrow or broad in his list of intrinsic goods, in view of the foregoing, especially the list of major concerns of different peoples?)

Other philosophers, from Epicurus to Bentham to Sidgwick to J. J. C. Smart and other contemporaries, have thought that there is one and only one state of affairs that is intrinsically good: pleasant (liked) *experiences* (and bad states: disliked experiences). This item, of course, is included in Griffin's list.

On reflection, it seems that there have recently been two main systematic traditions about what states of affairs would be wanted, for themselves, by a person whose desires (aversions) have survived careful appraisal in the light of full factual knowledge. Call these "desire theories" and the "happiness (or pleasure) theory."

But what is it for a desire to survive "careful appraisal"? So far, I have said very little about this. But let us consider the possibility that there are certain conditions that a desire might meet (such as compatibility with full factual information, including the known laws of psychology), and when the desire is known to fail to meet these conditions, then *all* (or almost all) persons initially having it tend to reject or modify it or at least be ambivalent about it – at least, they would if they were clear-headed and had a broad knowledge of human nature, including

---

[55] James Griffin, *Well-Being* (Oxford: Clarendon Press, 1986), pp. 67–8. A slightly different list appears in "Against the taste model" in J. Elster and J. Roemer (eds.), *Interpersonal Comparisons of Well-Being* (Cambridge: Cambridge University Press, 1991), pp. 63–4.

how desires are formed. Now if a given desire meets these conditions, I suggest there is no reason why we might not say that it "survives careful appraisal." (It does not follow that two persons might not have conflicting desires, or the same one with a different strength, even if both sets are carefully appraised.) It remains, of course, to explain what these conditions are and why, as I shall roughly attempt to do. The reader must judge whether the described tests must be passed in order to earn a corresponding evaluation by informed, thoughtful people.

The *first* of the two main contrasting theories – the desire satisfaction theory – about what is intrinsically good or better than something else (and, I am suggesting, about which desires meet the explained conditions) can take any of several forms, all considered in contemporary literature. One can hold that the conditions are satisfied – so the object is desirable (or *more* desirable than some other outcome) – if a person (1) *wants* (more) a certain state of affairs (for itself) *at the time* (of the choice or evaluation) or (2) if he knows he *would* want it (more) *at the time* if his wants were *informed* in ways to be specified (e.g., as in (5)). Or, (3) a restriction may be imposed that the only states of affairs to be considered be "global," that is, the total foreseeable difference a given event would make within the total span of one's life. (I might want the immediate effect of a shot of cocaine now but not want the total package of the high from the shot plus the prospect for addiction – here comparing two total strands of life for themselves but including the probable effects as part of a total package.) Or one might replace just "wants at the time" (in (1)) by (4) "has a disposition to desire (more strongly) over a lifetime, at past [but "past" could be omitted, since few persons think something is desirable just because one *did* want it in the past], present, and future moments." (In this last case, when a decision between two outcomes is being deliberated as to which is better, one should pay attention to the intensity of (the disposition to?) desire the relevant events at every moment of one's life and give the palm to the event that gets the higher score – the sum of the products of

37

intensity times the number of moments at which it occurs with that intensity. Or (5), a restriction may be added: that the person know the concrete form the wanted event will take (e.g., not just wanting, rather abstractly, to become a lawyer, but having the experiences expectable in the life of a lawyer represented in foreseeable detail). Obviously, a person needs as much of this information as she can get, for people want in advance mostly abstractly defined events but are often not clear about what their concrete nature will be – and one is much more likely to continue to want, and/or like when it occurs, what one initially wanted if one knows in advance what the target of wanting will be like in concrete form.[56]

A somewhat more demanding requirement of "information" is what Derek Parfit has called the "deliberative theory": that a desire for something is adequately informed only if wanting it stands firm in the face of a vivid representation of all available information about it that, if known, would tend to change the desire. (One can also appraise likings or pleasures as being "informed" on the same basis: that they would occur even in the face of all available information.) This proposal doesn't provide a simple formula for identifying which aims (or likings) are informed in this sense, but I shall shortly offer an account of some types of desire (liking) that I think obviously fail this kind of reflection.

So, according to the desire theories, the intrinsic goodness (or betterness) of an event is to be estimated in terms of the number and intensity of the desires it will satisfy in one or the other of these forms or some combination of them. "*Satisfy* a desire" here *means* only that "the event wanted *occurs.*"

But what is not required, according to all forms of this theory, is that the "satisfaction event" be *gratifying* or enjoyable – much less its intrinsic goodness determined by the strength of such

---

[56] These sorts of theory have been suggested by Derek Parfit, *Reasons and Persons* (Oxford: Clarendon Press, 1984). For criticisms, see Thomas Scanlon, "Value, desire, and quality of life," in M. C. Nussbaum and A. Sen (eds.), *The Quality of Life* (Oxford: Clarendon Press, 1993), pp. 185–200.

reactions – to the agent at the time it occurs, or that she will necessarily know about it then or later, or even be alive at the time. Of course, if a person *likes*/enjoys some event/experience, she will, at that moment, *want* it to occur; and so far, there is a minor confluence of the desire theory and its hedonistic opposite. (That this is so follows from a plausible conception of "pleasant.")[57]

A question that may occur to the reader is how it is possible to state consistently, as I did at the beginning of this chapter, that the main question about what is intrinsically good is what a *fully informed* person would *want* for itself, and then go on to question whether a desire theory should be accepted at all or whether a happiness/gratification theory should be used instead. The answer to this question arises from reflection on the

[57] For a view of this sort and an extended survey of other theories, see W. P. Alston, "Pleasure," in Paul Edwards (ed.), *The Encyclopedia of Philosophy* 1 (New York: Macmillan, 1967), pp. 341–7, who suggests that the theory is very similar to that of Henry Sidgwick, *Methods of Ethics*, Book II, chaps. 2 and 3. (See also C. D. Broad, *Five Types of Ethical Theory* [London: Harcourt, Brace, 1934], pp. 237–8.) On this view, an event is pleasant if it is (contains) an experience the felt quality of which is the differential cause (see footnote 74) of preferring it or wanting it to continue or be repeated *at the time*. Different qualities of experience, such as a taste or a glow of joy, can be parts of a pleasant experience in this sense. *How* pleasant an experience it is is fixed by the *intensity* of the *desire to continue or repeat it at the time*. This view allows that one might prefer (at a *different* time) one whole pleasant experience to another because of the quality (taste, joy, feeling) independently of how strongly each is wanted at the time; and it allows that an experience that one wants to continue (etc.) at the time might be regretted or its recollection found to be distasteful at another time. This view contrasts with the theory that pleasantness is some kind or tone of experience. For a somewhat fuller discussion, see Brandt, *A Theory of the Good and the Right*, pp. 35–42.

If this is what pleasure is, does that explain why a person will *want* pleasure for this future? This seems unclear. Perhaps Duncker's conception of "desire" (see the earlier discussion) gives a clue. Or if being pleasant is important for an experience's continuation or repetition to be wanted at the time, it could be that something like the experience will necessarily be wanted later – perhaps partly by conditioning. But we do manifestly want future experiences expected to be pleasant.

size of one's perspective. It may very well be that the desire of a fully informed person for the content of his life *as a whole* would not be directed solely at the occurrence of events wanted at one specific time (or more of them), but at something else. So, there is an important contrast between the target of a broadly informed desire – a preference for a kind of life (or a sequence of events) viewed as a whole – and the targets of specific desires. Therefore, if one desires something now but can foresee that fulfillment of the desire is or is not something one would later be *happy* about, one might no longer want it. Thus, one might say that a short-range desire, however well it stands up to criticism on the basis of information available at the time, may not be a long-range desire. Long-range *informed preference* for a whole life or a segment of it might come *close* to a gratification-type theory of "well-being" or at least might incorporate a hedonist component. It would not, of course, if "gratification" is identified with the occurrence of sensory pleasure alone. I come back to details of this in a moment.

The alternative view is hedonistic (but without the connotation of sensory pleasure); call it the "happiness theory." It holds that an event can be intrinsically good or the object, for itself, of someone's fully criticized desire if and only if it is a conscious *experience* – possibly a recollection. This pleasant experience could be either the occurrence of sensory enjoyment, like that of eating when hungry or drinking when thirsty or just the pleasantness of an odor or hearing a piece of music or seeing a sunset, or it can be *joy* from the awareness that an event of a certain kind has occurred, for example, that one has been helpful to an ailing mother. It is a mistake to think that "enjoyment" is one simple state of mind. An event being gratifying for a person, of course, implies that the event enters into the person's experience in some way and that he likes it in the sense that he wishes (not necessarily consciously) at the time to continue or repeat it.

A proponent of the happiness theory might present an empirical argument for her view. She might ask what an altruistic person would want for other persons. If we look back to our discussion of altruism, we find that one possible theory is that this involves extension, by conditioning, of our own native aversive or approach responses (e.g., escape tendencies, crying, autonomic changes) to occurrent states of the self like pain or the taste of quinine. The theory goes on to state that some stimuli (e.g., the sound of a child's cry) having become conditioned to unpleasant states of the self, like pain, will arouse the same aversive responses when they are not caused by one's own aversive states (pain). At a later level of development, the same aversive responses will be aroused by the mere representation of the internal states of another (like pain), just as they are aroused by hearing his crying. But which internal states of the other? The same kinds that are associated with expressive behavior of our own: experiences of pain, the taste of quinine, the taste of chocolate, the exhilaration of activity. These will arouse sympathetic responses in us. But there is no reason to think that pure satisfaction of a desire – an event the person perhaps doesn't even know about, even though she desired it earlier – will as such elicit any conditioned liking responses in the self; and hence there is no reason to think it will arouse sympathetic/benevolent motivation. So, what a benevolent/ sympathetic person will want for others is not just events that satisfy a desire of that person but internal states of joy/happiness.[58]

A major criticism of even such a broad hedonist theory is that many people find it difficult to believe that some facts, *not* about a person's mental states, are irrelevant to what we conceive to be his well-being (or what adds to the intrinsic goodness of his state of affairs). For instance, we may incline to think that a person who is overjoyed because he thinks he has made a great discovery is better off if he really has made the discovery, not merely enjoys thinking that he has; or we may think a woman who is happy because she thinks her husband loves her and is faithful to her is better off if her beliefs are correct than if she merely has this delightful fantasy. The happiness theorist can

[58] See Brandt, "The psychology of benevolence," especially 450ff.

reply that although it is true that we would prefer these things, we do so possibly for the reason that in real life such mistakes normally produce unhappiness later on. Moreover, he may ask: Are such events an intrinsic *benefit* to the person (irrespective of their being enjoyable in sum), that is, do they make a difference to him?[59]

Another criticism of the happiness theory has been put forward by Robert Nozick, James Griffin, and others:[60] the notion of an "experience machine." We are invited to consider whether we would want to accept an invitation to become a brain in a vat, with electrodes providing only enjoyable experiences – or any experiences we want. Griffin and Nozick predict that we would not wish to accept this invitation, that we want to do things and be things, in contrast to the hedonist, who is supposed to say: "What else can matter to us other than how our lives feel from the inside?" But it is not easy to see exactly what state of affairs is depicted by this conception. Indeed, it is not clear that such enjoyable experiences would occur if one were made aware of the fact that one is only floating in a tank! Nozick's real objection seems to be that the machines would be "living our lives for us." Griffin, too, explains that his objection is that he "wants control over his own fate." But is not having control over one's own fate making decisions after reflection on the consequences, including how much we would like them if they occurred, all this having the normal effect – as might well be the case if one adopts Nozick's suggestion that the machine might be a "result machine" that produces in the real world everything one thinks one is bringing about? It is true that we do want to *do* things; but in actual life, doing things is enjoyable and being unable to do them is frustrating: and if we attend to the theory of the source of desires described earlier, wanting to

---

[59] Some questions about all this are raised by Shelly Kagan in "The limits of well-being" in E. F. Paul, F. D. Miller, and J. Paul (eds.), *The Good Life and the Human Good* (Cambridge: Cambridge University Press, 1992), pp. 169–89.

[60] Robert Nozick, *Anarchy, State, and Utopia* (Oxford: Blackwell, 1974), pp. 42–5; Griffin, *Well-Being*, p. 9.

do something may just derive from past experience of discomfort when one was frustrated.[61]

How disparate are the implications of these two theories? Normally, if we desire a certain event and it occurs, we are pleased, and disappointed if it doesn't. (This is not so if the occurrence or nonoccurrence was fully expected or if the desire was weak; we may want to understand differential geometry or speak French intelligibly without expecting much of a thrill if we succeed.) There are, indeed, some cases of something's being pleasant apparently just because it was greatly desired in advance: perhaps finding yourself in the Kennedy Center waiting to hear a symphony, which you have longed to do. But sometimes having been desired and being pleasant do not coincide: You wanted very much to hear a performance by a certain orchestra but are bored by the performance, or you wanted to try a much-praised Manhattan but don't like it. And there are experiences we very much like that may not have been desired in advance at all – a lovely sunset, a cool drink, an unexpected visit by an old friend. (The continuation or repetition of the whole experience is, of course, desired at the time, and later one is glad to have had it.)

It may seem that these two theories are in direct conflict: One says that an event's being correctly expected to be enjoyable/gratifying is a necessary and sufficient condition of a desire for it (by someone) to be well founded, and that a life being so liked is the only thing that makes it worthwhile. The other denies this. Some philosophers wish to achieve an accommodation of the two theories, saying that each is right in part of what it affirms and wrong only in what it denies. Thus some believe that the hedonist theory can be right in saying that no state of

61 See J. J. C. Smart, "Hedonistic and ideal utilitarianism," in P. F. French, T. E. Uehling, and H. K. Wettstein (eds.), *Midwest Studies in Philosophy* III (1978), 247. Peter Railton has argued that experience-machine reasoning "draws upon intuitions about what we want for its own sake which were developed in settings where the drastic split the machine effects between experience and reality does not typically exist." See "Naturalism and prescriptivity," *Social Philosophy and Policy* 7 (1989), 151–74.

affairs is intrinsically good unless it is enjoyable/gratifying to some degree, but it can be wrong in thinking that *how* good some state of affairs is depends solely on its pleasantness.[62] Others think that some form of the desire theory may be right – that some things are good to the degree they are partly because desired – but wrong in thinking that just anything desired in the proper way is good, irrespective of whether it is liked when it occurs.[63]

There a third theory: that some state of a person, or act of hers, can be intrinsically good even if it is not desired for itself and is not pleasant for anyone. For instance, it has been thought that a state of character (or its exercise) may be intrinsically good or an altruistic act benefiting another person: so Aristotle. (This view is rather like Dworkin's conception of something being sacred or an inviolate good, mentioned earlier.) This view is not often defended today,[64] and I propose to ignore it. Not everything we *admire* need be intrinsically good.

Thomas Scanlon has recently criticized desire theories, I think only in the narrow, restricted sense, in favor of what he calls "substantive good" theories.[65] But I do not see that he offers an alternative, as a way of deciding what is an intrinsically good life, to considering what one would want or be glad about having occurred, given ideally complete factual information, taking the long view.

---

[62] Blanshard, *Reason and Goodness*, pp. 290–324; W. K. Frankena, *Ethics* (Englewood Cliffs, N.J.: Prentice-Hall, 1973), pp. 90–1; Parfit, *Reasons and Persons*, 501–2; but see G. E. More, *Principia Ethica* (Cambridge: Cambridge University Press, 1929), pp. 213ff., and *Ethics* (Oxford: Oxford University Press, 1949), pp. 146–54.

[63] For a somewhat similar suggestion, see Parfit, *Reasons and Persons*, pp. 501–2.

[64] But see Thomas Hurka, *Perfectionism* (Oxford: Oxford University Press, 1993).

[65] T. M. Scanlon, "Value, desire, and quality of life," in M. Nussbaum and A. Sen (eds.), *The Quality of Life* (Oxford: Clarendon Press, 1993), pp. 185–200; and "The moral basis of interpersonal comparisons," in J. Elster and J. Roemer (eds.), *Interpersonal Comparisons of Well-being* (Cambridge: Cambridge University Press, 1991), chap. 1, especially pp. 26ff. We still have to rely on someone's preferences to compare, for him, the worth of friendship, achievement, and enjoyment.

How might we justify a choice between the two main pure theories? Suppose we take the desire theory to concern not just desires with the longest-term perspective, with knowledge about whether their fulfillment will be liked, but specific dated desires coexisting with the kind of knowledge we are apt to have. The desire theory then faces a practical problem arising from the fact that desires are *dated* and that they can *change*, and this fact makes it exceedingly difficult for the theory to decide which of two actions will have better consequences. Suppose I wish to give my son a present that will maximize his well-being within the limits of my funds. Is how much his well-being is enhanced fixed by the relative strength of his desires at the time of discussion (at which moment he may most want a Greek lexicon, having recently acquired a yen to learn Greek), or when I make him the gift, or at some later (or earlier) time when he would much prefer to have something else, such as a ten-speed bike? (The gratification-type theory does not have this problem; its comparative conclusion is fixed by the sum of enjoyments for which the event is responsible from the time of the event on – or possibly including the joy of anticipation.) How will the desire theory enable us to compare the outcomes of two courses of action for their possible benefit? This problem of change of desires is more important than it may appear, since it is not just a report of intuitions about what we desire for the long run, but is also a difficulty in the theory's setting up an intelligible program for identifying the relative desirability of two events.

One way for a desire theorist to avoid this problem is by stipulations that reduce the likelihood of real change of desires. Earlier, I noted that some desire theorists aim to mitigate the problem by suggesting that a person should consider only her "informed" or "global" desires[66]; but a person's preferences about these, it seems, may also change, although doubtless less (some might deny that informed global desires change at all, but how about the desire to smoke?). If one adopted the stronger deliberative view, the changes in informed desires might be smaller still. I have described a different view that might avoid

---

[66] Parfit, *Reasons and Persons*, pp. 128, 149–52, 496–9.

the problem of change of desires altogether, proposing that what should be decisive is the sum of all (informed?) desires a person has had or will have – either actually, consciously or dispositionally – over her whole (or at least her postevent) lifetime, counting the intensity of a desire at each moment. It is clear that such sums, if we are comparing two events, may not vary from time to time, however much individual desires at different times may vary.[67] But making such a comparative calculation is a somewhat daunting project, even if it is theoretically possible to carry it out. This problem should be discussed more by those who advocate a straight desire theory.

Another and perhaps one main objection to this type of desire theory is that it implies that events *after one's death*, desired earlier, can make life better for one – or events about which one will never know. Would a fully informed person want to subscribe to this view? Would even the success of one's loved children – a major project of a person – *benefit* a person after his death? Aristotle may have thought so, but this view is very unconvincing.

We should bear in mind the possibility that informed reflection might discredit *every* general type of desire except that for happiness. For instance, a person may say that knowledge is desirable in itself, but we may wonder if this applies to true, justified beliefs that are not conscious or to all kinds of conscious knowledge, like that of the love life of others or the details of their dying moments. (A desire theorist might restrict intrinsic goodness – on intuitive grounds? – to some kinds of knowledge, like that of the theoretical part of some science.)

But are there cases of enjoyment/gratification, or at least *informed* enjoyment/gratification, that we should not want to say add to well-being? Perhaps one thing we need to do is specify more exactly what it is to be "gratifying." Suppose, for instance, we say that to be gratifying implies a pleasing awareness of an event or a recollection of it with joy, along with a favorable attitude toward the event. If we do this, there is the possibility

---

[67] See the discussion in Parfit, *Reasons and Persons*, 494, 496.

that some event gratifying at the time may not be gratifying in retrospect – perhaps like a woman greatly enjoying a big wedding at the time but being pained at the recollection of it years later. (But one might object that the original enjoyment was not fully informed.) Even the occurrence of an experience very pleasant at the time may be recalled with distaste. If so, this might raise a problem at least somewhat similar to the problem of change of desires. In order to know if some experience is really gratifying, must we speculate on whether all the future recollections of it will be gratifying? Perhaps this is a complication that we must simply accept. (Or, to make matters more complex still, should we include a *disposition* to take a certain attitude toward a recollection of the event that one might have later, even though in fact the person never thinks of the event again? And should we evaluate any specific occasion of gratification by how fully it was based on a full awareness of relevant facts?)

One might ask whether, given failure of gratification by a desired event, there is any importance at all to whether some kind of event is/was wanted. Why not just say that an event adds to one's well-being if and only if it is gratifying and forget about whether it was desired (even given full information)? Well, suppose one has had a gratifying experience but comes to *regret* it later. Suppose one wishes one had not enjoyed a particular sexual experience so strongly. Or suppose one was gratified by news that some professional rival has erred and lost status on that account, but on reflection wishes one had not been the sort of person to experience such gratification. Do such reflections not cast doubt on whether the initial gratifications increased one's well-being? (Perhaps these initial gratifications are tainted by not having been in a state of full information.)

I do not suggest that such considerations conclusively decide the sole importance of gratification for any agent in appraising goals and how fully a pure desire-satisfaction theory fails. In what follows, I shall for the most part attempt to leave open the possibility of some sort of combination theory, closer to commonsense views of the kind of life we should like to live for the long run. We might say that one would not *want* one's life to consist just in events that fulfill desires but with no gratification from (or even awareness of) these events; and we might say that, in retrospect, one would not feel satisfied with a life of sheer happiness if major ambitions about it were unfulfilled (although in that case the life could hardly have been of *pure* happiness). We might follow a suggestion by John Harsanyi[68] (and perhaps by Derek Parfit[69]) and say that what is intrinsically better for a person is a total segment of one's life marked by enjoyments *and/or* by satisfaction of desires, which one would *prefer*, from the long-range point of view, given full relevant information, so an *informed gratification* theory.

If we adopt this Harsanyi type of compromise, however, we are left with at least one problem, which will be considered in Chapter 7: how reasonably to make interpersonal comparisons of well-being. Suppose we know which combination of goods – enjoyments and others – one person would prefer from her long-range, fully informed position. How shall we decide whether that individual, in the light of her present state and future prospects, and her preferences, is better off, by this standard, than another person with her present state and future prospects and *her* preferences? Or, more precisely, as we shall see in Chapter 7, would the addition of $1,000 to the income of one person add more to her well-being, by this standard, than the loss of $1,000 from the income of another? There are two variables here: one what change the gain to one or the loss to another would make to the present state and prospects of each, the other how strongly the fully informed *preference* of each

---

[68] As Harsanyi put it: "a person's *informed-satisfaction* level" is "the degree to which his subjective experiences and the objective conditions of his life, as they are now and as they can reasonably be expected to be at various future times, given his own likely behavior at various contingencies, satisfy his present *informed preferences*." In "Utilities, preferences, and substantive goods," unpublished in 1992, to appear in a volume honoring A. K. Sen.

[69] In *Reasons and Persons*, pp. 501–2.

would respond to this gain or loss. We might get agreement on the first point but not be clear on the second – for example, if one sets more store by pleasant experiences, the other by achievement, knowledge, or good friends, and we cannot decide whose evaluation is correct since the preferences of the two persons may be different, on account of past experiences, by conditioning. I shall make an attempt to resolve this question for the purposes of a theory of distributive justice in Chapter 7.

Perhaps we can say that one major practical question is *which* kinds of desire to satisfy and *which* kinds of enjoyment to experience in view of all the knowledge we can assemble. We come to this in the following section. We shall return to the conception of a person's well-being in Chapter 10.

THE APPRAISAL OF DESIRES AND ENJOYMENTS

If a person wants to adopt *plans* of action that will either maximize his long-term happiness or the long-term satisfaction of desires that have been criticized on the basis of full information, obviously the first and most important thing to do is to identify the likely consequences of adopting one plan rather than others and consider how well the plan does, relatively, in probably increasing happiness or desire satisfaction. But the second thing to do, especially in the case of big decisions like choice of a vocation, is to subject actual desires to informed criticism and, where possible, substitute criticized desires for the actual ones. (The same may be done for types of enjoyment.) Why should this be done?

Before we deal with this, however, let us consider some simple points that will hardly be contentious. (1) Desires should be transitive: If I prefer X to Y and Y to Z, I may not prefer Z to X. A person with intransitive desires must lose money to a skillful gambler. (2) If I desire X and Y equally but the probability of obtaining X from an action A is greater than that of getting Y from action B, I should choose to do A. (I suggested earlier that in fact persons do this, on the whole; we may now add that it is rational that they do so; following this procedure is the most efficient way to get one's desires satisfied.) (3) Perhaps a person will not have desires for outcomes she knows it is impossible to bring about. Doubtless there are other rules, equally uncontentious, or supportable roughly by appeal to the instrumental conception of reasoning in action and planning.[70]

Earlier in this chapter, we considered some of the complexities in the sources of desires and likings, with the thought that this information might be useful in deciding which desires/likings would be embraced by factually informed people. We must now consider various facts that affect whether a given desire/liking meets such requirements.

The deliberative theory, as described by Parfit, about what it is to be fully informed, does not imply that a desire for something (or a liking of some event) is in the clear, as far as information is concerned, if it is merely *logically consistent* with the information. Such a requirement would exclude nothing. What the theory must say is that there may be some information that is *causally incompatible,* in the sense of a *differential cause,*[71] with the *persistence* of a given desire or liking in the person who gets the information. But how is this? This is not like a piece of evidence disconfirming a theory. The best answer, I think, is that *all* (or nearly all) persons who are clear-headed, with broad knowledge of human nature and of how desires are produced, would in fact lose or be doubtful about a desire/liking if certain information came to hand. (This might well be because such persons would know that having the relevant information, taken with known laws of psychology, would result in the questioned desire being impossible.) It may not be easy to identify and list

---

[70] Robert Nozick offers a list in his *The Nature of Rationality* (Princeton, N.J.: Princeton University Press, 1993), pp. 141ff.

[71] So not in the sense that the information alone is a necessary or sufficient condition for the effect, but that the information, plus conditions present before getting it (themselves insufficient), is a sufficient condition. Some other conditions might have produced the same effect, but in fact they were not present. See John Mackie, "Causes and conditions," *American Philosophical Quarterly* 2 (1965), 245–64; and Jaegwon Kim, "Causes and events: Mackie on causation," *Journal of Philosophy* 68 (1971), 426–41.

exactly which kinds of information are causally incompatible with certain desires in this sense, although I shall propose some criteria that I think would reasonably be included. For readers not convinced by this list, I shall later try to show, by a cost–benefit analysis, why an individual often does better by himself if he ignores desires/likings that are causally incompatible with certain information in the preceding sense.

The first kinds of case to be looked at do not specifically involve the theory of how desires (pleasures) are brought about; we come to those later.

1. There are cases in which a person strongly desires a certain kind of event expected to happen now but desires it much less strongly if it is expected to occur in an hour, or a week, or a year. Some economists think this is a universal human trait, which explains why interest is charged – one wants to enjoy now what one's money will buy.[72] Usually there is some extraneous explanation for the fact, such as uncertainty: I know that I might be dead within a year and hence cannot work up a desire for something to happen a year from now. But if all factors of uncertainty are set aside, including uncertainty about whether my tastes may have changed and I may like something less well a year from now, what pure time discounting overlooks is the fact that the experience of something nice now will be the same as the identical experience of something nice a year from now, no more and no less. Now two events that differ *only* in date can hardly be desired differently by a thoughtful person. It is no wonder that F. P. Ramsey thought that discounting later enjoyments "is ethically indefensible and arises merely from weakness of the imagination."[73] There is controversy among psychologists about why such things occur. One view, which seems to have much to offer, is simply that the effects arise from inade-

[72] See N. Georgescu-Roegen, "Utility," in *International Encyclopedia of the Social Sciences*, vol. 16 (1968), p. 250.

[73] F. P. Ramsey, "A mathematical theory of saving," *Economic Journal* 38 (1928), 543–59.

quate cognitive representation of future events.[74] (Why such underrepresentation should occur is a further question.) If this is the source of time discounting, removal of the cognitive defect will result in a change of desire. Evidently, thoughtful people would question a case of their own time discounting if they realized it was a result of relatively inadequate representation of the future. (For one thing, if adequate representation were present, discounting would not occur.) Such realization would be causally incompatible with continuation of the time-discounting phenomenon. It seems that such discounting is clearly subject to rational correction.

2. There is a somewhat similar phenomenon: failure to be moved by knowledge that I shall later have a certain desire but do not have that desire now. (This is different from wanting something in the future now, but only weakly because it is so far in the future.) It seems that knowledge that one will have a desire later (e.g., 20 years from now) will not automatically produce a corresponding desire now, although one might well think it should. Is there any fact that can compensate, to some extent, for the absence of interest in the satisfaction of foreseeable future desires? Well, aversions to anticipated frustrations are more reliably available, and if we can clearly understand how (and how badly) we shall be frustrated later from failure to satisfy a desire we shall then have, this may to some extent repair the absence of interest now in satisfaction of desires we

---

[74] I have summarized some data behind this controversy in *A Theory of the Good and the Right*, pp. 58–64. See the brief review in Heckhausen, *Motivation and Action*, pp. 169–70. See also Walter Mischel, "Cognitive appraisals and transformations in self-control," in Bernard Wiener (ed.), *Cognitive Views of Human Motivation* (New York: Academic Press, 1974), pp. 33–50, especially pp. 42–8; and with R. Metzger, "Preference for delayed reward as a function of age, intelligence, and length of delay interval," *Journal of Abnormal and Social Psychology* 64 (1962), 425–31; H. N. Mischel and W. Mischel, "Development of children's knowledge of self-control strategies," in F. Halisch and J. Kuhl (eds.), *Motivation, Intention, and Volition* (Berlin: Springer-Verlag, 1987), pp. 321–36; also K. J. Rotenberg and E. V. Mayer, "Delay of gratification in native and white children," *International Journal of Behavioral Development* 13 (1990), 23–30.

shall have later. (This is why hikers carry flasks of water!) Such rectification seems to be rational criticism.

A person who fully took into account the foregoing considerations might be said to be *prudent*, since imprudent behavior seems to consist mostly in ignoring some of these points. It seems that an ideally prudent person is one who makes plans with the long-range project of maximizing her pleasures, satisfaction of desires, and so on – in other words, in view of her future life as a whole. Of course, a person cannot be expected to have such a large vision in mind all the time, but when she is said to act imprudently, she has failed to do so in an obvious and spectacular way. In fact, all the criticisms of action surveyed here can be construed as recommendations of prudence. But we should be careful not to define "imprudence" too narrowly, as involving only self-interest, for everybody has desires directed at the states of other persons – either children, friends, or, in the case of benevolent persons, in other sentient beings generally. So, if we take the whole gamut of desires (and satisfactions) into account and order them according to their long-term importance to us, we arrive at an ideal of a whole good life for us (including our desires about others), in terms of which we may appraise particular plans for action. A person would need virtual omniscience to be able to derive such a whole picture. Our actual thinking will usually involve only plans and goals we happen to think of in our particular circumstances.

3. The strength of both desires and likings is influenced by temporary emotional or motivational states. For instance, if at a given time a certain type of desire has recently been satiated, a desire for the same sort of thing now may not show its normal strength. The opposite occurs in a state of deprivation.

Much the same can be said about how pleasant/unpleasant events are experienced to be. If one is satiated, one will be less pleased by an event one would normally like very much; the reverse is true after a period of deprivation.

Why should we care about these variations? Obviously, there can be no criticism of the lack of desire for food or liquid when one is already sated. But the strength of our desires affects not only short-range but also long-range planning. In the case of desires, a condition of satiety now may reduce the strength of desire for an event in the future, since the pleasantness of the idea of that event will be reduced by the absence of a "natural" boost from a present need state. So, the fact of this lawful phenomenon can have misleading results for future planning. In the case of enjoyable experiences, these misleading frames of mind (satiation or deprivation at the time) may result in associations that make the ideas/images of similar kinds of events more or less attractive than they otherwise would be. When these facts are pointed out, we can expect the strength of preferences to change; we realize that we normally would want something more (or less) strongly. This is rational criticism.

4. Very often, even perhaps normally, we acquire desires/aversions from personal experience with liked/disliked examples of the target object or things like it by conditioning. (This is not the case with desires/values obtained from identification with models, parental advice, or values expressed in television programs.) Desires/aversions with this sort of etiology we might call "authentic." When they have this etiology, acting so as to get what one desires is normally a way to achieve enjoyment or desire satisfaction, since we want something we have actually experienced as wanted or pleasant. But desires/aversions don't always arise in this normal way. Sometimes there is stimulus generalization from atypical events. There was a famous case in the psychological laboratories (of J. B. Watson) in the 1920s. A male child was playing with a rabbit; meanwhile, a gun was (intentionally) fired just behind him. He was very frightened. By conditioning, any contact with rabbits at once became aversive to him. And as a consequence of stimulus generalization, his aversion generalized wildly. (The law of stimulus generalization is that an attitude produced to one type of event will generalize to similar types of event.) Something was grossly wrong here, although the laws of association by conditioning and stimulus generalization presumably derive from considerations of survival of the fittest, and individuals not governed by these laws at all would do badly in the struggle for survival; for example, they wouldn't learn to eat nourishing foods. So what went wrong? One thing is that the conditioning

was to a very atypical event. Such aversions will diminish after more experience with the central objects (rabbits or dogs), since the law of inhibition[75] states that a response (here, aversion) diminishes as the object of the attitude is repeatedly experienced without the feature responsible for the aversion. (So, if one had a range of normal experiences, by this law the aversion would not occur.) Moreover, the same inhibition effect can occur merely as a result of thinking: reflection that similar events regularly occur without the aversive features. Thus, if we supplement the original experiences with reflection on a wider set of cases, the aversion will (normally) disappear. We thus see the force of a possible rule: Don't pay attention to aversions obtained from stimulus generalization from atypical situations. Change of preference from such reflection on the source of a desire is rational criticism.

5. Some desires/aversions can be affected not only by the process of extinction but also by counterconditioning. Suppose one is imaging something, like a tender moment with a beloved for whose affection one yearns (unfortunately, say, since the desire is no longer reciprocated). This reflection might be interrupted by a severe shock to the arm. I am told that after a few such shocks, delivered while one is daydreaming of an intimate moment with the beloved, one will no longer yearn to be with the beloved. This, of course, is not rational criticism but interference with a preference by causing a pain, which results in counterconditioning. But if one wants to fall out of love less painfully, one can take steps to associate the image of the beloved with thoughts of displeasing attributes or events involving her. This reflection will have the desired effect, and it is rational criticism if the beliefs are true/justified. This representation, taken with psychological laws, implies that the love attitude will disappear. (The reverse treatment associates a pleasant recollection with a thought or image hitherto phobic – a

---

[75] I have discussed the psychology of inhibition in *A Theory of the Good and the Right*, pp. 105–7. For a relevant recent paper, see R. P. Swinson and K. Kuch, "Behavioral psychotherapy of agoraphobic/panic disorder," *International Review of Psychiatry* 1 (1989), 195–205.

procedure called "desensitization," widely used by therapists in treating anxieties and phobias.) Again, therapists have treated a liking/desire for alcohol by encouraging thoughts of how sick one felt the last time one was drunk. Rehearsal of the unpleasant effects of some state of affairs can reduce the desire for it; and in the case of the alcoholic, the desire itself was partially the result of failure to represent these effects. So, if one is an alcoholic and wants to get rid of the desire to drink, one thing to do is to dwell on the bad consequences when one is tempted to drink and get the benefit of the association. This is not just criticism of a plan or intention; it is criticism that undermines the desire itself.[76] Failure to do this is a kind of cognitive mistake – failure to be moved by representation of the facts.

6. We have seen that stimulus generalization can spread a liking/desire very broadly. But an individual may combat this tendency by making discriminations. For instance, in one experiment, students widely generalized a galvanic skin response from having been shocked when a color word was read aloud. At first, the response came when *any* word was read. Then it was pointed out that the shocks came only after color words. Then there was a reduction, after six trials, of the galvanic skin response to non-color words, although it was not immediate or complete.[77] This effect of making discriminations can be utilized in treating psychological problems. Here is an interesting variant. Suppose one was a poverty-stricken newsboy during childhood who could not purchase nice things without real hardship. This fact generated a conditioned aversion to spending money on expensive, unnecessary items. But later the boy becomes a successful businessman and has no reason to scrimp on luxuries. Nevertheless, the purchase of a luxury item may

---

[76] Therapists have reported considerable success in changing some desires through stimulation of the patient by true statements: alcoholism, extreme craving for the approval of others, aversion to being alone, desire to achieve, concern about irritating one's employer by being assertive, even the desire to smoke. Cf. L. Birk and A. W. Birk, "Psychoanalysis and behavior therapy," *American Journal of Psychiatry* 131 (1974).

[77] S. N. Cole and C. N. Sippreth, "Extinction of a classically conditioned GSR as a function of awareness," *Behaviour Research and Therapy* 5 (1967).

arouse anxiety, as a hangover from boyhood days, and as an adult he is unable to buy, or at least to buy without anxiety and with pleasure, nice things he can now afford. If he could discriminate, and tell himself firmly and maybe repeatedly that his situation in life has changed, he would be able to overcome this disability. His problem arose from lack of vivid awareness of present facts. This is rational criticism.

7. I have pointed out that satisfaction of desires that arise from stimulus generalization can be expected to result in happy states of mind and the relief of bodily needs. These desires I have called "authentic." But as we have seen, many desires/aversions do not originate from specific pleasant/unpleasant experiences at all, but rather from imitation of models or parents, or preachments by either one, roughly in the transmission of societal values to the next generation – so not authentic. For instance, you may have acquired an aversion to engaging in a relatively low-prestige occupation like being a motorcycle repairman from expressions of dismay by your parents or your classmates, either from associating these unpleasant expressions of attitude with the idea of the activity or with vague anticipations of possibly very unhappy outcomes later. This aversion will be removed by personal experiment – if you find you like that kind of work. Or you may get testimony from motorcycle repairmen that they enjoy their occupation. Short of this, however, the same result may be obtained by reflecting on the infrequency of benefits from following parents'/classmates' advice on matters about which they have no expertise. Such aversions have no solid basis and will be modified by reflection on facts – rational criticism. Many values acquired in childhood learning have similar standing and are subject to criticism.

8. Some desires/aversions are brought about by unjustified beliefs about fact. For instance, you might have acquired an aversion to enjoying yourself, say boating on a Sunday, because you have been taught to believe that a loving God wants the Sabbath to be kept holy, devoid of fun. Here a false or unjustified belief is the source of an attitude that prevents happiness and general desire satisfaction. When this belief is replaced by true or justified beliefs, the anxieties tend to go away, partly

because this activity is no longer viewed as a special case of respect due to a loving God, partly by extinction, and partly by counterconditioning. Again, this is rational criticism.

This list might be extended if we ran through a list of our aspirations for living or a list of our strong likes or dislikes. One thing we tend to forget is the importance to us of interactions with other people and how important their well-being may be to us. Or do we perhaps care too much about the well-being of others, perhaps total strangers? Should we apply the foregoing types of criticism in appraisal of these attitudes – say, the level of one's benevolence? The answers could be doubtful.

One might ask: Why bring all this knowledge to bear? I suggest that the propriety of doing this will hardly be doubted by a reflective person. We shall think: If bringing to bear thoughts about *facts* will "fumigate" our likes/desires, so be it. This is one value judgment that seems secure, at least for most people.

But to some extent, we might also support paying attention to these results by a kind of cost–benefit analysis. For being guided by desires/aversions/likings of the criticized kinds is not apt to lead to maximal satisfaction as one now is – either in enjoyments or in events that in sum are most desired. The aversions acquired because of expressions of dismay or misleading religious teaching by parents or classmates are apt to prevent a sensitive reaction to various aspects of the world – to lead one to invest one's energies in projects/avoidances not gratifying maximally in the long run. Obviously, the same is true for desires/aversions resulting from stimulus generalization from atypical experiences in the past, like an aversion to having a dog as a pet. A similar case holds for action on desires influenced by being or having been in an abnormal frame of mind, or for failure to make discriminations or failure to represent relevant facts vividly, and so on. So, thoughtful, informed people would not consider such desires/aversions as ones to guide behavior for this reason alone. So, it might be said that many of these criticisms are, after all, only applications of strategies about how to maximize actual desire/satisfaction or enjoyments as we now are.

But it is not clear how far this kind of cost–benefit analysis can take us. For instance, an argument of this sort against time discounting supposes that the discounted future events have equal value and are not to be ignored – although they are not valued now. The dismissal of desires based on misleading states of mind supposes that our normal desires are the ones to be catered to – not the ones we actually have. The same holds for stimulus generalization from unusual contingencies. Why disallow these, although they are perfectly good desires/aversions? It is true that a *strategy* of ignoring desires/aversions arising from stimulus generalization from unusual experiences will maximize enjoyment and desire satisfaction. But this assumes that we already have confirmed an ideal of maximizing enjoyment or desire/satisfaction in the long run. This is different from starting with desires/aversions we already have and criticizing an action plan solely on the ground that it is not a good instrument for achieving these goals.

The acquisition of desires/aversions and values, then, is a lawful process, and some of the causal links – conditioning and stimulus generalization – are very important for living. But it also seems as if many effects of this process are also subject, in a lawful way, to being undermined by vivid reflection on facts. So far, at least, there can be rational criticism of desires. On this matter, at least, it seems that Hume was mistaken.[78]

One might ask whether the kinds of criticism I have described can really be counted as rational. On this perhaps we

---

[78] When he said "It is only in two senses that any affection can be called unreasonable. . . . Secondly, when in exerting any passion in action, we choose means insufficient for the designed end, and deceive ourselves in our judgment of causes and effects. Where a passion is neither founded on false suppositions, nor chooses means insufficient for the end, the understanding can neither justify nor condemn it. It is not contrary to reason to prefer the destruction of the whole world to the scratching of my finger. It is not contrary to reason for me to choose my total ruin, to prevent the least uneasiness of an Indian or person wholly unknown to me. It is as little contrary to reason to prefer even my own acknowledged lesser good to my greater, and have a more ardent affection for the former than the latter." *Treatise*, Book 2, Part 3, Sec. 3.

should not be dogmatic, considering the scope of disagreements about the nature of rationality (including noncognitive analyses). We should admit that the corrections called for do not involve mistakes in logic or scientific reasoning alone. But it may be that for a change of state of mind to be described as "rational," it is enough if it derives from careful reflection on *facts* or *justified beliefs* and is a change that all (or almost all) thoughtful, psychologically aware people generally would go through as a result of such reflection.

Suppose everyone subjected all his desires to these forms of criticism. Would the result be that all differences of valuation would disappear – for example, that a Hopi would lose his aversion to violence or to being singled out as an important or accomplished person? Perhaps the Hopi and the traditional Alorese would reach a reconciliation. Or would Griffin's list of intrinsically good things become acceptable to everyone? Or would all of us become equally benevolent/altruistic? Is it being unduly optimistic to expect so much? Perhaps we have to reconcile ourselves to a bit of relativism about basic values – or perhaps support of careful thinking will lead us all to the same results.

The foregoing cases, of course, are only examples of types of thinking that may result in rational criticism of desires.

CONCLUSIONS ABOUT WHAT IS INTRINSICALLY DESIRABLE

There are some further questions to be kept in mind. (1) What total set of requirements would thoughtful, fully informed persons demand that a desire/liking meet if it is to satisfy them? I have presented some plausible candidates for rejection, but is this list complete? And will my listing of some as objectionable sustain thorough criticism? (2) Which of our own desires/likings meet these requirements? One needs a catalog of personal attitudes, and an examination of each, in the deliberation on important decisions.

Chapter 3

The varieties of norms for behavior

The preceding chapter ignored a major complication: that human behavior takes place in a social setting and that some aversions are comprised of or arise from social constraints, so that a person is not free to do what would have maximized expectable utility in the absence of these constraints – constraints of custom, etiquette, law, codes of honor, and a host of moral prohibitions: of incest, adultery, lies, abortion, and usually any behavior typically harmful to others or risking harm to others. We need to understand at least the more important such constraints and how they work; and eventually, we want to find out whether some of them are justified in some important sense. The results of the preceding chapter, however, apply to all kinds of motivation, including the aversions involved in these social constraints.

SOCIAL NONMORAL CONSTRAINTS ON BEHAVIOR

One type of social constraint is legal. If I overpark, I may receive a ticket and be required to pay a fine. If I break a contract, I shall be required to make good the loss to the other party and perhaps pay punitive damages as well. It is important to compare and contrast these constraints – and others – with what we would call "moral" constraints. Are all these things the law penalizes me for doing/not doing things that I am *morally* bound to do/not do in any case? No: Conscientious objectors contrast legal duties (e.g., to serve in the armed forces) with moral obligations. Again, the law prohibits us from giving assistance to a person who wants to commit suicide, and it may prohibit a physician from giving a lethal dose of a drug to a seriously defective newborn. Clearly, the legal requirements do not settle all issues about moral requirements. Law and morality differ in other ways as well. Why do people conform to the requirements of the law? A strongly motivating factor (not the only one: Most people desire to be law-abiding, often on moral grounds) is the desire to avoid legal sanctions. But a person will not necessarily be disturbed by guilt feelings about breaking the law; he may just believe the law is wrong about something and feel quite cheerful about the conflict.

There are nonmoral norms, however, not enforced by the penalties of the law. Some of these might be called "social norms." Consider the rule about how to eat – which instruments to use – or the rule forbidding men to wear a hat while dining in a restaurant or (except for Jews) during a religious service. These rules seem to be purely conventional. In these cases, those who notice discrepant behavior may think the agent just does not know the standards, perhaps may be mildly irritated, but may think no more about it – hardly rebuking the offender. But there is no indignation at failure to conform. The agent herself will feel a bit embarrassed if she finds she has publicly breached a known and recognized standard of what is done at least in polite circles, ones in which she'd like to be included – what is the case for many matters of etiquette. In the case of these rules, there will hardly be a claim that they are justified. Does every *custom* imply a rule of this sort? Doubtless what we should say depends on how we use the term "custom," which the *Oxford English Dictionary* defines as a regularity of social behavior but which others think implies a normative component, so that regularity of social behavior does not count as a custom unless it does imply a norm. John Ladd wrote that custom is an explicitly acknowledged norm, binding only on members of the group, and its force deriving from long-standing practice in the group.[1] But there are nonlegal social norms that we would hardly call matters of custom, so that "custom" and "social norm" do not coincide. Suppose my son has accepted hospitality when traveling in a far-off place; then I feel bound to invite his hosts to dinner when they visit my city. Should my feeling be viewed as a matter of custom? Another example comes closer to being a matter of custom. Suppose my daughter is being married; I shall feel obligated to pay the expenses of the wedding (unless both parties have been married before). In this case, known convention (other societies expect the bride's or groom's family to be paid) is important – although one may need to consult a handbook of etiquette, at least in the United States, to find out what it is, since who pays the expense of a wedding is not rigidly defined. But in both cases there is a recognized "proper" response. I feel cheap if I do not meet the standard, and the other party will at least find it strange if I do not. I think most people would hardly call either of these behaviors "morally obligatory," although some people might regard them as rather trivial forms of moral obligation. What we should probably say is that they are matters of etiquette, where "etiquette" refers especially to informal rules or expectations of society, especially polite society. So, regularity of behavior, the expectations of polite society, and the presence of some motivation to conform are often involved in social nonlegal rules for action but are related only in a complicated way.

Somewhat similar are norms of friendship. Friendship is primarily a relation of mutual affection, concern, and trust. There is the feeling that a friend is a person on whom one can count in trouble and be counted on for judicious, impartial advice. One of the things one does for a friend is to make at least small personal sacrifices to meet his needs, such as visit him if he is sick in a hospital, something one would not do for a casual acquaintance. Why does one do this? Because one cares, not because of some recognized rule of moral duty or even eti-

[1] John Ladd, "Custom," *The Encyclopedia of Philosophy*, Paul Edwards, ed. (New York: Macmillan, 1967), vol. II, pp. 278–80.

quette, although expectations grow as the friendship matures. Yet there is something a bit like social norms: a person who fails to visit will feel somewhat uncomfortable; the ill friend will wonder why his friend does not appear; and others will wonder what kind of friend he is after all.[2]

Another social norm, fortunately diminishing in importance, is "codes of honor." So, if one person – usually belonging to the aristocracy – is insulted or demeaned by another, he may challenge the other to a duel, and the second person is "honor bound" to accept. The writer once observed an episode in a German restaurant: A young man thought that someone across the room was staring at his girlfriend. He stood up, approached the other person, gave the Hitler salute, and challenged him to a duel. The other party stood up, saluted, and accepted the challenge. What was going on here? I find it difficult to empathize with either party, and so, I think, would most Germans today. (Somewhat the same holds for a famous lethal duel in American history, that of Alexander Hamilton and Aaron Burr, who accused Hamilton of besmirching his character.) Those who sympathize appear to be members of a small circle of the elite – in the case of the challenge between the two Germans, probably just members of some old-line German fraternity – who are concerned about maintaining their status and reputation. The insulter doubtless feels bad about what he has done and does not wish to engage in even a nonlethal duel, but the attitudes of his particular elite group being what they are, he believes that to maintain status and reputation, he must accept the challenge. Somewhat the same feelings characterize the insulted person. So, each feels bound to do what he would otherwise prefer not to do because his status and reputation are at stake – at least with the elite group that each respects. Doubtless the code of

---

[2] Conceptions of friendship appear to differ from one society or age to another. See, e.g., Aristotle on friendship or the very careful account by Henry Sidgwick in *The Methods of Ethics* (London: Macmillan, 1922), pp. 257ff. Sidgwick concludes that many questions about what to do for friends are more matters of "good taste and refined feeling" than of morality. See also M. J. Meyer, "Rights between friends," *Journal of Philosophy* 89 (1992), 467–83.

honor has some social function; the risk of being open to challenge to a duel prevents some sorts of antisocial behavior. But surely there is no *moral duty* to issue or accept a challenge. (This is very different from "debts of honor," which a person with a delicate conscience feels morally bound, although not legally bound, to pay, e.g., debts of a father who failed in business – or, like Sir Walter Scott, who paid off the debts of his bankrupt publisher.)

It seems as if there are also informal norms in business, for better or worse. An officer of a firm may be supposed to put his firm and its profits first. For instance, when business is poor, a manager might lay off 2,000 employees with many years of service to the company, without taking steps to cushion the impact on them (if they are not protected by a union contract). Would failure to do this reflect on the agent? Well, if he did fail, some of his associates would think him weak, indecisive, unable to recognize what is "good business," and unsuited for a managerial job in a capitalist society. Profits and efficiency are the basic criteria for management of a company. How would the manager himself feel if he failed to act in the expected way? At least embarrassed and uncomfortable, and probably worried about his position. He has conflicting aversions: to not doing his job and to doing a morally questionable thing. But the manager's "duty" is hardly a *moral* duty unless one thinks that, in accepting his job, he has made moral commitments to the company that it is now his duty to discharge.[3]

All of these, by the way, are to be distinguished from habit: A person may have a habit of drinking tea at 5 P.M. each day, or of postponing reading the morning paper until evening. These are habits only, and while one might debate with the person whether such habits are rational, there is no social pressure to act differently. Habits may be functional for a person, saving on time of deliberation. But such behavior is not failure to conform to any kind of social rule. In all cases where there is a social rule,

---

[3] Henry Sidgwick seems to have recognized something of this sort; *Methods of Ethics*, pp. 167–9. See the account in John Braithwaite, *Crime, Shame and Reintegration* (Cambridge: Cambridge University Press, 1989), pp. 30–1.

there is at least a slightly negative attitude toward the nonconformer on the part of a group to which she belongs or would
like to belong, and there is some discomfort and embarrassment
on the part of the nonconformer, perhaps at the thought of
being disdained by an elite group.

In all these cases, we need to understand what motives an
individual has for following a norm (perhaps just wanting to
conform to a social standard, or caring for a friend, or maintaining status with a group), how other persons will react if they
learn that he has failed to follow the norm, and who they are –
say, the elite in the case of a code of honor, or friends, or others.
Differences on any of these points may identify a different kind
of social norm. There are many types of social norms other than
moral norms.

THE NATURE OF MORALITY

In the preceding section, I referred to "moral" norms without
explaining what sort of things they are. We must now look at
this. In drawing the parallels I am about to draw, it should be
noted that I am not supposing that morality is essentially a
cognitive matter: that one first just apprehends – sees the truth
of – principles about what one is obligated to do, or would be
wrong to do, and then infers the moral status of an individual
past or projected action by noting its logical relation to the relevant principles. (Alternatively, a cognitivist might hold that if
one attends carefully to the nature of a past or projected act, one
can just *note* its property of wrongness or obligatoriness.) Although these cognitive conceptions have been quite influential,
they fly in the face of all we know about the learning of morality
by children, as well as the variation of moral norms and the
sociology of changes in such norms. They also create insuper-
able epistemological problems about the sources of such purported knowledge.

In contrast, I shall pursue a *motivational* view of morality,
which is more in line with what we know, and was espoused by
J. S. Mill when he wrote that "the essence of conscience . . .
consists in the existence of a mass of feeling which must be

broken through in order to do what violates our standard of right, and which, if we do nevertheless violate that standard, will probably have to be encountered afterwards in the form of remorse."[4] So, for Mill, personal morality consists in an intrinsic (not self-interested) *aversion* to *acting* in certain ways[5] and (Chapter V of *Utilitarianism*), a disposition to feel remorseful (or guilty) about acting contrary to this aversion, and a disposition to disapprove of those who do.[6] (Of course, these features may obtain to a lesser or greater degree, depending on the kind of behavior involved.) And, as we shall see, we should add: The person believes that these attitudes can be *justified* in an appropriate way, but Mill does not say it would be *irrational* (in the sense of contrary to self-interest or in any broader sense of "irrational") to be without them. But we can consider whether such attitudes have a social function and ask what it is. For these features of a person's morality, we should admit that it is normal and proper to *express* it by saying things like "Doing *A* is *morally* wrong." I shall follow this pattern.

One might ask why one should define "personal morality" in this way. Is it supposed that this is a correct dictionary definition of the term as it is commonly used? Surely that would be to claim too much. However, we may note that most people often *do* have such aversions toward *types* of action, along with the disposition to feel guilty if they act contrariwise and disapprove others who do – and also believe that their attitude is justified.

---

[4] J. S. Mill, *Utilitarianism*, first published, 1863, many editions, chap. 3.

[5] One might ask what kind of aversion this is: Is it like an aversion to eating a banana? Maybe it is like an aversion to the thought of the unpleasant taste of a banana or to bringing about such a taste – in the case of morality, an aversion to a state of affairs such as harming another or being the author of such a state of affairs.

[6] *Utilitarianism*, chap. 5: "the idea of penal sanction, which is the essence of law, enters not only into the conception of injustice, but into that of any kind of wrong. We do not call anything wrong unless we mean to imply that a person ought to be punished in some way or other for doing it – if not by law, by the opinion of his fellow creatures; if not by opinion, by the reproaches of his own conscience. This seems the real turning point of the distinction between morality and simple expediency."

Further, there is some reason to think that the motivational features (aversions, etc.) are causally connected and so belong together.[7] Moreover, I suggest that if someone said some action was wrong, but it was pointed out that one of these features was missing in her, we should not think her attitude was one of morality. This collection of facts about a person is important for explaining her behavior. And if we construe personal morality in this way, we can assimilate what we know about children's learning of morality and how moral codes in a society get changed.

How do moral norms differ from other social norms? Some have thought that moral rules concern more important matters and that the reactions of other people to breach of such rules are relatively severe, to the point of taking the form of criminal punishment, and that the rules are not subject to deliberate change, as they are in the case of law. Doubtless there is some truth in the matter of importance, but some acts forbidden by morality are venial. It is right that moral norms, like some other social norms and unlike laws, are not subject to deliberate change. More important, however, is the suggestion about the form of "sanction" for the breach of moral rules. Apart from the agent's aversion to behaving in certain ways, he will himself feel remorse, guilt, or shame[8] if he misbehaves. How about the

---

[7] Some psychologists (M. L. Hoffman, "Empathy and justice in society," *Social Justice Research* 3 [1989], 283–311, and "The contribution of empathy to justice and moral judgement," in N. Eisenberg and J. Strayer [eds.] *Empathy and Its Development* [New York: Cambridge University Press, 1987], pp. 47–80) think that remorse is a causally fixed response to causing injury to someone one is disposed not to injure – a "combination of empathic and sympathic distress and a self-blame attribution."

[8] Gabrielle Taylor explains guilt as a response to awareness of one's action being a case of what is authoritatively forbidden, not necessarily involving harm to anyone, e.g., some sexual offense or not going to church on Sunday. (See *Pride, Shame and Guilt* [Oxford: Clarendon Press, 1985], p. 88; also see the contrast with remorse on the following pages.) "Shame" is somewhat differ-ent. I include it as an alternative to allow for the possibility of an allegedly "shame society" like Japan. The suggestion by Taylor (*op. cit.*, chap. III) is that shame (possibly as in the heroic codes of the *Iliad*) is primarily "a self-directed adverse judgment of the person feeling shame" in which awareness

reaction of others? Some philosophers have held that their reaction is a distinctively moral feeling, disapproval, but this view probably has few supporters today. We probably need to flesh out the concept of "disapproval" in terms of anger, contempt, a feeling of coolness, and so on. We do not find it admirable or funny if we learn that someone has underreported his income for tax purposes; we have a negative attitude toward him of some sort. When a person is said to "think" that some sort of action is wrong, motivational theory says that he has a syndrome composed of all these properties, *and* he thinks all of these attitudes are *justified* in some appropriate way.

We should, however, note a certain complication. Suppose a person's morality opposes her doing a certain thing, such as telling a harmful lie. This fact is compatible with her morality's *not* being opposed to an act of that sort in its *total context*. For instance, a person may tell what is in fact a harmful lie but may do so because of nonculpable lack of information; or she might be acting under duress. So, there are excuses in morality, just as in criminal law:[9] The law may prohibit doing a certain thing, but the agent will not be punished if her illegal act was unintentional, done under duress, and so on. What I suggest is required for justified remorse or disapproval of others is an objectionable *act*: one we would be averse to initiating in the normal case (although there are complications if a person *intends* to perform such an act but fails through clumsiness, etc.) that *also* shows a *defective* level of intrinsic aversions on the agent's part, a defect

of the appraisal of an audience plays a causal role. What she suggests is true of a "shame culture" is that public esteem is thought the greatest good, so that loss of public respect leaves nothing of value to the individual (pp. 34–5). (One might add that the ashamed person wants to disappear from the public gaze, not to make amends, as when he feels remorse.) Bernard Williams has recently questioned whether the *Iliad* represents an essentially shame society. See footnote 27.

[9] See my "A utilitarian theory of excuses," *Philosophical Review* 78 (1969), 337–61; "Traits of character: a conceptual analysis," *American Philosophical Quarterly* 7 (1970), 23–37; and "A motivational theory of excuses in the criminal law," *Nomos* 27 (1985), 165–200. All are reprinted in *Morality, Utilitarianism and Rights* (Cambridge: Cambridge University Press, 1992).

of "character." When we ask, in prospect, whether a certain action would be wrong, I suggest that what we are asking is whether it *would* be wrong in the full-fledged sense – the object of disapproval by others and of the agent if she/they are well informed – if there were no *excuses*. It is true that we should probably have no *aversion* to doing something under specifically excusing circumstances, but when we are asking in advance what we ought to do – say, tell a hurtful lie – we are normally asking whether we have a justified aversion to doing something and would feel guilty for doing it, or would disapprove of others for doing it, assuming *no* excusing circumstance is present.[10]

There is another complication. A person will often have a moral objection to two kinds of conduct but, in a given case, the requirements for action are conflicting. Thus, one might have a moral aversion to telling a lie but also an aversion to harming another person. Suppose, then, that one can avoid harming another person only by telling a lie, and that the aversion not to injure in the relevant way is stronger than that not to lie. In this case, it is best to say that the person has a prima facie obligation not to do either but that, everything considered, his more pressing obligation is to avoid this kind of injury. One will say, then, that although he has a prima facie obligation not to lie, his real obligation in the *total* circumstances is not to cause the injury. This terminology was introduced by W. D. Ross[11] and marks a distinction that it is necessary to make.

Ross also pointed out a somewhat puzzling feature of our

---

[10] It is something of an oversimplification if we think that we always disapprove of conduct in others about which we ourselves should feel remorse. Some (earlier) studies have shown that some young people have (had) a strong moral aversion to premarital sex but are disinclined to criticize others for their sexual behavior. Is this possibly because they consider it an excuse that a person does what his own conscience permits him to do? This explanation would not apply to all areas of morality; if a person's conscience permits him to do some things, we think his conscience is defective, not that it is an excuse for what he does. If a person has an ambivalent attitude about sex, we might ask: Is a prohibition of unmarried sex a part of his morality or not? The right answer seems to be: In a sense it is, and in a sense it isn't.

[11] In *The Right and the Good* (Oxford: Oxford University Press, 1930).

morality: If there is a conflict of duties and the agent decides to perform the action more strongly obligatory, the moral requirement to perform the here avoided action is not just wiped out; we feel, in Ross's terms, "compunction" about having neglected the weaker requirement[12] – at least, often or even normally so. We can see why this might be so when we look shortly at the psychological sources of personal morality. For if, say, we learn an aversion to acting in a certain way or feel remorse if we do by conditioning (perhaps associating the breach of a rule with pangs of sympathy), there is no clear reason why this effect should be expunged in the context of a stronger rule that outweighs it. And perhaps it is a good thing that this is so, for the discomfort of failing to abide by the weaker obligation will prevent the obligation from being weakened in other situations. Somewhat the same may be said when a person does something she is clearly obligated not to do because of a mistake, duress, and so on. As has often been pointed out recently, if a motorist runs down a child through no fault of her own, she will feel more than just regret at the accident; rather, she will have a pained feeling of personal responsibility rather like remorse. This phenomenon seems to contrast with the view of both morality and the law that a person is culpable for an act only if it manifests a defect of character – of motivation. Why, then, should she feel quasi-remorse for doing something unintentionally that her moral code forbids, or why should she feel compunction at having done what was her overriding duty just because there was a weaker obligation she could not fulfill in the total context? What we can say is that clearly neither law nor morality should condemn a person for doing what was overridingly her duty, but the desirability of doing the other thing still manifests itself in the conscience of a considerate person.[13]

There is another element that should be added to the conception of a moral system (perhaps not included in the ordinary concept of "morality"), beyond the aversion, remorse, and dis-

---

12 Ibid., p. 28.
13 See Bernard Williams, *Moral Luck* [Cambridge: Cambridge University Press, 1981), pp. 27ff.

71

approval parts, and that is *admiration* or *praise* of acts the motivation of which is not required by the system – normally, acts that aim at enhancing someone's good and that would have been required except for the personal cost to the agent of performing them. For instance, a doctor decides to go to a plague-stricken area to treat patients at great personal risk. We might say that this element concerns "acts of supererogation" or "morally preferable" acts. It does not follow that these acts are *intrinsically good*.

This syndrome does not hold for the various nonmoral "social controls" mentioned. Except where the law embodies morally justified requirements, we feel only a minor aversion to breaking the law or disapproval of others who do. (But we may feel we should respect the law, and have some aversion to breaching it, just because it is the law.) The law may forbid smoking pot or committing suicide, but do we necessarily feel seriously guilty for so doing or condemn others who do just on that account? And if there is to be justification, it seems the justification must be moral – perhaps an appeal to some moral obligation to obey the law as such (see Chapter 9). Somewhat the same holds for matters of custom or etiquette. We may feel irritated if a man wears his hat in a restaurant or in church, but (unless he is deliberately trying to disparage the religion of others) we would hardly take him to task for this, and no one would claim that the rule is justified. And would we attempt a serious justification of the conventional view of who should pay for a wedding or disapprove of a couple who decided on some other arrangement? And as for codes of honor, we cannot take seriously the attitudes involved or the claim, which may be made, that they are socially beneficial.

So, morality seems to be a distinctive kind of social norm.

THE SOURCES OF MORALITY

Information from anthropology and sociobiology

We know next to nothing about the historical origins of morality in this sense. We can draw some inferences from what we know of evolutionary processes and the conditions of life among early humans – who lived in groups of perhaps a dozen and survived by gathering and hunting. There are cave drawings that show an interest in the supernatural and raise the possibility of a belief in supernatural sanctions for some kinds of conduct. What we do know is that the existence of these small groups was precarious and that lack of control of in-group violence would likely result in the disappearance of the group. *Possibly* the same is true for incest: The absence of the prohibition of incest *might*, over the long term, result in genetic defects, not to mention encouraging tension and conflict within the family. (There is another view, proposed by E. Westermarck, that very young children who have been housemates have no sexual interest in each other; there is a good deal of evidence for this view.)[14] Much the same holds for the rule of exogamy (marriage outside the group), for this fosters peaceful relations with neighboring groups and opens the possibility of communication of new ideas or techniques. Again, if mothers are not disposed to protect their children during their long period of dependency, obviously the group would die out very quickly. So something – perhaps some motivation developed in our remote ancestors – must move the mother to provide protection and care and to relieve manifest distress. How far will such evolutionary thinking take us?

A question about these matters is whether an evolutionary explanation of moral norms is to be understood as a biological/genetic process, determining which types of genes survive, these again fixing what behavior (or at least the tendency to behavior) is *native*, that is, unlearned. Or is it to be understood as encompassing cultural facts, in view of the fact that some cultural forms may be socially destructive, so that societies with certain defective cultures are eliminated? The latter might imply that the survival of the fittest is construed to mean that societies without a certain tradition (e.g., of teaching morality) will simply not survive. So, it might be that a tradition of condemnation

---

[14] See A. P. Wolf, "Westermarck redivivus," *Annual Review of Anthropology* 22 (1993), 157–75.

of in-group violence is necessary for a group and its successor groups to survive. On this view, negative reactions to in-group violence need not be native. Possibly the evolutionary process can operate at both biological and social levels.[15] Possibly. It is far from clear why attitudes of this and other sorts might not be native; if one's genes determine the color of one's eyes or one's susceptibility to a heart attack or colon cancer, why might they not bring about a tendency to avoid sex with others raised in close proximity or to care for one's offspring?[16]

Suppose it is held that some parts of morality are native, or at least are based on native dispositions, such as dispositions to empathy/sympathy. The nativist explanation, then, must face the fact that some individuals seem to be devoid of it. How? Could it be that some family strains lack the requisite genes? (There is some evidence that women are more sympathetic/empathic than men.)[17] Or may it be that some such tendency

[15] For a discussion of the relative role of biological evolution, with survival value affecting the frequency of genes with a tendency to produce organisms of a certain kind, and the relative role of cultural evolution, with socially adaptive features being transmitted by imitation and indoctrination, see Donald T. Campbell, "On the conflicts between biological and social evolution and between psychology and moral tradition," *American Psychologist* 30 (1975), 1103–26.

See also articles by Crawford, Noonan, and Krebs in C. Crawford, D. Krebs, and M. Smith (eds.), *Sociobiology and Psychology* (Hillsdale, N.J.: Erlbaum, 1987). See also Richard Alexander, *The Biology of Moral Systems* (Hawthorne, N.Y.: Aldine de Gruyter, 1987).

[16] See W. Arens, *The Original Sin: Incest and Its Meaning* (Oxford: Oxford University Press, 1986); Joseph Shepher, *Incest: A Biological View* (New York: Academic Press, 1983); and G. Stent (ed.), *Morality as a Biological Phenomenon* (Berkeley: University of California Press, 1980). See also N. W. Thornhill, "Evolutionary theory and rules of mating and marriage pertaining to relatives," in Crawford et al., *Sociobiology and Psychology.*

[17] See the Maccoby–Jacklin study showing that women are less aggressive and more empathic/sympathetic than men. This is reported by Diane N. Ruble in M. H. Bornstein and M. E. Lamb (eds.), *Developmental Psychology* (Hillsdale, N.J.: Erlbaum, 1984), p. 334.

But another survey of the literature points out that verbal reports do not distinguish between the sexes, and much the same is true for physiological responses to depicted situations. The suggestion is made that women are

is present in virtually all human beings, but that its development requires certain conditions and that other life situations, such as life in a ghetto, are countervailing?

It has been claimed by some not only that not even part of morality is *native*, but that some societies have no morality at all in the sense explained. For instance, Colin Turnbull, writing of the Ik,[18] said he saw no sign of love, willingness to sacrifice, affection, or loyalty. However, one must observe, in extenuation of the gruesome details he gives of many things (like mothers dropping a small baby while they gather food, not minding that the baby might be eaten by predators), that this group was in a state of utter starvation. And many items that he himself notes indicate the survival of at least some morality: that there is a custom of sharing with others; that children in gathering bands will eat their fill but share rather than hoard; that if a gift is accepted, one is bound to make some repayment (e.g., in services); that adultery is disapproved of, as is incest; that members of the same clan may not marry; and that there are sworn friends who have an obligation to help one another for the rest of their lives.

In contrast to such queries about the universality of morality as such, however, is the view of the anthropologist Meyer Fortes, who wrote of all observable peoples: "Every social system presupposes . . . basic moral axioms. They are implicit in the categories of values and of behavior which we sum up in concepts such as rights, duties, justice, amity, respect, wrong, sin. Such concepts occur in every known human society, though the kind of behaviour and the content of the values covered by them vary enormously."[19]

---

just better at decoding the internal states of others. See Nancy Eisenberg and Randy Lennon, "Sex differences in empathy and related capacities," *Psychological Bulletin* 94 (1983), 100–31.

[18] *The Mountain People* (New York: Simon and Schuster, 1972).

[19] *The Web of Kinship among the Tallensi* (London: Oxford University Press, 1949). See also Clyde Kluckhohn, "Ethical relativity: sic et non," *Journal of Philosophy* 52 (1955), 663–77. A. MacBeath, *Experiments in Living* (London: Macmillan, 1952), as a result of a survey of the anthropological literature, generalized that a society's "ways of life, which their institutions in their interrela-

This view gets some support from the similarity of very early reports of moral codes to present ones. As early as 3,000 B.C., some Egyptian inscriptions over the dead pharaohs contained appeals to a divine judge about the afterlife in terms that sound very familiar to modern morality: "I have committed no sin against people . . . I have not done evil in the place of truth . . . I did not report evil of a servant to his master. I allowed no one to hunger. I caused no one to weep. I did not murder. I did not command to murder. I caused no man misery . . . I did not commit adultery . . . I did not diminish the grain measure . . . I did not load the weight of the balances . . . I did not take milk from the mouth of the child."[20] And if we tentatively assign the basic ideas of the Ten Commandments to the time of Moses (the thirteenth century B.C.), we find: "Honor thy father and thy mother: that thy days may be long upon the land which the Lord thy God giveth thee. Thou shalt not kill. Thou shalt not commit adultery. Thou shalt not steal. Thou shalt not bear false witness against thy neighbour. Thou shalt not covet they neighbor's house, thou shalt not covet they neighbor's wife, nor his manservant, nor his maidservant, nor his ox, nor his ass, nor any thing that is thy neighbor's."[21] And in the Psalms[22] we

tion constitute, explain and justify both the rules and the exceptions to them which different peoples regard as right" (p. 100). "The rightness of the rules themselves . . . , the ways in which they are construed, the exceptions to them which are regarded as justified, and the relative order of urgency which is assigned to them, are explicable by, and derive their authority from, the way of life of the people concerned" (p. 370). "[The rules] are regarded as obligatory because, in view of the beliefs these people entertain, the rules seem to them to be conditions of a way of life which they regard as good" (p. 376). I believe we may suppose that MacBeath construes these "rules" as covering the various concepts listed by Fortes.

[20] James Breasted, *The Dawn of Conscience* (New York: Scribner, 1933), pp. 255–6.

[21] Exodus 20:3–17. The last of these commandments sounds rather ridiculous if we translate "covet" as "desire eagerly." Is it possible not to be a bit envious of another's possessions, and is there any harm in it, except perhaps to one's own peace of mind? Of course, to covet to the extent of being inclined to seize is a different matter. See Deuteronomy 5:7–21.

[22] Psalms 15:1–5.

read: "He . . . who speaks truth from his heart; who does not slander with his tongue, and does no evil to his friends nor takes up reproach against his neighbor; . . . who swears to his own hurt and does not change; who does not put out his money at interest, and does not take a bribe against the innocent. He who does these things shall never be moved." Not all the laws were humanitarian – for example, the religious requirements to observe the Sabbath day and not to worship any god but Yahweh and the "eye for an eye" thesis (Exodus 21:23),[23] and the death penalty for various sexual offenses, including bestiality. When the Israelites fought with the Amalekites, we are told that the Lord commanded them, through his prophet Samuel, to slay all men, women, children, and cattle, and that they were rebuked by the prophet, who deplored the saving of cattle and of the Amalekite king, whose head he unceremoniously sliced off himself.[24] Judges 11, 29–40, reports that Jephthah sacrificed his daughter as a burnt offering to Yahweh for victory over the Ammonites.

Here we find several humanitarian themes: (1) not to do violence (except in war), but on the contrary to be kind, especially to children and the poor; (2) not to engage in usury; (3) to be truthful, and especially not to lie in a court proceeding; (4) to be honest about property – no theft and no use of dishonest measures; (5) to avoid adultery; and (6) to respect and cherish one's father and mother.

One question to consider is whether most of these forms of moral prohibition arise because of innate empathic/sympathetic attitudes.[25] It has been suggested that the Israelites did not

---

[23] This is deliberately excluded in Hittite law. See H. W. F. Saggs, *Civilization before Greece and Rome* (New Haven, Conn.: Yale University Press, 1989), p. 167.

[24] I Samuel, chap. 15.

[25] Does the trait of being empathic (or sympathetic) correlate with actual altruistic behavior? Studies show only a low correlation (.10 to .39), although there is reason to think that the actual correlation is higher. See Nancy Eisenberg and Paul Miller, "The relation of empathy to pro-social and related behaviors," *Psychological Bulletin* 101 (1987), 91–119.

practice morality in our present sense but instead had only a concept of God's law and fear of divine sanctions.[26]

The earliest report of Greek morality (around the tenth century B.C.) is found in the works of Homer. There is controversy about what morality for them amounted to; it seems possible that for warriors like Achilles, remorse/indignation was replaced by shame/disdain, and that behavior was primarily motivated by an interest in preserving one's reputation. Morality, as depicted by Homer, expresses the attitudes of warrior chieftains; the *main* requirements are (1) courage, acting so as to have a good reputation (fame); (2) protection of guests and suppliants; (3) loyalty to one's friends and relatives (*philoi*); (4) not displaying arrogance or demands beyond one's due (*hubris*); (5) telling the truth and respecting agreements, including the marriage vow (the adultery of Paris and Helen being condemned even by Hector); (6) returning favors; and (7) self-control in the sense of acting wisely in view of the probable consequences for oneself. The highest words of praise are reserved for the competitive virtues. *But* Hector was rebuked for not revering the corpse of Sarpedon and Aeneas for not defending his brother-in-law; Nestor rebuked Agamemnon for ignoring the army's decision to give Briseis to Achilles as a prize; Achilles was con-

---

[26] By Reinhold Niebuhr in conversation. We may note the large literature regarding the various forms of the Law in Exodus, Leviticus, and Deuteronomy. I am assuming that since obviously no God appeared to Moses to give commandments, these various writers were expressing their own morality, as explained earlier, and therefore we are free to use psychological explanations of what was going on. Many of the commandments, however, involve theological beliefs and requirements of respect for and worship of Yahweh. (For a survey of some of the literature, see Michael Walzer, "The legal codes of ancient Israel," *The Rule of Law, Nomos* 36, 1994), 101–9.

Peter Railton has suggested that "moral evaluation has begun to emerge as a distinctive category of assessment [as compared with etiquette or prudence] only in the last century or so." I doubt this. Why should we not think these (and other early) writers were not expressing their morality in my explained sense? See Railton's chapter in John Haldane and Crispin Wright, *Reality, Representation, and Projection* (New York: Oxford University Press, 1993), p. 282. See also p. 319.

demned for treating Hector's body as he did; and Eumaeus the peasant was praised as "noble" for preventing his dog from attacking the disguised Ulysses. The real sanction for behavior of these more humane sorts was apparently not suppositions about the attitudes of the gods, but primarily the respect of common people. So, early Greek morality not only praised competitive virtues but also made certain demands, including the defense of the unprotected.[27]

In the writings of Hesiod (about the eighth century B.C.) we get a fuller picture of the morality of the ordinary (nonmilitary) Greeks. Here there are added condemnations of (9) violence, (10) susceptibility to bribes and crooked dealing, and (11) being unkind to fatherless children or to an aged father.[28]

If we sum up all the foregoing, we get requirements (1) to do no violence (except in war) and to be kind to the poor, children, the hungry, and especially suppliants and guests (in Greece); (2) to be honest in property dealings: not to steal, break contracts, or cheat by using false measures; (3) to speak the truth, especially when much turns on it (in a court proceeding); (4) to show respect and kindness for aged parents; and (5) not to commit adultery (or incest?). The Greeks would perhaps add (6) courage and doing what will secure one's future good reputation, (7) returning favors, and (8) self-control based on reflection on what will promote one's own long-term good – although these may have been viewed as more prudential than matters of morality in our present sense. At least the first four of these might

---

27 See Michael Gagarin, "Morality in Homer," *Classical Philology* 82 (1987), 287–306, and the reply by A. W. H. Adkins, "Gagarin and the 'Morality' of Homer," ibid., 311–22. See also A. A. Long, "Morals and values in Homer," *Journal of Hellenic Studies* 90 (1970), 121–39, and especially Bernard Williams, *Shame and Necessity* (Berkeley: University of California Press, 1993), chap. 4.

28 I am indebted to Gailann Rickert for guidance and advice about early Greek ethics.

For another view that discloses the similarity of widespread popular moral views of a slightly later date to our contemporary attitudes, see K. J. Dover, *Greek Popular Morality in the Time of Plato and Aristotle* (Indianapolis: Hackett, 1994).

be explained by native empathy/sympathy, and so far there is support for the view that empathy/sympathy is a psychological basis of many moral norms.

Most of these requirements seem to have worldwide respect even today.

In a monumental work, Edward Westermarck[29] described an enormous number of differences among cultures about homicide (especially the killing of parents, children, the sick, women, fetuses, and slaves), blood revenge, dueling, charity, hospitality, the subjection of wives, slavery, property, regard for truth and good faith, altruism, suicide, diet, cleanliness, marriage, celibacy, adultery, regard for animals, and cannibalism. Westermarck thought that many of these variations were a result of differences in external conditions: hardship, necessity, economic circumstances (relating to slavery and the treatment of laborers) or the proportion of men to women (related to forms of marriage). He hardly touches, however, on an important question: how far all these variations (some of them exceptions to normal rules, others concerning the relative order of weight) can be traced to differences in the *conception* of the act in question.

The psychologist Karl Duncker[30] (along with Solomon Asch[31]) contended that such variations are only apparent: that when we hold fixed the "meaning" of an action for a person, the moral appraisal is uniformly roughly the same. For instance, he affirmed that whereas charging interest was prohibited in the Middle Ages but is take for granted today, in the Middle Ages loans were mostly used for personal consumption, whereas today they are mostly used for investment. (One might wonder about the high interest rates on credit card purchases!) In general, we might consider the possibility that if one person shared the understanding of another about the nature of an action, the two would agree morally. This question has considerable importance, for if the thesis is correct, then all moral disputes can be

29 *The Origin and Development of the Moral Ideas* (London: Macmillan, 1906).
30 "Ethical Relativity?" *Mind*, (1939).
31 *Social Psychology* (Englewood Cliffs, N.J.: Prentice-Hall, 1952), chaps. 11–14.

resolved, in principle, by science and conceptual clarity, that is, by ascertaining the correct description of some projected action.

It is not easy to be certain whether the Duncker thesis is true or false. The anthropologist Clyde Kluckhohn once urged that we simply do not have the information to be sure. However, the thesis is difficult to believe. For instance, there seems to be widespread disagreement about the treatment of animals. In some parts of Latin America, a chicken is (was) plucked before it is killed on the theory that this makes it a more succulent dish. Again, Hopi children are sometimes allowed to do as they please with captured birds; with a string tied to their legs, they are played with, their legs broken, their wings pulled off. The writer inquired into the Hopi view about the mental life of animals and found that they viewed them, if anything, as more like human beings than would philosophers. Is this case not a counterexample to the Duncker thesis? Indeed, we need not go so far afield: Hunters, trappers, and fishermen among ourselves are not known to minimize the pain of those they kill. Is it possible that there are also such basic disagreements today on the morality of abortion, euthanasia, and the killing of severely defective neonates?

Relevant to an appraisal of the absolutism of the Duncker thesis is what is known about the processes that apparently influence the moral values standard among groups. For instance, the anthropologist G. P. Murdoch[32] suggested that the psychological principle of stimulus generalization explains how an incest prohibition for the *nuclear* family may generalize to persons socially most like these; for example, where the mother's sister's children have the same social relation as one's own siblings (e.g., are called "sister" and "brother," live in the same house or in proximity), the prohibition is apt to extend to them. Not necessarily, but often.

Again, when two cultures are (more or less) in contact, one culture may change its standards as a result of knowing about the standards of the other. The history of successful missions is

[32] "The common denominator of cultures," in R. Linton (ed.), *The Science of Man in the World Crisis* (New York: Columbia University Press, 1945).

a case in point. When and why does this occur?[33] A change is more likely to be accepted if it fits in with other standards already accepted. Further, prestige seems to play a role: The white civilization may have the reputation of being more civilized or more successful, so that a receptive attitude is fostered.[34] This process is accelerated if some prestigious figure (e.g., a chief) is baptized and accepts Christian values. Again, H. G. Barnett[35] has shown that the process may be accelerated if some individuals in the recipient group are frustrated and motivated to identify with another group. The anthropologist E. Z. Vogt[36] studied the values of Navaho veterans. He found that the following factors tended to affect receptivity to white values: the extent of connection with older and more conservative relatives, the orientation of one's father, the extent of contact with the white world and its friendliness toward Indians, and whether a traditional belief has utility in resolving psychological problems (e.g., the belief in witchcraft).

Other changes, however, are the result of internal dynamics. Note, for instance, the effects of the resistance of blacks to racial discrimination, resulting in altered laws and marked modification of public attitudes. Similarly for the introduction of the contraceptive pill, which fostered an increase in sexual activity that doubtless resulted in a corresponding change in moral standards. When a new situation motivates behavior in conflict with accepted norms – for example, more sex – and if this happens often enough, the norm is modified. As Llewellyn and Hoebel put it:[37] "What comes to be in the way of practice produces in due course its flavor of felt rightness. . . . This takes no planning, no preaching, no thinking; it just happens. Change of

---

[33] See S. E. Keefe in A. M. Padilla, *Acculturation: Theory, Models, and Some New Findings* (Boulder, Colo.: Westview Press, 1980), p. 86.

[34] See J. W. Berry in Padilla, *Acculturation*, pp. 10f. and 49ff.

[35] "Personal conflicts and culture change," *Social Forces* 20, 160–71.

[36] "Navaho veterans: a study of changing values," *Papers of the Peabody Museum of American Archaeology and Ethnology* (Cambridge, Mass.: Harvard University, The Museum), 41 (1951), no. 1.

[37] E. A. Hoebel and K. N. Llewellyn, *The Cheyenne Way* (New Haven, Conn.: Yale University Press, 1941).

practice changes the base line of standard."[38] The introduction of money into Africa resulted not only in widespread interest in monetary gain, but also in changes in the institution of marriage.[39] The appearance of domesticated reindeer among the Asian Chukchi resulted (possibly because of increased wealth) in the adoption of polygyny among reindeer-breeding groups and abatement of the practice of killing the aged.

Most of these facts seem to be contrary to the Duncker–Asch thesis that where the conception of an action is the same, there will be identical moral appraisal. For they, in most cases, exemplify a change in moral norms in a society without any change in the *conception* of the behavior. Surely the process of stimulus generalization, the mere frequency of transgression, contact with another group, especially a prestigious one, and the economic feasibility of contrary behavior hardly count as changes in the *conception* of once prohibited behavior, except perhaps in a very broad sense of "conception."

Information from individual psychology

Let us now turn to what is known about the acquisition of a morality by individuals: the development of intrinsic aversions to acting in certain ways; reactions to one's own transgressions by remorse, guilt, or shame; and the response to transgressions of others by anger, contempt, disgust, and so on. Some anthropologists call this part of "enculturation." We should state at the outset that psychologists may not all agree with the preceding descriptions of what it is for a person to have a certain morality.

[38] Could this be the explanation of standards on the "duties" of friends? First, people somehow, after a significant amount of interaction, form attachments to one another. They perform services for each other, e.g., visit one another in the hospital. Gradually, each comes to expect certain sorts of behavior from the other. Other people become aware of this, and then come to view such behavior as standard and speak of the "duties" of friendship.

[39] See R. Thurnwald, "The psychology of acculturation," *American Anthropologist* 34 (1932), 557–69.

A child's earliest educational contact in life is with his parents (and siblings). From their encouragement or punishment the child first learns what he may or may not do, whether not to play in the street or not to hit his baby sister. Since there is not much that very young children can do that is strongly objectionable, encouragement/mild punishment will normally have the desired effect. Slightly older children acquire simple rules or standards. How can parental praise and punishment have this effect? Partly by conditioning, but one's view of how this works depends on one's predilection for a particular type of psychological theory. According to one theory, praise for an act arouses positive feelings that become associated with the act and involve the motivation to repeat acts like it, whereas with punishment, negative feelings are associated with an act and tend to prevent its recurrence. Or we could just say that praise "positively reinforces" an act and punishment "negatively reinforces" it. Any kind of reinforcement is apt to be more successful in the presence of explanations (e.g., that one should not play in the street because one might be hit by a car or do a certain thing because it is likely to injure others). The verbalization is likely to teach the child a rule – not merely avoiding one behavior, but avoiding a whole category of behaviors that the rule formulates. Punishment is most effective if it occurs soon after the behavior to be avoided. A special form of punishment is a parent's withholding of love if the child acts in a forbidden way. Punishment seems to be at least part of the source of guilt feelings about misbehavior; guilt feelings may be partly a psychological residue of anxiety about the pain of punishment, even at a later stage when the likelihood of punishment is very small – but, as noted earlier, we shall see that there is another theory about the source of guilt feelings.[40] Also important are rela-

---

[40] For a survey of the evidence on the effects of reward/punishment, see P. H. Mussen, J. J. Conger, Jerome Kagan, and Aletha Huston, *Child Development and Personality*, 6th ed. (New York: Harper & Row, 1984), especially pp. 174–5, 388–94.

tions of fairness and love between parents and child and parents' willingness to listen[41] to the child.

This kind of "conditioning," or shaping of behavior, is sometimes regarded as less important for the development of a child's standards than is imitation. Children tend to imitate especially parental behavior. The imitation may involve not only specific actions (the mother picking up a telephone) but also more general traits of behavior, idiosyncrasies, motives, attitudes, and values. All this, of course, may be gratifying to the parents, who reward the child for it.

This process is emphasized by "social learning theory," which stresses the importance of observation of "models" of all kinds (not just parents), whose behavior and verbalization can make various morally relevant features of situations salient, express morally different weights of various factors in a situation, and present justifications for these weightings. Modeling is provided not just by individuals but also by the mass media, especially television.[42]

The term "identification" is often used to refer to generalized imitation of admired persons such as parents, with whom there is also a strong affective bond. Identification is the motivation to be like (and being pleased if one succeeds in being like) the individual with whom one identifies. In the case of children, the prime object of identification is a parent, usually the parent of the same sex. (It may also be a teacher or some other person the child comes to admire.) And the scope of "being like" can be the totality of the figure's attributes, including his system of motivation and values.

---

[41] See Thomas Likona, "Parents as moral educators," in M. Berkowitz and F. Oser, *Moral Education: Theory and Applications* (Hillsdale, N.J.: Erlbaum, 1985), chap. 5.

[42] See Albert Bandura, "Social cognitive theory of moral thought and action," in W. M. Kurtines and J. L. Gewirtz (eds.), *Moral Behavior and Development: Advances in Theory, Research and Applications* (Hillsdale, N.J.: Erlbaum, 1988), vol. 1. Also see Martin Hoffman, "Moral development," in M. H. Bornstein and M. E. Lamb, *Developmental Psychology: An Advanced Textbook* (Hillsdale, N.J.: Erlbaum, 1984), pp. 297ff.

What is the reason for this motivation to be like the admired figure? Various suggestions have been made. One is that the child desires strength and competence and thinks she attains these by becoming like the parent (or other object) in all respects, including values. Another suggestion is that a child tends to be anxious in the absence of a nurturant parent, and then finds she can make herself feel better by behaving like the parent, thus becoming a kind of parent substitute, which reduces her anxiety. She succeeds most fully the more she acts like the parent, including taking over the parent's value system. If her behavior does not conform to the parent's values, she will feel guilty and anxious. The process obtains only if the child sees some similarity between herself and the object of identification, who must also possess attractive features: being nurturant, warm, loving, or competent.[43] The concept of identification originated with Freud, who wrote: "The role, which the super-ego undertakes later in life, is at first played by an external power, by parental authority. The influence of the parents dominates the child by granting proofs of affection and by threats of punishment, which, to the child, mean loss of love, and which must also be feared on that account. This objective anxiety is the forerunner of the later moral anxiety; so long as the former is dominant one need not speak of super-ego or of conscience. It is only later that the secondary situation takes the place of the parental function, and thenceforward observes, guides, and threatens the ego in just the same way as the parents acted to the child before. . . . The basis of the process is what we call an identification, that is to say, that one ego becomes like another . . . ; it imitates it, and as it were takes it into

---

[43] A useful survey of how these processes work, and of the evidence for them, can be found in Mussen et al., *Child Development*, especially pp. 391ff. For a critical experimental study, see M. L. Hoffman, "Identification and conscience development," *Child Development* 42 (1971), 1071–82. See also Ervin Staub, *Positive Social Behavior and Morality* (New York: Academic Press, 1979), vol. II, pp. 23–34. Other important factors are parents' fairness and love and their willingness to listen to the child. See Thomas Likona, "Rewards as moral education," in Berkowitz and Oser, *Moral Education*, chap. 5.

itself. This identification has not been inappropriately compared with the oral cannibalistic incorporation of another person."[44]

There is reason, however, to think that marked *changes* in moral standards within a short period of time must be explained not by identification with or punishment by parents, since changes can occur fairly rapidly, much more rapidly than can be explained by exposure to the moral standards especially of an earlier generation – that of the parents. It seems as if we must allow wide influence by institutions like education, interaction in institutions that presume responsible role taking by participants, the mass media, and court decisions, with the result that a child's standards at a given time may be an amalgam with diverse sources.[45] For instance, college students are apt to change their opinions on social and moral issues when they learn that these are espoused by prestigious persons in their environment. In a famous study of Bennington College students some years ago, it was found that students rapidly changed their views in the direction of liberalism, a view they attributed both to the faculty and to the majority of students. It was found that receptivity to this change depended on the student's success in college, the absence of strong family ties favoring clinging to traditional values, motivation to achieve a position in the college community, and intellectual energy (incidentally, not what they had learned in classes).[46] A retest 20 years later showed these new attitudes still to be firm. It does not follow, however, that a student can be moved to approve of murder, dishonesty, or anything the social undesirability of which is obvious. The issues about which (liberalism) the Bennington students were queried were complex, and it was not

[44] S. Freud, *New Introductory Lectures on Psycho-analysis* (New York: W. W. Norton, 1933), pp. 89–90.

[45] Bandura, "Social cognitive theory."

[46] T. M. Newcomb, *Personality and Social Change* (New York: Dryden Press, 1943); T. M. Newcomb, L. E. Koenig, and C. Morris, *Persistence and Change: Bennington College and Its Students after Twenty-Five Years* (New York: Wiley, 1969).

shown that opinions can be moved contrary to basic moral standards with equal facility.

Some psychologists believe that punishment and withholding love, imitation, and identification with admired figures, and even empathy/sympathy, are not the whole explanation of the development of a child's moral thinking. They have claimed to find a natural progression from the earliest to later stages of moral experience/thought. Thus Piaget[47] and Kohlberg[48] hypothesized stages of development. Piaget said that from the beginning, when parental dicta are received as universally binding laws, there follows a stage in which children pay attention to the consequences of actions of a certain type and to matters like intention and equity, forming their own opinions, which may be quite different from those of their parents. Kohlberg postulated six stages. Each also thought that a person cannot attain one of the higher stages unless he has already gone through the lower stages. Kohlberg's view was that a child progresses through the following stages: (1) "moral" behavior is just a matter of being guided by expectations of unpleasant consequences for him, such as punishment; (2) acting so as to gratify his own needs (and sometimes also that of others); (3) doing what pleases others and is approved by them (having good motives, showing concern for others, loyalty, etc.), taking intentions into account; (4) being morally motivated to follow the law, defer to authority, meet well-defined obligations, and support societal institutions by not doing what it would be bad for everyone to do; (5) being moved by the idea of contractual commitment to laws and institutions identified by their contri-

---

[47] Jean Piaget, *The Moral Judgment of the Child* (Glencoe, Ill.: Free Press, 1948).
[48] Lawrence Kohlberg, "Stage and sequence: the cognitive-developmental approach to socialization," in A. Goslin (ed.), *Handbook of Socialization Theory* (Chicago: Rand McNally, 1969); "From is to ought" in Theodore Mischel (ed.), *Cognitive Development and Epistemology* (New York: Academic Press, 1971), pp. 151–235; "Stages of moral development as a basis for moral education," in C. M. Beck, B. S. Crittenden, and E. Y. Sullivan (eds.), *Moral Education: Interdisciplinary Approaches* (Toronto: University of Toronto Press, 1971); "Moral stages and moralization," in T. Likona (ed.), *Moral Development and Behavior* (New York: Holt, Rinehart & Winston, 1976).

bution to the general utility, with rights like life and liberty deserving adherence in every society and espoused after following agreed-upon democratic procedures; (6) viewing morality in terms of the individual conscience, based on recognition of universal abstract principles respecting the equality of human rights and the dignity of individuals, as in the theories of Kant and Rawls.[49]

There is, however, only modest empirical support for the allegedly necessary sequence of Kohlberg's stages. In fact, the stages are so loosely defined that it is hard to see how they can be described as an empirical psychological *theory* at all. The theory was based on an initial study of 75 boys, beginning at ages 10–16, at 3-year intervals up to ages 22–28, ascertaining their replies to questions such as whether it is right for a man to steal a drug from a druggist who has grossly overpriced it in order to save the life of his wife. Some of the descriptions of allegedly typical stages seem to coincide with observations of young people, but it is clear from Kohlberg's data that persons sometimes regress from a higher stage to a lower one; and many persons score differently on various items in the test.[50] However, evidence from cross-cultural surveys suggests that an order of roughly this sort is present in different moralities around the world.[51] Actually, much of the discussion of the later stages is really a philosophical argument about what kinds of reflections could amount to a reasonable moral system. Moreover, although some psychologists think that there truly is some kind of cognitive development of standards corresponding to the cognitive maturation of the child, the *motivation* to follow such standards may depend in part on earlier warmth

---

[49] See the summaries by Bandura, "Social cognitive theory," and Hoffman, "Moral development."

[50] J. R. Rest, "Patterns of preference and comprehension in moral judgment," *Journal of Personality* 41 (1973), 86–109; "Longitudinal study of the defining issues test of moral judgment: a strategy for analyzing developmental change," *Developmental Psychology* 11 (1975), 738–48.

[51] John R. Snarey, "Cross-cultural universality of social–moral development: a critical review of Kohlbergian research," *Psychological Bulletin* 97 (1985), 202–32.

and love of parents and identification with them, as well as guilt (perhaps anxiety related to the pain of punishment of transgressions, such as loss of love or anxiety about its possibility) resulting from failure to conform to their standards in some way. If so, the stage theory does not tell us all, or very much, about morality. There are also serious questions about the mechanism that is supposed to bring about acceptance of a later stage. I propose to leave this "theory" at that and consider what would be a reasonable form of morality later in this book.[52]

There is another line of thinking about the development of morality that has received a good deal of recent attention, although parts of it go back as far as David Hume and Francis Hutcheson. This concerns the source of morality in empathy/sympathy and has been developed by Martin Hoffman, primarily on the basis of observation of young children.[53] He uses "empathy" to refer not primarily to awareness of the feelings of others (e.g., grief, joy, fear) and the production of feelings matching these emotions, but rather to an affective reaction, particularly distress, *appropriate* to the situation of another – not just mimicking the emotion the target expresses, facially or otherwise. As suggested earlier, Hoffman believes that empathy/sympathy for the distress of another is a native disposition, probably a result of the process of evolution, because when the disposition is directed toward relatives (normally those in the vicinity, in groups in very early times), the helpful-

---

[52] For some general evaluations, see the first half of Bandura, "Social cognitive theory"; R. S. Peters, "The place of Kohlberg's theory in moral education," lecture at the University of Leicester, August 1977; R. E. Carter, "What is Lawrence Kohlberg doing?" *Journal of Moral Education* 9 (1980), 88–102; W. P. Alston, "Moral attitudes and moral judgments," *Nous* 2 (1968), 1–23; Staub, *Positive Social Behavior*, pp. 38–57.

[53] See Martin Hoffman's writings, including his "Development of prosocial motivation: empathy and guilt," in N. Eisenberg (ed.), *The Development of Prosocial Behavior* (New York: Academic Press, 1982), pp. 998–1212; "Is altruism part of human nature?" *Journal of Personality and Social Psychology* 40 (1982), 121–37; "Conscience, personality and socialization techniques," *Human Development* 13 (1970); "Moral development"; and "Empathy and justice in society." See also J. A. Piliavin and H. W. Charng, "Altruism: a review of recent theory and research," *Annual Review of Sociology* 16 (1990), 27–65.

ness to the targets reproduces genes like those of the agent (which were the cause of the disposition), the disposition thereby being selected by the process of survival of the fittest. On this view, the disposition to have sympathy for others in distress is native. (There is another possible – but less likely – source of empathic distress: that infants experience distress at the crying of others, shown by the fact that in a nursery, if one child cries, all the others chime in – a disposition possibly learned by conditioning from the association of the infant's own distress with hearing itself cry. This tendency is evident among adults, who may feel sad when they hear someone crying. This disposition, however, is learned, not native.) According to Hoffman, the features of empathic/sympathetic distress vary, depending on the cognitive development of the child. At first, the response is a kind of global distress; the child responds as if the hurt of others were his own, running to his mother if someone else is hurt. At a later stage, the child becomes aware that it is someone else, not himself who is in trouble, so that the empathic response is on a higher level, and the child will do what he thinks will alleviate the distress of the other. Thus, we may use "sympathy" to refer to empathic distress plus the tendency to help remove the condition of its source and to be pleased by its removal – but not just to remove one's own empathic distress (although a tendency to do this may be involved). At a later stage of development, the child can respond to the feelings of others based on awareness of a range of their internal lives, of their needs and expectations (e.g., anxieties). Later still, the child becomes aware of the fact of others as continuing people with separate histories and identities, and he experiences emotional reactions not just to some immediate event but to the larger life experience of the other, like a child playing happily but having cancer or no prospect for escape from poverty. Girls, incidentally, appear to be more empathic than boys, although this may not be native but a result of different experiences and ordinary processes of reinforcement and modeling.[54]

---

[54] See Diane N. Ruble, "Sex role development," in Bornstein and Lamb (eds.), *Developmental Psychology*, pp. 345ff. For a contrary investigation, see footnote 18.

These responses are not merely emotional but motivational, to give help, and not just to relieve personal empathetic distress, although both motives may be present.[55] Further, according to Hoffman, if one knows that some other person was the cause of still another person's distress, anger at the agent may be aroused (unless one learns that the agent had previously been harmed by the patient or there are other considerations). If one attributes the distress of another to one's own action, there will be a combination of empathic distress and a negative attitude to oneself (guilt or remorse) as being the responsible agent.[56] If these causal connections between empathy and anger at others who are sources of distress are as Hoffman represents them, there is a partial explanation of the practices of punishing and blaming, in addition to the fact that such practices presumably have beneficial effects in strengthening the motivation not to harm others – a utilitarian account justifying punishment and blame when an agent's motivations are deficient in morality.

This general theory developed by Hoffman has been criticized, for example, by Dennis Krebs.[57]

According to Hoffman, research shows that the most successful form of adult teaching of specific moral norms is by "induction," that is, by pointing out the normally harmful effects, on self or especially others, of various forms of behavior (e.g., telling lies, breaking promises, or treating people un-

---

[55] Mussen et al., *Child Development*, pp. 169–70, 311–13, 360–2.

[56] Hoffman, "Empathy and justice in society."

[57] In "The challenge of altruism in biology and psychology," in Crawford et al., *Sociobiology and Psychology*, pp. 81–118. He questions whether the sympathetic behavior is really altruistic; it may really be aimed at reducing the discomfort of the *agent*. Moreover, he suggests that the disposition might be learned by interaction with the mother. Krebs agrees that empathy/sympathy is probably heritable (and, if so, is presumably native). He also agrees that such helping may be "irrational" and "impulsive" – say, to risk one's life to save another person who is known not to be related. Research also suggests, he thinks, that perception of similarity is involved, so there is a greater disposition to help members of the same ethnic group.

I think we have to view the Hoffman theory as fairly well supported by observation.

equally). So, "moral rules," on the empathy account, turn out to be the requirements for forms of behavior that would result from applying the principle of sympathy to various types of behavior.[58] The effectiveness of appeals to empathy seems to increase with age.[59] On this view, practice in role playing, that is, putting oneself in the place of another, should foster moral development.

It is obvious, as Hume noted, that empathic reactions are more pronounced if the victims are familiar or similar to the observer, or if the distress is nearby rather than occurring elsewhere (in space or time) and directly observed rather than just heard about. It seems consistent with the general theory to suppose that if several persons are involved (e.g., both agent and patient), one may empathize multiply, with vivid enough images to produce sympathetic responses to each. Presumably full-blown awareness would involve sympathizing with the situation of everyone involved, resulting in some holistic reaction, as Adam Smith insisted.

This conception of moral norms and guilt feelings (plus disapproval of those who breach the norms) fits closely with the conception of what a person's "morality" comes to be, as explained earlier in this chapter, although we shall see that other processes also play a role.

Empathy/sympathy, however, does not necessarily explain action motivated by a sense of justice (e.g., giving a student the grade she earns rather than giving her a high mark out of sympathy). In issues of this sort, wider reflection seems called for – for example, about the incentive effects of a system in which rewards are allocated according to accomplishment.

Of course, empathy/sympathy cannot explain various fea-

---

[58] Some recent neurological evidence presented by Drs. Antonio Damasio and Hanna Damasio may support the view that morality derives from a segment of the brain involved in social decision making and emotional experiences. The ideas that empathic reactions are native and feed into the development of morality would fit this concept very well. *New York Times*, May 24, 1994, pp. B5, B8.

[59] J. C. LaVoie, "Type of punishment as a determinant of resistance to deviation," *Developmental Psychology* 10 (1974), 181–9.

tures of traditional moral codes: the objection to incest or besti-ality, the requirement of marriage outside the group, the require-ments of property morality/law, the objection to suicide, and respect for the dead. Thus, it seems that some parts of morality must be acquired in some way, as reviewed earlier, different from the "inductive" application of empathy/sympathy. But native empathy appears to play a large part in the explanation of normal moral experience.

The system of personal morality can be very complex, per-haps as complex as language. W. D. Ross identified only seven moral principles of duty as self-evident, but he allowed a much larger number of "intuitions," partly about the relative strength of moral claims. The Ten Commandments are far too simple as a summary of serious morality, as is the injunction to "Love thy neighbor as thyself." When we think of the scope of our atti-tudes about harming others, truth speaking, breach of promise, euthanasia, abortion, the treatment of severely defective new-borns, charity, the treatment of women or other races, property and the just distribution of income, adultery, respect for the dead, and cannibalism, we become aware of a vast number of aversions, but with various exceptions allowed and quite differ-ent in degree of strength. But all of these involve restrictions of behavior (aversions) and sanctions for misbehavior (guilt and disapproval of others).

If we try to enumerate such "rules" of morality, however complex, we shall fall short of the actual complications. For, as noted earlier, simple rules may conflict; for example, the obliga-tion to keep promises may conflict with the obligation not to harm another person. What are we then to do? What we seem to do is follow our stronger feelings or, as we shall see, possibly follow the rule that seems socially more important. We can say a few things in general, such as that the obligation not to kill another person is weightier than any other obligation. More-over, the various rules must be construed as having various exceptions attached; for example, we ought to keep our prom-ises, but how about a promise made on the basis of a gross misrepresentation by the promisee? And how about novel situ-ations, such as being faced with the problem of whether, when

94

shipwrecked and unlikely to be rescued immediately, one person may be killed and eaten to ensure the survival of the others? And what do we do if we come to think that some well-learned rule is defective and needs to be altered? It seems as if some general philosophical *normative theory* of morality is needed in order to respond to such cases.

How can the psychological framework of learning, discussed earlier, explain all of this learning? Some of the distinctions noted previously – the exceptions, the ordering of rules in terms of strength, and the distinction between a wrong act and a blameworthy agent – may be in the parent's (or other model's) mental framework and may be passed on as the child observes individual cases and what is said about them. Or perhaps, when faced with a particular situation, the prospective agent's/observer's native empathic attitudes somehow combine to produce a holistic response. But irrespective of how all this is learned, what is needed is a systematic moral philosophy that explains the necessity of the distinctions and justifies them. In this, preceding remarks are only a beginning.

Chapter 4

The justification of moral statements

When people talk about the moral status of actions or types of action, they obviously do not *say*, "My moral system is opposed to (or favors) *this* (or this kind of) action, everything considered." They *say* things like "It would be morally wrong to" or "You have a moral obligation to" or "That action was morally wrong (or blameworthy)." Much the same effect can be achieved by a statement descriptive of an action or its motivation, for instance by saying that an act was cruel, deceptive, unsympathetic, insensitive, and so on, here describing the act/motivation more specifically but with the implication, since it is generally believed that these kinds of action/motivation are wrong/blameworthy (and these words would hardly be used unless the speaker thought so), that the particular action was wrong or blameworthy. These latter terms are sometimes called "thick moral terms," since they describe the action (or motivation) in a certain way while at the same time, partly by implication, expressing an unfavorable moral appraisal, just as if one had added "That was wrong" – although "was wrong" is called a "thin moral term," since it does not imply any description of the action/motivation. (Not everyone would agree with this characterization.)

What is the relation of statements like these to the moral aversions (etc.) described in the preceding chapter? One an-

96

swer, which I shall accept but with some additions, is that moral statements are somehow *expressive* of these aversions.[1] In what sense of "expressive"? This is not a matter of agreement, but I think the most plausible suggestion is that moral statements such as "*A* is wrong" are *expressive* in the sense that normal speakers of the language, on hearing one of these statements and supposing the speaker to be speaking sincerely, would take it that the speaker embodied a corresponding moral system relevant to and directed at *A* (and perhaps that his moral system is a partial cause of his making the statement). And the normative statement will not be used sincerely by a speaker of the language unless he does (or thinks he does) embody this corresponding aversion (etc.). So, if I say "It is normally wrong to steal," auditors will infer that unless I am speaking insincerely, I have an intrinsic aversion (etc., as described earlier) to standard cases of theft. Sometimes, alternatively, it is said that moral statements are essentially "prescriptive" in the sense (although there is a question about the sense of "prescription"[2]) of being *directives* about what to do (or not do), essentially functioning like imperative sentences. But a prescriptivist function seems to be implied by expressing a moral attitude, since if a statement can be taken as expressing a person's negative moral attitude (etc.), say to theft or deceit, his statement can be taken to imply that the speaker disapproves of stealing of the standard sort, and wants auditors to avoid stealing (and will be indignant if they don't), and so will have a directive impact on the attitudes/behavior of others, depending on the respect in which the speaker is held. It is sometimes added to the prescription theory that the prescriptions expressed by moral language ("You morally ought . . .") have overriding force in the sense

---

[1] J. J. C. Smart has suggested that one might come to this conclusion in a "radical translation" of evaluative statements. See his *Ethics, Persuasion, and Truth* (London: Routledge and Kegan Paul, 1984), p. 41.

[2] This use does not seem to be identical to the medical use of "prescription." I might say to a student, "If you want to do better work, I prescribe a lot more careful study." This is a kind of counsel. In what sense of "prescribe" could "You morally ought . . ." be said to be a prescription?

that the favoring expressed is implied to be stronger than any competing attitudes of the speaker. On either of these theories as so far explained, however, a moral statement will not be true or false in the sense of statements in science (namely, the appraised act having an objective property that corresponds to independent facts).

Is any purpose served by being able to express one's moral attitudes through the availability of such expressions – say, just the thin ones? The most obvious one is that they tell other people, in a concise manner, what you think – what your moral system consists of. Doing this may result in influencing others to take a similar view, depending on your reputation/prestige with them. (Of course, you might not think this is a good thing.) Moral attitudes also play a role in moral decision making, for a "conscientious" person is one who has a special (and strong) aversion to doing what she is convinced is, everything considered, morally wrong. So, when it becomes clear, after suitable reflection, that one of these terms (e.g., "It would be morally wrong for me to . . .") is to be applied to a projected action, the conscientious agent will be especially motivated not to perform it, over and beyond any aversion the agent may have to specific features of the proposed action. (The moral statement expresses a conclusory attitude toward a complex action as a whole.) Moral terms are also helpful in teaching moral views to children. A father may say: "Don't hit your little sister; you know that's wrong!" Here the "wrong" statement is very similar to the "Don't" directive, but at the same time carries a special sanction against the anticipated action, since it obviously expresses the moral attitude of the parent, and children soon learn that it is bad to run afoul of the moral aversions of their parents. The child thereby acquires special motivation to avoid this act and, by conditioning, if all goes well, develops a relatively long-term disposition not to do similar things.

Historically, philosophers have been concerned about how to construe these moral predicates. They have wanted to construe them so that moral statements, in their ordinary meaning, are true/false in the correspondence sense, correctly (or incorrectly) affirming a moral fact. Thus, most historical philosophers have rejected altogether the idea that such terms normally simply express the speaker's attitudes (even with various qualifications attached). They generally think that such statements can be appraised by methods appropriate to ascertaining facts. I have stated and dismissed these proposals in Chapter 1.[3]

This view, so far, may seem to imply that moral statements are not literally either true or false, or perhaps even justified, at least in any clear sense of "justified." For *expressions* of an attitude are not, as such – that is, as utterances caused at least partly by the speaker's moral attitudes or believed by auditors to be controlled by his moral attitudes – assertions with a content that can be either true or false (except in a use of "true" such that to say that "It is true that P" is the same as to say "P!"). But there may be other facts to be taken into account, which may bring them closer to the status of true/false or being justified. For instance, it is possible that uttering an ethical statement may *imply* certain commitments, just as my assertion that "P" implies that I (the speaker) believe that P. Why do I *imply* that I believe what I say? The *American College Dictionary* defines "imply" as "suggests, as something naturally to be inferred." So, I imply that I believe what I say because generally people do believe what they say, and if we are to think that a person is departing from the norm, we need a special story – say, an explanation for his wanting to lie. If a person doesn't give a warning sign – say, a wink – he is encouraging us to go along with the natural inference. Some background such as this must be assumed if we are to say that making an assertion "implies" that one believes what one said.

Now something like this seems true of moral statements: The speaker knows full well that when moral terms are used, auditors will suppose that she in fact has a corresponding attitude. So that, at least, is implied. But more than this will be supposed. I pointed out earlier that part of a person's moral system

---

[3] See also my *A Theory of the Good and the Right* (Oxford: Oxford University Press, 1979), chap. 1.

is that she thinks, perhaps only vaguely, that her moral attitudes can be *justified* (or defended) in some appropriate way. Why should this be? One answer is that the question "Why?" is always, or almost always, accepted as appropriate when a moral statement has been made or a moral attitude expressed. People think that, if asked, their moral attitudes call for a defense.[4] So, every thoughtful person who understands the language and has had experience with the give-and-take of moral discussion will consider a moral speaker to be prepared to defend her moral commitment of some appropriate kind. If we could only specify what these "appropriate kinds" are, the types of justification recognized as permitted (or not), then we might be in a position to identify some more specific implications of moral statements. A given person may have somewhat definite ideas, perhaps consistent and systematic, about what is required for justification. Whichever it is – crude or systematic – the types of reason a speaker would naturally offer (provided auditors consider her to stand ready to offer it) can be tacked on to the expressive theory as part of what the person's expressive statements may be taken to imply. Indeed, if there are implications thus closely connected with the making and defending of moral statements, what is implied in this sense could possibly be said to be part of what the moral statement means, not just what it implies.[5] A subtle distinction has to be made in deciding whether one is holding an expressive theory (with certain implications) or a form of meaning naturalism, say like the ideal observer theory, holding that "is wrong" *means* "would be dis-

---

4 See John Locke, *Essay Concerning Human Understanding* (1690), Book 1, chap. 3, no. 4: "I think there cannot any one moral rule be proposed whereof a man may not justly demand a reason."

   A person offering a defense is making his moral stance more coherent with his total thinking and moral commitments; that is one reason why trying to justify one's moral attitudes is useful in moral reflection.

5 I am not convinced that what I wrote some years ago was a mistake. See "The status of empirical assertion theories in ethics," *Mind* 61 (1952), 458–79, especially 468ff.

approved of by anyone factually omniscient and without emo-tional/motivational ties to any individuals."[6]

We must see where this takes us. Can we decide plausibly what being "justified in an appropriate way" might include or come to? As a first approximation, one might suggest that the points offered in defense of a moral statement be ones that will be favorably received and convincing to an actual objector or critic. But this suggestion is much too loose; all sorts of points might move some sorts of people in one direction or another. Somewhat stiffer requirements are needed.

Suppose one gives an appropriate justification only if one's expressed reasons for or against his moral view are ones that would tend to induce agreeing moral attitudes in (nearly) every person who is factually informed, with broad knowledge of morality and its normal impact on social living, about human nature and psychology. Identification of the considerations that would move such persons would seem to be a large order, but as we go on, I shall explain why factually informed (etc.) people would be moved toward agreement by certain sorts of consider-ations. Of course, we should not expect the average person to be articulate about what these "appropriate" defenses are. Cer-tainly the average person will not have a list of them and may hardly recognize them even when pointed out. (So far, what is implied for one auditor may be different from what is implied for another.)

How can we say that moral statements imply that the attitude expressed meets conditions sufficiently complex that the average person might not even understand them, even if they are under-

---

[6] So it might be held, as it was in a closely related theory presented by E. Westermarck in *Ethical Relativity* (New York: Harcourt, Brace, 1932), that these expressions be construed as assertions like "*I* have a disposition to feel impartial resentment at . . ." Then moral statements would be true or false, depending on the dispositions of the speaker and on whether they are impar-tial. This view will not satisfy most people, however, because when two speakers are in ethical disagreement in the ordinary understanding, both might still be speaking the truth. Some people will want to avoid this con-struction partly for that reason.

stood and moving to informed, clear-headed people? Well, we can show that the attitude is "ideally implied" if we can demonstrate plausibly how the plain person can be led, step by step, to see the force of certain requirements, so that she winds up approximately where I shall suggest she ought to be. At least when a person follows this explanatory reasoning, she will find that it is natural to infer that the moral attitudes of a responsible speaker meet these conditions and that such a person who expresses a moral attitude thinks they do. We must see how this works out.

What would be examples of "approved" reasons (either pro or con), ones that would be accepted by the informed people I have suggested are the test of a justification's being appropriate?

To begin, such persons will think that an attitude one has toward a *particular* action must be based on an adequate conception of the action in its setting. If someone points out to me some fact about an action that I had not thought of, information about which modifies my attitudes, I will then change any earlier *expression* of attitude. Why should a person not be taken to imply, when he says a particular act A was wrong, that his aversive (etc.) attitude to it is based on knowledge of the kind of action A is, so that more information about it will not cause this attitude to be changed? How could a person think a particular action is morally objectionable if he doesn't even know what kind of action he is talking about, at least in relevant respects? Admittedly, such a point is more likely to be made by a philosopher than by the average person, but when it is put before an average person, he can hardly fail to recognize its force.

Another appropriate requirement is that a person is not to commend one action but condemn the same action by others in comparable circumstances. Call this the "principle of universalizability." (Sidgwick thought this principle of "justice" is *self-evident* – that what is right for one must be right for all others – but this account belongs to the framework of non-naturalism.) According to this principle, if someone points out to me that I condemn in one person an action that I regard as permissible for another, I shall feel called upon to change one of these attitudes or at least find some significant difference between the cases.

Why this demand? Some (e.g., R. M. Hare) think it is part of the *meaning* of moral terms ("morally wrong") that *moral* attitudes are in this sense universalizable – a view defended by urging that we should be very puzzled about what was meant if a person said that to treat her a certain way was right but wrong for her to treat others the same way when all the circumstances are the same – puzzled just as we would be by the statement, "The two figures are exactly the same shape, but one is triangular and the other not."[7] How might an explicit definition of "morally wrong" look, so that universalizability can be said to follow from it? Hare once offered one: that "*A* is morally wrong" be construed as "I hereby proscribe, with overriding force, the doing of any action exactly like *A* (including the circumstances) for absolutely everybody." But there are other possible theories to the same effect, short of offering an explicit definition like Hare's. The first thing to note is that I explained the "*morality* of a person" in terms of the person's intrinsic aversions (along with guilt feelings and disapproval of others) to "certain *types* of behavior" – like telling lies and injuring others. Now if a person's morality is explained in terms of attitudes to *types* of action, it seems as if, given that a person morally disapproves of a certain type of action by one person, she is also bound to disapprove of that same type of action by another person if the situation is the same.

But the question may still arise: Why define a person's morality in terms of her attitudes toward actions of a *certain sort*? This conception seems to carry (at least part of what Hare defines as) universalizability with it, for a person could not be expressing his *moral* attitudes by "That's wrong" talk if he appraised the act of one person in one way and the identical act by another person in a conflicting way. (I am taking it as a fact that our moral aversions are to act-types; so, in discussing this issue, we are only bringing out the implications of a fact about what we call "moral" attitudes.) So, a person who questioned universalizability must in effect be questioning the preceding definition of "personal morality." How might he do this? Possibly by modifying the sense of "acts of the same *type*." He could do this consis-

---

[7] R. M. Hare, *Moral Thinking* (Oxford: Clarendon Press, 1981), p. 81.

tently while rejecting universalizability if he allowed that two acts are not of the same type if different persons are involved (the situation otherwise remaining the same), that is, if proper names are allowed in the specification of an act-type. So it seems, in effect, that the requirement of universalizability is a demand that this definitional move not be allowed, that an act-type be described in terms of universal properties.

Why would a factually fully informed person, with a broad view of morality and its contribution to social living, accept this requirement? Well, for one thing, if a person applied *non*universalizability to herself, thereby permitting her moral statements to express what Charles Stevenson called "self-excepting attitudes," other people would pay very little attention to her moral statements,[8] so that it would be pointless to issue them. Her statements would be taken to be merely disguised expressions of self-interest. Moreover, I suggest that everybody knows that moral aversions (etc.) and the expressions of them are parts of a social system of direction of behavior, a device that, among other things, normally reduces the incidence of harmful interpersonal conflicts. Now if a person rejects the requirement of universalizability, she is in effect abjuring the right to view her morality as part of such a social system. Why so? The answer is that such a person would hardly be supporting an identifiable *standard* at all, one to which one could appeal in adjudication of particular behaviors.[9]

One might reply that the belief that moral standards are part of a desirable general system of behavior control that can sensibly be argued about is itself a moral judgment. If so, it is at least a judgment that persons who understand what morality is and its relation to society will surely underwrite. So, I think it is

---

[8] Charles Stevenson, "Value judgments: their implicit generality," in N. E. Bowie (ed.), *Ethical Theory in the last Quarter of the Twentieth Century* (Indianapolis: Hackett, 1983), pp. 17ff.

[9] This requirement, it should be noted, is so far very weak: It does not exclude the color of a patient as relevant to an act-type or whether the patient is an animal.

justified to accept the requirement for the reasons stated. Moral "principles" are unacceptable if their statement requires the use of proper names.

It should be noted that this requirement is not met by some types of *egoist* moral principles. For it does not permit a moral *judge* to affirm that it is always morally permissible for anyone to do what will benefit *him* (the judge) in particular. But it does not exclude the egoist thesis that it is morally permissible for an agent to do whatever will benefit *that agent,* since no proper name is required to state the principle. Thus, the requirement leaves open whether an agent can be morally free to do what will benefit himself. (It is another question whether sensible persons would want a moral system in which agents have so much freedom, since they could do much better by themselves by supporting an alternative moral system.)[10]

There is a third requirement on the *weight* of reasons that may affect a decision: The individual must be willing to weigh the same features in any situations that she may have occasion to appraise and give them the *same weight.* This is manifest if my account of "moral systems" is acceptable; for if a person has a moral system at all – intrinsic aversions (etc.) to certain act-types – the system will presumably manifest itself in the *same way* and with the *same weight* (degree of aversion, etc.) on all occasions. So, if I have a moral aversion to situations with the feature F, then whenever some situation (action) has the feature F, I shall be aversive to it to the same degree. (This does not imply that whenever I have a certain reaction to a feature F, I may not have a somewhat different reaction when it appears in the combination F and some countervailing G.) The reason for this demand is somewhat similar to the demand for universalizability. Permitting a consideration to have different weights in different cases is like allowing proper names into the definition of "same type"; a person need not have a definite aversion

---

[10] See my "Rationality, egoism, and morality," *The Journal of Philosophy,* 1972, reprinted in my *Morality, Utilitarianism, and Rights* (Cambridge: Cambridge University Press, 1992), pp. 93–108.

(moral system) at all to which she could appeal in the appraisal of particular moral issues.

Is there any further restriction we should lay on the concept of "same act-type" beyond specifying that proper names are not to be included? Is an act-type different if it involves an animal, so that it might be all right to treat an animal in a way it would be wrong to treat a human being? Or does it make a difference if the individual involved is male or female, or black or yellow, or poverty-stricken or rich?

Hare has aimed to meet this challenge by stating that moral judgments must be understood to apply to all *logically possible* worlds, "all logically possible" including all worlds in which, taken together, *everyone takes on the position of whoever is affected* by a given action. So, if I think it morally acceptable to treat a given person in a certain way, I must also regard it as morally acceptable for me to be treated in exactly the same way, which I may be very much disinclined to do. (Here Hare's view of the prescriptivity of moral judgments plays a role.) The same holds for treatment of animals if a *possible* world includes one in which *I am an animal*. So, the judgment that it is all right for me to treat another in a certain way must be retracted if I my-self cannot prescribe that others treat me in that way in log-ically possible situations – such as my being an animal, a woman, a Japanese, and so on. Is this argument sound? Or must morality be thought to apply to all possible worlds in quite so strong a sense?

I think we shall agree that a given moral judgment holds in any possible world in which the situations are the same; the question is whether the situations are the same when certain changes are introduced, such as one party's being an animal.[11]

---

[11] Hare might claim the authority of Kant, who said that the imperative of duty is to "Act as if the maxim of your action were to become through your volition a universal law of nature." *Groundwork of the Metaphysic of Morals,* H. J. Paton, trans. (New York: Harper Torchbook, 1964), p. 89. Also, *Werke,* Ernst Cassirer ed. (Berlin: B. Cassirer, 1922), p. 279. It is not clear that the omission of animals in the scope of duties is inconsistent with this concep-

For instance, we do think that, were I an animal, it would be proper to submit me to the life-threatening risks of medical research (not to pain, which can be relieved by analgesics in animals as well as in human beings) when it would not be proper to submit children to the same risks. Why so? I suppose the answer is that we think an animal life has not – taking the long view of a life with all its qualities – the same value as a human life, so that it is acceptable to raise animals to provide food but not human beings. I suggest that Hare's view that moral principles must apply to all logically possible worlds in his sense is too widely framed to carry the burden placed upon it.

Aside from this, Hare has a more specific line of reasoning. As I see it, Hare's view is that a full account of practical moral reflection must be as follows: (1) When I am contemplating doing a certain thing to someone else, I first identify how this will affect the individual's experiences, directly or indirectly. (This may seem too narrow; do all moral judgments turn just on the impact on the experiences of others, e.g., incest?) Then (2) I determine how strongly this individual will, for one reason or another, wish this not to occur to him. (3) Then, according to Hare, if I *fully understand* the experience of the other (including how it may feel to be an animal used in an experiment), *including* his following *motivation* that the action not be done to him, I shall find in myself a negative reaction *now* to being in the position of the other party with his objecting motivation. This reaction will be equal in strength to the motivation of the other person. (This proposal seems to be a factual assertion – and dubious, since it places an infinitely high demand on empathic sympathy – and has sometimes been called the "principle of conditional reflection."[12] In any case, it appears not to cover cases of *painless killing.*) (4) Then I may not be able to prescribe that what is done to the other be done to me; so, by univer-

tion. The "universal law of nature" seems to mean "universally characteristic of human volitions," but it does not imply that this universal law of nature is to make no distinctions between human beings and animals.

12 Allan Gibbard, in D. Seanor and N. Fotion (eds.), *Hare and Critics* (Oxford: Clarendon Press, 1988), pp. 6off.

salizability, I cannot say that it is morally proper to do what I am contemplating. So, the equal status of animals (etc.) seems to be preserved as a result of my equal motivation not to be hurt as they are hurt.[13]

Unfortunately, there seems to be some difficulty with this view. For to take first Hare's principle of "conditional reflection," is it true that I shall in fact have a negative reaction *now* to some projected action equal in strength to the actual one of the party (e.g., an animal) I am proposing to injure if I fully understand this situation? (This is different from questioning whether, if I *were* exactly *like* him and *in* that situation, I would react to it negatively, just as he does – a necessary causal truth.) But must my motivation be identical to his? (This reasoning seems not to apply even to the case of my own future: I may know I shall strongly dislike being fat a year from now, but this awareness need not produce in me an aversion to that future state *now* sufficient to get me to restrict my present diet.) Moreover, the person I am proposing to injure might have a negative reaction that is at least partly irrational, say, a strong aversion to any degree of pain. Shall I duplicate the other's preference, however irrational I think it to be?

In any case, there may be further considerations that are morally relevant, beyond how the affected party feels about what is happening to him. For instance, I may feel free to kill an enemy soldier because of his status as an enemy soldier, although he does not want to be killed. Is this then to be condemned? Hare might reply, as he did earlier in the case of a judge handing down a nasty sentence, that many persons are actually involved (e.g., those who want to be protected from crime and possibly, mutatis mutandis, for the case of the sol-

---

[13] Hare thus differs sharply from David Gauthier, who views morality as essentially a matter of mutual beneficial agreement among rational persons, since animals are not in a position to provide benefits to us. See his *Morals by Agreement* (Oxford: Oxford University Press, 1986), e.g., pp. 17, 268, 285.

Hare reasonably supports his position by an appeal to facts of psychology, although the alleged fact apparently is a mistake.

dier). This may be so, but it would seem at most to be the case that the soldier's not wanting to be killed is *a* fact to be taken into account as negative toward the action. Moreover, there are other moral issues that may not easily be fitted into this two-person conflict relationship: those having to do with sexual freedom (e.g., wrongness of incest), property rights, promises ("A promise is a promise" even if breach involves no injury), suicide, and cannibalism (in the sense of eating the body of someone already dead). One might, of course, suggest that the real moral issue in all such cases is how much hurt one does to someone, directly or indirectly; and Hare sometimes says that his conception fits only cases of conflict of interest. That morality applies only to such cases, however, must be shown.

Is there any other line of reasoning, besides Hare's, that can show that informed, thoughtful people would not be racist, or sexist, or speciesist in their attitudes? Perhaps a fully informed, thoughtful person *could not possibly* be moved, in her moral attitudes, by knowing that a patient (or agent) is female, yellow, or an animal if what is behind her moral attitude (appraisal) is that she knows that someone has been *hurt* (or in some way mentally impacted) and a negative attitude to *this* is either native with her or has been a result of her moral training. To say this, of course, is to come somewhat close to Hare's principle of conditional reflection, but only close; it is not asserted that one who merely *understands* the motivation of someone's act will automatically share that negative motivation. I shall have more to say about this in Chapter 5, where I discuss how we may identify an optimal set of moral attitudes and determine how far sound reasoning can take us in these directions.

So, making a moral statement does seem to imply that the speaker has knowledge of the kind of action he is appraising, and that he is prepared to make the same judgment for all other cases like it (but this specification leaves open what counts as "like it") and with the same weight. If a person's moral attitudes can be shown not to conform to these requirements, that is a reason against them. Conforming moral judgments can be said to be justified so far in an appropriate sense.

So far, so good. We must see if we can go further.

UNIVERSAL REQUIREMENTS FOR
JUSTIFICATION OF JUDGMENTS OF
PARTICULAR CASES

Let us begin by inquiring whether, if we assume that adults have moral systems that meet the previously listed requirements for justification, there are necessarily certain modes of reflection for specific cases. Later, we shall consider other difficulties with the appraisal of general principles.

Let us consider an example of what a person equipped with a moral system may do to decide how it is right to behave in a certain situation. Suppose that a year ago I owned a Dodge minivan of recent vintage and you owned a Toyota of the same vintage. And suppose you have a family and would like to have a minivan, whereas I am single and have no need for so much space. At this time, you propose that we trade cars (their market value being about the same). I reflect on the matter, look up the repair records of the two types of car in *Consumers' Reports,* and decide, in view of this and given my belief that a sporty red Toyota would suit my image better than a black minivan, to go along. Subsequently, things go well for me. But you begin having troubles: You start using a great deal of oil and may possibly incur a large repair bill. So, you then come to me and propose that we trade back (perhaps with a $100 "sweetener" for me), and you claim that I have a moral obligation to accept this proposal, since I have traded you a defective car. Should I go along?

First, as far as personal preferences are concerned, I do not want to. But I also have moral principles, aversions (etc.) to certain act-types, and these naturally motivate me in deciding what to do. So I, in effect, consider whether my aversions to act-types (my moral principles) require me to do what you say I am morally obligated to do. (If I think they do and are justified, I shall say that I "am morally obligated" to act accordingly.) To decide this, I consider the situation carefully, picturing its various features as vividly as possible so that all my relevant moral aversions are engaged, prepared to go along if any (important one) of them would be offended if I refuse. First, I consider what kind of act-type a refusal would be. It would, of course, be a failure to help a friend out of a difficulty, and that consideration makes some appeal to my principles. Also, I did trade you an imperfect car. However, I did not know it at the time, and in good faith entered into what I thought was a fair transaction. So, the fact that the trade turned out badly for you does not seem, at least to me, to be a moving consideration, one that engages my moral aversions.

Therefore, I ask myself whether I can think of some moral principle that might be relevant to the case and require me to do what you propose: perhaps a principle requiring that if one trades something to another that subsequently turns out defective for the other party, one must accede to a request to revoke the agreement. This suggested "principle" leaves my moral aversions cold when I reflect that if such a principle were really instated in the moral (or legal) systems of everyone, trading (and selling) would be a vastly more complicated business which nobody would want. (Note that I am here paying attention to the social desirability of a moral code with a certain feature; in Chapter 5, I shall return to the question of whether social desirability is a decisive factor in defense of a certain moral code.)

I then try to think of other "types" into which this act would fall, counting on my moral system to make me uncomfortable if any of them contravenes that system. I can think of no more. So the real question becomes: Is the obligation to help you sufficiently weighty to require me to make this sacrifice? I conclude that it is not; my moral aversions moving me to accede to your request (in this case, only one) are relatively very weak. Acceding to this request has essentially the status of acceding to a request to give to charity, except for the fact that you are my friend and that I am, to a certain extent, responsible for your being in the situation you are in. (It would make a difference what kind of friendship there is between us and how my alleged responsibility for your problem is spelled out. If these reflections turned out in a certain way, important aversions of mine would be engaged.) And I think that if I were in your position, I would think the various considerations insufficient to justify making such a request to me on moral grounds. We can, if we like, regard this final weighing of considerations – the judgment of the weakness of an obligation of friendship in this situation – as an intuition or something like it.[14]

I suggest that most of us analyze practical moral problems this way. Various features of a situation move us one way or the other on account of our moral aversions (which are themselves open to critical evaluation, as we shall see shortly), and our conclusion is a holistic or intuitive response of our principles, or aversions, to the situation as envisaged – doubtless supported by reflections on what would be the socially best system.

I do not suggest that deciding in this way is all that easy. An overall response does not present itself if there are moving considerations in contrary directions. Moreover, probabilities can enter in: One course of action will probably offend against a certain aversion, and an alternative course of action will probably offend against a different one. If I have a choice between helping an injured person and missing an important engagement, it seems I must make a decision about the probability of the injury's being serious. If I am deciding which person to employ, and one candidate is a better philosopher but white and male, the other a less promising philosopher but black and female, my moral aversions are not apt to speak with one voice. In many cases, I may have to fall back on deliberations about how relatively weighty a moral aversion it is best to have ac-

---

[14] See Smart, *Ethics*, pp. 60, 80, 102. Also see W. D. Ross, *The Right and the Good* (Oxford: Clarendon Press, 1930), chap. 2.

Some philosophers would eschew all talk of "principles" in describing such moral thought, rather saying that we must carefully go over the facts of the case and then find ourselves either agreeing or disagreeing. They might ask how my own position differs from theirs, since in the end I have to appeal to a kind of intuitive judgment about weight to settle matters in a particular case. Such a story, however, omits the role we actually give to the thought of general principles and the testing of these principles themselves. It also permits no story of how a person learns his basic aversions, how he comes to be moved pro or con by certain features of a case.

For the "no principles" view, see David McNaughton, *Moral Vision* (Oxford: Basil Blackwell, 1988), pp. 192–204. Also see J. Dancy, "On moral properties," *Mind* 90 (1981), 367–85, and "Ethical particularism and morally relevant properties," *Mind* 92 (1983), 530–47.

cepted in my society. If we are lucky, the seemingly superior strength of one aversion will be paired with the principle it is socially best to have weightier in the society.

If I am right in this, a person must come to a moral appraisal of particular problems on the basis of *reasons* – features of the problem that are morally significant because, when represented vividly, they engage his system of (justified) moral aversions (etc.). For appraisals of individual cases, it is obviously necessary that a person have one or more moral principles of a relevant sort in his system of morality, although he may not be able to formulate them verbally. (But in some cases, we may need to start from scratch and decide which kinds of moral principle we *ought* to internalize.) To think this way is part of what it means to give a "reasoned" defense of a moral stance on a particular issue. Is there a serious alternative?

I think we must concede that two persons with somewhat different basic principles may differ in the moral appraisal of a given issue. Moreover, intuitive weighting is a delicate process, so that two persons with substantially the same principles may appraise a given situation differently. This may be regrettable, but that is the way things are.

So much for how we must reflect on individual cases.

JUSTIFICATION OF MORAL PRINCIPLES OR ABSTRACT SYSTEMS

But is there any way of justifying our whole set of moral principles – our intrinsic aversions (etc.) to certain act-types – as distinct from justification of appraisal of a specific situation based on balancing aversions to relevant act-types? We must concede in advance that any justification we may offer in the appraisal of general moral principles may leave some space for variation/disagreement (just as may reasoning about particular cases) about the moral principles thus appraised.

I have already suggested that there are several requirements for acceptable moral principles, the most important being that they concern act-types (with "type" understood not to permit definition by the use of proper names). But suppose a person's moral aversions meet these conditions.

There seem to be some further requirements for moral aversions/thinking. In order to get a clear conception of what more can be done to criticize moral *principles,* let us again consider how reflection and argument work in real-life cases – only, in this case, about general principles. In this chapter we can only begin on this task.

Suppose, on the matter of abortion, one person is pro-choice and another is equally fervently pro-life. What can be done to justify either stance?

Obviously, if we are debating with someone, we shall try first to identify common ground, thereby sharpening the area of disagreement. For instance, participants in a debate on abortion might (but might not) agree that an abortion is justified if it is necessary to save the life of the mother. Suppose so much is agreed. Now what is the area of disagreement? The pro-life person states a basic principle to guide particular decisions: that, this exception aside, we may not kill anything alive and potentially a human being, as distinct from the criminal law (in the United States), which defines murder as the killing of a person who has been born. We can then ask why he thinks this – we agree with Locke that the affirmation of this principle requires some defense. But the pro-life person may think it needless to give a reason and misleading to do so, since his principle is basic (thus possibly disagreeing with Locke). But can he seriously claim that such a moral principle is to be accepted as basic, with no supporting argument? (We must concede that some moral principles are basic in the sense of not being defensible by inference from other moral principles; thus, there are some moral aversions that are justified – like not needlessly injuring other persons – and are *not* dependent on some other moral principles. We shall shortly see how the acceptance of these basic principles can be justified. The pro-lifer's principle *could* be one of these.)

He might, however, offer a reasoned defense by appeal to a more general (and seemingly more basic) principle. But then he may be in trouble. For instance, the pro-life person might say that adults normally lead happy lives, that we are obligated to do what we can to promote happy lives, and that abortion is an infringement of this obligation. (Pro-choicers would agree that normally human life is fairly happy; so far, so good.) But if he relies on this argument, he runs into difficulties: Suppose there is reason to think that a particular child, if born, would not live a happy life because his mother will be an irresponsible teenager who has no financial resources to care for him and no desire to do so. (In any case, the clear prospect of an unhappy life seems, intuitively, a point prima facie favorable to permitting an abortion.) What are we then to say about this type of case? (The pro-life person may suggest adoption as a way out. The reply will be that adoption may be a good thing but hardly feasible as the only way of taking care of the million and a half fetuses aborted each year in the Unite States). Further, it may be asked, are we really obligated to produce (and sustain) happy lives, and if one says we are, then are we not obligated not only to make substantial sacrifices to avoid general starvation, but also to produce as many babies as possible in order to maximize the number of happy lives? This would be absurd, and no pro-life advocate would go for it (I think: although Hare comes very close to it, suggesting a duty to produce until the optimal population size is reached.)[15] He would say that it is one thing to be obligated to produce a fetus but a very different thing to prevent a fetus, already started on the way to birth, from continuing to exist; his basic principle applies only to the latter type of case. So far, then, it seems that the pro-lifer's attempt to justify his principle by appeal to a more general one is unsuccessful, although wider use of adoption in conjunction with much broader sex education and education in the use of contraceptive methods might go a long way toward reducing the importance of abortion (unless contraception itself is viewed as a form of abortion).

Is there no other, more general principle to which the pro-lifer can appeal in support of his view on abortion?

One thing he may do is affirm that every human being (inno-

---

[15] See his *Essays on Bioethics* (Oxford: Clarendon Press, 1993), chap. 5.

cent of any wrongdoing) has a moral right not to be killed. But this position is purely a terminological one. For what it is to say that a person has a moral right to something is no more and no less than to say that some person(s) have a strong moral obligation not to prevent his having that thing, or to assist significantly in providing it for him, primarily because of the importance to his well-being of having that thing. But our present discussion is precisely concerned with inquiring under what conditions persons can be said to be morally bound to do a certain thing. To offer having a moral right as a decisive reason for doing a certain thing is therefore, in effect, to assume that we already know what people are morally bound to do, which is precisely the question we are discussing. To offer having a moral right as a reason for something, then, is not to offer us a new reason for viewing something as morally obligatory but rather to affirm a conclusion. So, it is no help to our reflections about whether it is morally justified to have an abortion.[16]

The pro-life person might offer a different supporting argument: that if in principle we authorize terminating a human life, then what is there to stop us from killing anyone whom it is inconvenient to have around or is not very bright, particularly if it is a small child? To this it may be replied that lines can be drawn, and it would be absurd to suggest that there is no line between the welfare impact of killing an adult or a child and extinguishing something with no feelings, anticipations, thoughts, or interests of its own. It is true that a fetus will later have interests, but it does not have them yet.

Still, it seems that although the pro-lifer must be ready to answer (how?) the charge that unwanted babies are apt not to live happy lives, he may stick with his basic principle and claim that it has not been refuted, even though it is not derivative from a more basic principle.

There is a problem for the pro-life person: His basic principle, of prohibiting abortion except in the rare cases where he per-

---

[16] See my "The concept of a moral right and its function," *Journal of Philosophy* (1983), 29–45, reprinted in my *Morality, Utilitarianism, and Rights* (Cambridge: Cambridge University Press, 1992), pp. 179–95.

mits it, is a somewhat narrow, special principle; one is inclined to think that there must be some more general line of thinking that leads to it. One would like to know what this is. Why do pro-lifers affirm their principle?

One possibility is that their attitude stems from a religious tradition. Consider the influential encyclical *Casta connubii* (1930) by Pope Pius XI, which reads: "But can any reason ever avail to excuse the direct killing of the innocent? For this is what is at stake. The infliction of death upon mother or upon child is against the commandment of God and the voice of nature: 'Thou shalt not kill.' The lives of both are equally sacred." The claim that the prohibition is a commandment of God seems to rest on the biblical commandment "Thou shalt not kill." But this fact is not enough to support the thesis of the encyclical. For was this kind of killing intended? The biblical injunction might be taken to forbid killing of animals, action necessary for self-defense, or euthanasia to relieve extreme pain. So, the question remains whether abortion may fall among admissible exceptions. Thus, if the attitude of pro-lifers is based solely on interpretation of Scripture, it seems to require elaborate exegesis. Abortion, incidentally, is not mentioned in the *New Testament*, although it is forbidden as early as the time of the Didache (c. 80 A.D.) and by the early Church Fathers. It is not forbidden by the Jewish tradition. Of course, persons who think historical religious traditions are not evidence for any moral principles will be unmoved by appeal to them.

The encyclical also says that abortion is contrary to the "voice of nature," but this contention is too obscure to provide serious support. Perhaps the claim is nothing more than the affirmation of a strong moral intuition, an appeal we have already found some reasons to set aside.

The pro-lifer may, however, take a more substantial stand: He may go back and question the claim that the pro-choice thesis is consistent with some of the requirements of an acceptable moral system, as mentioned earlier, specifically the requirement of universalizability.

Hare, for instance, has held that the principle of universalizability is offended by most types of abortion, so that we should hold that abortion as a general rule should be prohibited morally.[17] Hare argues, in essence, that every happy person will proscribe abortions in cases like his own (for he does not want to have been prevented from being born) and, unless there are relevant differences, must in consistency proscribe the same for all other cases. (The happy person will presumably not be bound to proscribe for the cases of prospectively *un*happy lives.) Consistently, Hare is prepared to admit that it is highly relevant whether a given fetus is likely to be unhappy, perhaps because she will be the child of a teenager who will be very displeased to be saddled with her. And it seems Hare must admit that postponement of childbirth by a woman whose career would be damaged by having a child now but who plans to have one later has a relevant ground for an exception. (And is the pro-life person not prepared to count the general well-being of the mother as something to be weighed in deciding what is morally permissible?) Again, Hare appears to admit that the necessity to limit the population is also a possibly relevant ground. It seems as if the force of Hare's argument is simply that the future well-being of the individual who will live if the fetus is not destroyed should be counted in deciding on a course of action. Whether that is a good reason for regarding abortion as morally wrong as a general rule needs to be argued.

Ronald Dworkin, who holds that something has moral *rights* only if it has interests (which a preconscious being cannot have at the time), points to an error in Hare's reasoning. It is true that a person who is alive may be glad he was not aborted; for that to have happened would be contrary to his *present* interests. But it does not follow that when an abortion occurs, there *is* anyone whose interests *then* are infringed. The real question is whether the fetus has interests *at the time* of the abortion, not whether interests will develop if the abortion does not take place. But

---

[17] See his "Abortion and the golden rule," *Philosophy and Public Affairs* 4 (1975), 20–22, and his "A Kantian approach to abortion" and "Abortion: reply to Brandt," *Social Theory and Practice* 15 (1989), 1–14 and 25–32; and "Preferences of possible people," forthcoming, read at a conference in Saarbruecken in July 1992. See his *Essays on Bioethics*.

Dworkin thinks that one might still argue that the fetus should be protected because "human life has an intrinsic, innate value; that human life is sacred just in itself . . . [and that] abortion is wrong in principle because it disregards and insults the intrinsic value, the sacred character, of any stage or form of human life."[18] We need not deny that probably many persons share Dworkin's view on this, but Dworkin does not support his contention by absorbing it into any general theory about what is good – or absolutely good, independently of what anybody wants or would want if fully informed (see Chapter 2, footnote 1). I suggest that one might reasonably withhold agreement with Dworkin until this argument is supplied.[19]

Suppose it were argued, in contrast, that society would be better off – including the lives that would be lived if there were fewer abortions – if some moral prohibition less stringent than the pro-lifer's avowed principle were prevalent, everything else remaining the same, at least partly because it is clear that many social problems have arisen from the recent vast increases in population.[20] Suppose it is argued that something must be done to restrain population growth. For this, wide use of methods of contraception would be ideal, but realistically this does not seem a complete solution to the problem (although with possible newer methods, this problem might be resolved). Might it

18 Ronald Dworkin, *Life's Dominion* (New York: Alfred A. Knopf, 1993), p. 11.
19 For a careful review of both moral and legal issues, see Nancy Davis, "The abortion debate: the search for common ground," *Ethics*, 103 (1993), 516–39 and 731–78. The paper essentially is an extended review of recent volumes by Faye D. Ginsburg and Lawrence Tribe.

A careful discussion of many issues relevant to the morality of abortion is found in F. M. Kamm, *Creation and Abortion: A Study in Moral and Legal Philosophy* (New York: Oxford University Press, 1992), reviewed by Jeff McMahan in "The right to choose an abortion," *Philosophy and Public Affairs*, 22 (1993), 330–48.
20 It is not clear that the increase in population in the developing countries is solely a consequence of failure to use birth control methods; to a large extent, it is a result of improvements in medicine, so that people live longer, especially to a reproductive age. See Mark Sagoff, "Doing the numbers: demographic trends and global population," *Philosophy and Public Policy* 13 (1993), no. 4, 3ff.

then not be best to have some weaker moral prohibition against abortion than the pro-lifer would allow? It could be a moral principle rather like the legal principle enunciated in *Roe* v. *Wade* but more subtle – but not so subtle that intelligent people could not decide, on the basis of it, which abortions are permissible. Suppose such a principle were proposed. Would the pro-lifer change his stance? My guess is that a thoughtful pro-lifer who became convinced of the force of such an argument might at least find himself with conflicting feelings.

Thus, we see how appeals to various general principles a person will accept (either ones that support or ones that conflict) and more information about facts (e.g., the annual abortion rate in the United States) may cause a person to modify her original view. And if support is provided by some general principle that may itself have implications that are either acceptable or objectionable, some major reconsideration of views may be in order. Suppose we are morally averse to abortion but also to condemning babies to very unhappy lives. Something must give. Thus, if a person sorts out her principles and their interrelations, and considers relevant facts, she may have made some progress in appraising her initial principle.

These reflections illustrate one general requirement for a person holding a moral principle (aversion, etc.): It must be consistent with his other principles (taken along with knowable facts). If it is not, some revisions are called for. I think we all take this requirement for granted, and we could view it as another and obvious implication of language about "right" and "obligation."

If principles are inconsistent, it seems that at least one of them must be rejected or bracketed (or perhaps both modified). But how? Consider deciding between "You ought not to have sex outside of marriage" or "You ought not to commit suicide" on the one hand and "You are free to do anything that doesn't harm others" on the other. How are such questions to be answered? Writers who discuss these issues are usually rather coy in describing exactly how to decide which principle to follow. We are often asked to choose the principles that are coherent or in "reflective equilibrium," but it is not clear how (or why) we are to go about using this procedure to arrive at an order of weight. Sometimes it is suggested that we adopt the principles about which we feel more strongly (have stronger aversions, etc.); sometimes it is thought that the favored principle is the one least in conflict with our most numerous intuitive judgments about particular cases, real or hypothetical – so consistent with most possible counterexamples. A question may be raised, however: If this is all we are to do, may we not be throwing away good principles because of inconsistency with a host of bad ones? Is there not, then, some other line of thinking that might enable us to make a justified choice among such conflicting principles?

One possible answer to this question is that there is: It is the power of the conception of a certain moral system in society to recommend itself to informed, thoughtful persons, that is, to make them *want* to incorporate it in their society. But an exact formulation of this conception, the reasons behind it, and its implications are better left for separate treatment later, in Chapter 5.

So, where do all these reflections leave us? With the proposal that moral statements are expressions of the speaker's moral system (or, if one prefers, statements that the speaker's moral system is so and so, thereby expressing his attitude), along with the implication that this moral system is justified – satisfies certain types of criticism that would be moving to thoughtful people with a broad view of morality (etc.), types of criticism that generally will be familiar to the speaker and his society. Which requirements must be met? (1) An attitude toward a particular action must be informed about the action in its setting and in view of its effects; (2) the person must be willing to apply to all similar cases the moral aversion (etc.) he applies to one; (3) the aversion to a given property of an action must be given the same weight in particular cases that share the identical property; (4) in forming an attitude toward a particular action, all of one's relevant general moral aversions should be involved and, if possible, produce a holistic response; (5) some changes should be made, if necessary, to avoid inconsistency among one's general aversions; and (6) principles must contain no proper names.

Suppose we agree that the foregoing requirements would be set by thoughtful persons – conditions to be satisfied by serious moral reflection. What sort of status does that give them? It does not follow that, from being so weighed, a consideration has the force it would achieve if it were supported by observation and the methods of science, as is true of the principles of physics. But we should not forget the force of the particular pragmatic reasons given for the various considerations. If it is generally known that these requirements would be set by all factually informed, thoughtful (not insane or sociopathic, etc.) persons, then I suggest we can say that only a moral code that satisfies them is so far justified (but allowing for the possibility that there are further requirements that would be set by factually informed persons), and perhaps also that it is an implication of moral statements that these requirements have been met.

Chapter 5

Optimal social moralities

The reasoning presented in Charter 4 establishes only some necessary conditions of a person's moral statements being justified – "justified" in the sense of meeting conditions that would be imposed, for acceptance of moral statements, by factually fully informed persons. For conditions like the properties of being adequately informed about some action being appraised, the universalizability of one's moral statements, and their consistency do not tell us specifically which general kinds of moral statements are justified. To this end we must do more: perhaps identify an *optimal* moral system. Thus, so far, what would be the specific content of an optimal moral system has been left open.

THE GENERAL STRUCTURE OF AN
OPTIMAL MORAL CODE FOR A SOCIETY

What more can be done, in appraisal of a set of moral judgments/motivations, beyond showing that it meets the conditions stated in Chapter 4? At least a partial answer is that there may be some way to *recommend* to people one or more fairly specific moralities (or parts thereof) *for their society* – not just *one*, since the morality we want to recommend for a physician is apt to be slightly different from that we want to recommend for a lawyer or a housewife. That is, we want to find considerations that will engage *support* for *teaching* or defending one or more packages (or parts) of moral motivations, and thereby hopefully also, to some extent, motivate the relevant persons to share the aversions appropriate to them (and corresponding dispositions to feel remorse and to condemn others). We saw in Chapter 2 that people can be motivated to *do* what will tend to bring about a certain state of affairs (here "do" is taken as including support of certain moral systems for relevant statuses) only if that is something they have come to *want*, either for itself or in view of its consequences. So, to see what moral system(s) can be recommended and how, we must clarify what *antecedent* desires/aversions we can count on in the persons we address that will lead them to want, instrumentally, to have certain moral systems in their society, with their expectable consequences, when these are pointed out to them. If we can show that certain kinds of morality would be instrumentally favorable to satisfaction of people's actual (better, carefully appraised) desires, we shall have recommended them.

We should be clear, however, about what we are attempting to do. What we ultimately want to do is recommend *sets* of *moralities* for different people, along with a justification of them. The objects of each such morality will be classes of *actions*. Each such morality will presumably contain a central core that will be the same for everyone in the relevant society. The list of basic core aversions will presumably include something like Ross's list of prima facie obligations, presented later in this chapter. But how we should spell out the content of any of these sets for particular social subgroups (like lawyers or physicians), perhaps by showing their importance for general well-being, is another matter. What we need to work out now is a strategy for how such thought must develop.

I do not suggest, however, that showing a person that some morality for him (or his subgroup) would be optimally instrumental in maximizing social well-being as a whole will by itself produce in him intrinsic aversions (etc.) to certain types of action. That would be too much. Some of the various causal factors (described in Chapter 3) involved in the acquisition of moral aversions may be necessary for this. On the other hand, if a person *wants* a certain set of moral systems for his society as a whole and thinks these would be a socially good thing, it seems he needs some explanation for why he should not think it good for him to share in such a system relevant to his status. Can he complain if the sets of optimal social moralities make certain demands on him if he wants these types of demands made on everyone in his society (or his subgroup)? (We shall return to these questions in Chapter 10.) What we shall now try to show is that a person will *want* certain moralities *for his society*.

In considering how to recommend some basic moral aversions for a society, should we pay attention to the moral aversions a given person already has, such as about adultery? Such aversions must, for our purposes, be ignored. I do concede, however, that some philosophers are "contextualists" about this: They think it justified to take for granted moral aversions that are not currently in dispute for the appraisal of ones being evaluated. This view, however, raises epistemological problems about how the aversions not in dispute are to be justified, and in any case are of little practical value unless there are many such moral aversions that are accepted by everyone. It seems more promising to avoid any such assumption if we can get somewhere without it, as I shall show we can.

So, our question is: Which moral commitments for everyone in society (the core) or for special groups would all (or nearly all) people agree in wanting (or wanting if their wants were carefully appraised) for a society in which they expected to spend a lifetime, previous moral commitment aside, if they were *factually* informed and considered the matter? If we can give a substantive answer to this question, we shall have solid ground to build on.

In order for a person to decide which specific moral codes – packages of aversions – she prefers, she must obviously get an idea of the costs and benefits (from the point of view of her own nonmoral values – but these motives or values may well include some degree of benevolence) of such a moral code existing and being maintained. For example, consider a society in which it is thought morally proper to reward people economically solely on the basis of productive performance, which might as a result be a society where there is much poverty, serious dissatisfaction

125

with one's lot, and envy of the better off – especially if the resulting state of affairs seems a result of the socioeconomic position of one's family. If one does not wish this outcome, then, except insofar as there are countering considerations, one will not want moral codes that permit this principle of economic reward. (This argument assumes that deliberators may care somewhat about the distress of others or at least be concerned about the distress they themselves might experience in a society with such a code.) It was for this general reason that I urged, in Chapter 4, that we pay attention, in deciding what is a right action, to the *social desirability* of codes with certain features. The reason is that people being as they are, social desirability is central to the possibility of recommending a certain kind of moral code.

There is a special benefit of the prevalence of *specific* moral codes: To the extent to which the moral codes of a society succeed in producing conforming behavior, persons in the society will know, reliably, which kinds of conduct to expect of various types of moral individuals in typical situations, and so can count on the ability to execute plans the success of which depends on such predictable behavior. A moral code will *not* be very helpful in this way if it simply calls on people to act so as to bring about the "best" consequences. What is needed is one or more codes with relatively specific prohibitions/requirements.

Before turning to the more detailed content of the moral system that can be successfully recommended, let us look at some further considerations relevant to its general structure. Bearing in mind that morality is a syndrome involving intrinsic aversions to act-*types*, and corresponding dispositions to feel guilt and to disapprove of others, the first question is how complex such a system can be. For such motivations/dispositions can be learned, primarily (not wholly: consider punishment by parents, influence by prestigious models, and identifications) through the existence of empathy/sympathy and self-interest and through the inductive method of teaching aversions to act-types by showing that such aversions are called for by these desires/attitudes. This requirement for learning seems to argue for fairly simple rules (for each relevant type of social status).

But we should not go too far in this: In the course of a lifetime (or of growing up, say, to age 18), everyone must come across many complex situations that many initially learned simple rules just won't fit – when, for instance, they are in conflict with such basic desires as a sympathetic wish for the well-being of others or for protection against injury to self. Thus, one may be taught that it is bad to lie but then come to see that in many types of case it is hurtful to say exactly what one thinks. Or one may be taught that it is wrong to break a promise but come to feel differently about promises extracted by lies the promisee has told you in order to get you to give him an unwarranted advantage over you, or when keeping a promise would make impossible the fulfillment of some stronger moral demand. As a result, our earlier moral motivations (with guilt feelings, etc.) will normally be displaced by something more complex. (Not only such experiences but also tutorial explanations will play a role.) It may be that the older, simpler moralities will be more salient (e.g., immediate guilt feelings more pronounced), but the results of the learning will make some difference when we need to compare our motivations (etc.) about what to do, as explained in the preceding chapter. So, it appears that something as complex as ordinary commonsense morality (variant for persons in different statuses) can be learned as a complex package of aversions (etc.). But we shall see that even a disposition to follow such a "corrected" package of developed conscientious aversions may not always be an optimal guide for what to do in concrete situations, and we shall, in important cases, want some further thinking to back it up – as we shall see we can have.

There is a second question about the structure of the moral systems we might recommend: how *strong* these aversions/dispositions should be. The aversions recommended for a moral system will surely be strong enough to compete with motivations to act contrariwise that we *want* moral motivations to overcome. (Otherwise, what would be the point?) It is sometimes said that to say an action would be *wrong* is at least to imply that the optimal motivation not to perform it has overriding moral force, although what is mostly intended is that the motivation is stronger than any competing *nonmoral* motivations. But since there can be conflicting *moral* motivations (e.g., to tell the truth but also not to harm others), in almost all cases any learned moral motivations may not be strong enough to override all competing moral motivations unless deviation from the motivation in question is one labeled "conclusively wrong." But need every moral motivation be so strong as to overcome all competing *nonmoral* motivations? It would seem not: like "duress" in the law, when following the law would be very oppressive, surely not every moral motivation must be strong enough to overcome all conceivable contrary motivations. When not the latter? Well, perhaps, a motivation to help others so strong as to require giving a kidney to help anyone who needs a kidney to stay alive – or, even more, to give *both* kidneys to help two persons, each of whom needs one to stay alive. (Humans, being what they are, it may not be possible to teach successfully, or at least widely, even the former obligation!) So, there is no point in trying to teach moral motivations of infinite strength – it would not be possible. What we want to teach is motivations of optimal strength, of strength sufficient to override contrary non-moral motivations we want them to override, in view of the costs of teaching.

There is another complication. So far, I have written as if the moral aversions, guilt feelings, and disapprobation of others are roughly parallel in strength. This may not be defensible. For there are costs in having guilt feelings and displaying disapproval of others, and this may need to be taken into account. In the law, I think (and shall explain in Chapter 9) a person is not punished unless the level of her pro-legal *motivation* falls below what is expected of the average law-abiding person. Possibly the same consideration should obtain in moralities, and "excuses" will obtain in them just as in the law. For instance, I may have a satisfactory *strong* aversion to doing a certain thing but still do it – either out of clumsiness or because I nonculpably believe that what I do is not an act of the forbidden sort. Then guilt feelings will hardly make sense, since the major function of the pain of guilt is to remedy a person's defects in motivation. (Somewhat the same is true for indignation at others.) Where there is aversion to performing an act of a certain type, there will be *some* disposition to feel guilt/remorse if one fails and to disapprove when others infringe, but with exceptions and qualifications.

It will be helpful to draw out further parallels between morality and the law, pointing out that criminal law is intended to prohibit typically harmful behavior, but that it nevertheless does not punish a person for action that is contrary to the law but justified because precise conformity to the law would in a given case do harm rather than good; and morality may say the same. (But it does not follow that it would be desirable, either in the law or in morals, that an action that the optimal package of first-order moral aversions, or the law, forbids is to be permitted if performing it would produce only a marginal benefit.) Again, sometimes the statutory requirements of the law conflict, and there is no super-rule that explains what is prohibited in such cases. In law, in "hard" cases, matters are left to the judgment of the appellate courts. What they do is roughly formulate rules to decide such cases, as ones they would like to set as precedents for the future (prospective costs and benefits taken into account, along with preserving analogies so that the law as a whole is left a coherent system). They then follow this rule. The same may be said for morality. Where no aversion has been built into the optimal package of first-order aversions that provides for a novel type of case (or when two rules apply, the directions of which conflict, but neither moral aversion is notably stronger), the individual person can be enjoined (as part of his learned morality) to reflect, and thereafter (it is hoped) to think of a relevant new rule, which he sees can be recommended as a rule it is desirable to have taught to and followed by persons in his position in the future, precisely for the considerations underlying his choice of a social morality as a whole. As a result of reflection on this, the person will presumably follow that rule – and in time find that it has been incorporated, doubtless not saliently but at least in a somewhat muffled form, into his package of intrinsic aversions.

So much for preliminaries. Now if we are to go on and draw a picture of what substantive moral codes thoughtful individuals will want to support for themselves and others, we need information about what states of affairs people in general want (or are averse to) before forming moral attitudes. A preliminary answer is that at least most sane people do have firm nonmoral aversions to certain types of events: such as being injured by other people or being submitted even to the risk of injury, having their property taken or threatened by others, or having career prospects unnecessarily jeopardized by others (and the same things for their children). The same holds roughly for all the major "selfish" aversions of a person. The motivation that arises from this reflection will be the same as that for a system of protective laws and a police force to implement them. So, one wants to live in a world with protection against intrusion by other persons in ways causing injury or preventing satisfaction of major interests. If certain kinds of social morality are essential for this, virtually everyone will want them. So, virtually everyone will want a system of law/morality protecting one from murder, assault, rape, theft, deceit, slander, and so on. We may take it as a given, then, that harmful or interest-frustrating behavior will be opposed by the intrinsic nonmoral attitudes of most normal persons out of self-interest but also, in at least many cases, from empathic altruism; certain kinds of behavior that *usually* lead to events that are harmful or interest-frustrating to human beings will also be opposed.

Obviously, these various interests are not protected if there is only a system of police for law enforcement. There is no point in having police if the members of the force do not themselves have *moral* commitments. It is not enough for a policeman to be part of an institution charged with enforcing the law if he has no moral commitment to doing his part. (He may threaten to arrest a person unless he is given sexual favors.) Moreover, the law is rather a crude instrument; there are many kinds of undesirable behavior it does not condemn – for example, merely demeaning behavior. I suggest it is obvious that nearly *everyone* will want the protection both of the criminal law and also of *complementing* (and *expanding*) social moralities. For much of social morality we can count on nearly universal agreement.

One might ask how such considerations can be brought to

bear on the subject of abortion, discussed in the previous chapter. Of course, here as elsewhere, the various alternatives need to be compared for public benefit and consideration given to the social need for population control, the benefits of choice for the mother, and whether the nonsentient fetus has "interests" in its prospective future. Reflection on these and other matters will make a difference to a person's *wanting* a particular regulation of abortion in the morality of the group (not to mention the intrusion on privacy of any *legal* regulation).

It must be conceded that not everyone can be adequately motivated by *self-interest* to support even a protective kind of law or social morality; some persons may have sufficient power, strength, money, and so on (e.g., an influential racketeer), so that the appeal to one's nonmoral interests in support of a moral code may not be successful. So, there may be a limit beyond which the well placed person cannot be moved by nonmoral selfish interest for the protection of parts of either law or morality. Moreover, more of us belong, to a certain extent, to such well-placed groups than we may think. For we are not animals, members of future generations, poverty-stricken citizens of Third World nations, young children, fetuses, and so on. How might one recommend optimal moralities to all of us (a relevant one for each of us) in these circumstances?

The late Gregory Kavka recently pointed out why even a relatively selfish person will want a morality extended in some ways traditional utilitarianism advocates, independent of the extent of any rational altruism. He stated that wealthy nations benefit in various ways from giving aid to poor nations, with poor nations presumably eventually offering markets, and their better position benefiting others by avoiding political turmoil and regional wars. And he pointed out that present conservation of resources for the sake of future generations tends to benefit the present generation, not to mention the fact that people do care about the well-being of their children and grandchildren, who will clearly benefit. Kavka also said that many people have "self-transcending" interests, like concern for the arts, religion, democratic government, and the prospering of the human species. Promoting these interests gives meaning to their lives and expands the protection they will support for otherwise unprotected groups.[1]

In the case of such advantaged individuals, moreover, we may normally (although not always) count on *some* degree of empathy/sympathy that will motivate them to help protect those less well off. (One might add that many persons wish to have the reputation of being *decent* persons.) In *most* cases, self-interest and empathy/sympathy will tend to support the same social moral codes: Behavior that some do not want because it may put their well-being at risk others will not want because they do not wish still others to be frustrated or injured. But it would be too much to suppose that empathic altruism (etc.) is universal, or at least universal with a high degree of strength. Doubtless even *native* empathy/sympathy occurs in different degrees in different persons. Of course, caring about the well-being of others need not be native; it can have other sources, such as past identification with or teaching by parents and others. In either case we can ask how much such *altruism* is *rational* that is, how high a degree of it might not be subject to the criticism of desires outlined at the close of Chapter 2. (To the extent to which it is *native*, presumably it will not be subject to such criticisms; but if it is not native, one might doubt its force if one became convinced that one was altruistic only because of the coaching of parents or teachers, especially if their teaching was laden with misrepresentations. One might well ask oneself, "*Why* am I benevolent to the degree that I am?") Altruism of any sort is clearly a force, and to a considerable extent it will support moral codes forbidding injury (and promoting benefit) to people generally, just as, to some extent, will self-interest. But the argument does not show that a beneficial social morality can be recommended to *everyone*.

Is there no way we can justify a moral system that protects the interest of *all* sentient creatures, including animals, with a force depending on the strength of the interests involved? (But

---

[1] Gregory Kavka, "The reconciliation project," in David Copps and David Zimmerman (eds.), *Morality, Reason, and Truth* (Totowa, N.J.: Rowman and Allanheld, 1984), pp. 297–319, especially pp. 310–17.

it does seem that if we have to choose between the death of several animals and several children, we should sacrifice the animals; for instance, if it is necessary to test a new medicine, we should put animals at risk rather than human beings. This is not to say that we need not go to the same expense to save animals suffering that we would to save equal suffering for human beings.)[2] The reasoning I prefer for extension of the protection of the moral codes we want for persons in our society to nonprotected groups (animals, future generations, etc.) is a showing that it would be accepted by persons who have a *vivid* idea what life would be like (e.g., for animals), *and* had whatever degree of sympathetic altruism is "rational" for them in the sense of avoiding the mistakes specified in Chapter 2. This does not go as far as to guarantee equal treatment for animals, as we saw (in the preceding chapter) R. M. Hare's theory would go. But if a person's level of empathic altruism does not reach that far, I know of no good argument that shows that, as she now is, she must change her moral stance. It may be, therefore, that the kinds of moralities we can recommend to people in our society will not be fully *utilitarian* in the traditional sense that acceptable moral codes are the ones that will do most good generally for *every* sentient creature affected.

When we bear these points in mind, which substantive moral principles can we recommend? A first *approximation* is this: The best-justified moralities will contain prima facie prohibitions of all acts of types that characteristically injure other sentient creatures in body, property, or status or characteristically prevent others from attaining happiness or getting what they seriously want ("external preferences" aside; see later). This sounds as if an optimal morality would comprise only protection against harm and providing benefits *to* persons (or animals). But it is *logically possible* that there is more: For instance, it might be argued that factually informed people would favor principles that protect *equality* of well-being or of resources, or of opportunities, or *fairness* in the distribution of sacrifices, at least partly

---

[2] See David DeGrazia, "Equal consideration and equal moral status," *Southern Journal of Philosophy* 31 (1993), 17–32.

independently of the benefits *to* persons – but not wholly, for a desire for equality/fairness must surely depend to some extent on recognition of the bad position of the worse off.

Should we want to extend this umbrella of protection to the satisfaction of *every* desire of persons for their own net welfare or to *every* kind of happiness they might experience? It would seem not. For one thing, as I have argued elsewhere,[3] we are inclined to be interested in satisfaction of the desires of other people only when we think frustration will result in distress (or the satisfaction enjoyable), and even then only if the desire is deemed sensible. Moreover, I suggest that society, for obvious reasons, will hardly have an interest in protecting sadistic desires or satisfactions. Further along the same line, I think we need not be concerned about satisfaction of a person's ("external") desires about the states of others' lives. For instance, suppose I want you to paper your house in certain colors, or suppose I even derive satisfaction from the thought of how your rooms are painted. Or suppose I want you not to enjoy reading lewd literature and am displeased if I know you are reading it. I do not know of any general argument by which to justify exclusion of protection of all these latter desires/satisfactions beyond the fact that the actual satisfactions derived from protection of these preferences will be relatively small, smaller than the costs of their protection and the loss, in satisfaction of autonomy, to the other persons. It seems clear that most thoughtful persons would want to exclude them.

Note that I am not here proposing to justify any morality by appeal to any intellectual "intuitions" about the necessary truth of its principles. What I am doing is pointing out the possible benefits of the prevalence and teaching of certain kinds of morality – say, of living in a society where there is mutual trust – among self and others, relying on the effect provided by the vision of these benefits for bringing about the support of moral codes necessary to obtain them. Is this too weak a kind of sup-

---

[3] For instance, in "The psychology of benevolence and its implications for philosophy," *Journal of Philosophy* 78 (1976), 429–53.

port? But if we are to make a rational appeal for support of law/morality or some parts of them, it seems that we have to use the route I am proposing.

What would a complete list of the features of optimal moralities look like? Presumably they would all be near variations of the core of *ordinary morality*, criticized along the *quasi*-utilitarian lines suggested – where the "core" refers to the principles to be taught to everyone. (I say "quasi," since I am not saying that the code we can *successfully* recommend to everyone is exactly utilitarian, being fitted to maximize the good of everyone, including animals.) At the least, scrutiny of ordinary "core" morality will be apt to draw our attention to problem areas where some kind of moral regulation is needed.

Since ordinary morality is complicated, the suggestion that our optimal moral code will be substantially a version of ordinary morality criticized along utilitarian lines may seem disheartening. Do we really need to know so much (or more) – rather after the fashion of Sidgwick?

The work of some recent philosophers may seem to reduce at least the basic principles of commonsense morality to a smaller set. For instance, W. D. Ross proposed that there are just seven distinct, basic, self-evident moral principles: to keep promises; make reparation for injuries wrongfully caused to others, reciprocate services rendered us by others; assist in bringing about a distribution of happiness in accordance with merit; make others better off in respect of virtue, knowledge, and pleasure; improve ourselves in respect of knowledge and virtue; and not injure others. This proposal, however, does not take us very far; it does not tell us what to do when these principles give conflicting directions, nor does it fill in the details – for example, on which promises we are obligated to keep (e.g., ones made because of a misrepresentation of the facts by the promise?) or when to conceal facts (as a lawyer might have an obligation to do for his client). In such situations, Ross thought we must judge which duty is *more pressing* in the case; but we have no self-evidence here. Moreover, Ross made no attempt to show how even the basic principles can be recommended to thoughtful persons (although most of them obviously can be); he simply affirmed that they are self-evident, a conception we have set aside for purposes of moral criticism.

Another view, which might, with numerous apologies to its author, be posed as a simplified formulation of an optimal social morality, is that of Kant: that an act is morally right if and only if its guiding prescription (such as the prescription "let me do A in circumstances EFG") is one the agent can choose to be a guiding motivation for everyone. Thus, it is wrong to borrow money on a promise to repay that one has no intention of fulfilling because it is logically impossible (so Kant thought) for everyone to succeed in following such a rule (since, if everyone did, sensible people would refuse to lend!). But it is also wrong to refuse to make any gifts to charity, or to refuse to develop all of one's talents because there would be a defect in one's self-interested motivation and reflection if one did – since, for the case of charity, one must know that one conceivably could need charitable giving oneself and, for the case of developing talents, one must see that failure to develop one's talents could prevent one from achieving many goals.[4] However, these proposals face difficulties. Among the difficulties is that it is rarely possible to show that it would be logically impossible for everyone to do a certain thing, and that it is far from clear why there would be a defect in one's motivation if one failed to develop one's talents. (We shall shortly see, incidentally, that Kant supported various moral principles that are by no means obvious implications of his general principle.)

Historically, the most widely represented, systematic key to the basic principles of optimal moral systems has been utilitarianism, the theory roughly affirming that the prohibitions or requirements of optimal moralities are fixed by their capacity to maximize the intrinsically good in some way. In some forms

---

[4] Kant says: "as a rational being, he necessarily wills that all his faculties should be developed, inasmuch as they are given to him for all sorts of possible purposes." *Foundations of the Metaphysics of Morals,* trans. L. W. Beck (New York: Liberal Arts Press, 1959), p. 41f.; also p. 48; Akademie edition, 424f. and 430.

"intrinsically good" is construed very broadly, but more convincingly, the "intrinsic goods" considered may be restricted to the goods *of persons* (including animals), as identified, for example, by some version of the happiness or desire satisfaction (or "informed satisfaction") theses formulated in Chapters 2 and 10. The optimal moral system is then identified as the one the implementation of which maximizes the intrinsically good in one of these senses. In what follows, I propose to defend the form of quasi-utilitarianism[5] that holds that *optimal* moral systems are *roughly* those that maximize the intrinsic good of *individuals*, actual or future, directly or indirectly. I shall, in the end, opt for the *indirect* form.

It is perhaps obvious how moralities of this sort can be recommended, with some force, to informed persons by appeal to self-interest, empathy/sympathy, or both.

But to theories of this type there has been a great deal of objection; it has been claimed that such views are far too simple. Some kinds of moral principle have been widely supported by significant moral philosophers, which the previously suggested kind of theory seems to reject.

Begin with some simple principles, hardly supported by philosophers today but doubtless with some popular appeal. Thus, one might propose a moral principle like that of Kant, who, in his *Lectures on Ethics*,[6] castigates various sexual practices (particularly onanism – *Genesis* 38:9) on the ground that they are contrary to nature and especially because they "degrade" a person to the level of animals and make him "unworthy of his humanity. He no longer deserves to be a person." Somewhat similarly, Hastings Rashdall[7] affirmed that even an occasional drunk is

---

[5] I am using the term "*quasi*-utilitarianism" in order to contrast what I shall support with a pure utilitarianism to permit deviations from the traditional view that the target of morality must be the actual good of *all* sentient creatures. I am conceding possible deviation from this view on the part, e.g., of persons with defective empathy/altruism.

[6] New York: Harper & Row, 1963, pp. 169ff.

[7] *The Theory of Good and Evil* (Oxford: Oxford University Press, 1924), vol. 1, pp. 156–8.

intrinsically "disgusting." But one can ask how they came to hold these views. Surely not by personal experimentation or observation and finding that acts of these types have displeasing results. Doubtless they acquired these aversions in the process of culture transmission, from the preaching of puritanical parents. Perhaps they might have justified the aversions, but that would necessarily have been a longer story. (It is possible that a person is opposed to drunkenness because he has frequently been annoyed by the attention of drunks, or because drunks are dangerous, especially if they drive; but surely this is not what Rashdall had in mind.) Intuitive principles like these will hardly be taken seriously at present; they are obviously wanting in ability to be recommended.

Consider again a principle forbidding suicide. About this Rashdall wrote: "A strong feeling against suicide seems to be the spontaneous deliverance of the moral consciousness, wherever the Christian view of life, with its ideas of discipline, education, or moral probation, and its sense of responsibility to a divine Father, is accepted."[8] Much the same is stated by Kant: "We have been placed in this world under certain conditions and for specific purposes. But a suicide opposes the purpose of his Creator; he arrives in the other world as one who has deserted his post; he must be looked upon as a rebel against God. . . . Human beings are sentinels on earth and may not leave their posts until relieved by another beneficent hand."[9] In both these cases, however, an aversion to suicide has evidently been produced by false or at least highly questionable theological beliefs. Doubtless suicide is normally unfortunate, but is it something thoughtful, factually informed people would want the moral code to oppose as such?[10] (Perhaps, if that might prevent irrational, impulsive suicides.)

Somewhat similar things may be said in criticism of the view

---

[8] Ibid., vol. 1, p. 210.   [9] Ibid., vol. 1, p. 154.

[10] See my "The morality and rationality of suicide," reprinted in Brandt, *Morality, Utilitarianism and Rights* (Cambridge: Cambridge University Press, 1992), pp. 315–35; also "A moral principle about killing," in Marvin Kohl (ed.), *Beneficent Euthanasia* (Buffalo, N.Y.: Prometheus Books, 1975), pp. 106–16.

that criminals should be punished according to the heinousness of their offense, with relatively little regard to the utilitarian concern about whether such a system of criminal punishment is to the public benefit. This view has a long history: "An eye for an eye" (*Exodus* 21:24–5). Again from Kant: The standard of justice is the "principle of equality. . . . Whatever undeserved evil you inflict on another person, you inflict on yourself. . . . [This] is possible only through the rule of retribution . . . only then is sentence pronounced proportionate to internal wickedness. . . . If a person has committed murder, he must die."[11] (Kant did not explain how a given offense is a mark of "internal wickedness," or how he would propose to punish prostitution, or why it is the duty of the state to punish internal wickedness.) There are better ways to prevent a criminal from repeating and to get at the causes of crime, as we shall see in Chapter 9; but we shall also see that there are contemporary supporters of essentially a Kantian-type view.

In all these cases, condemnation of a form of behavior or a person who behaves in a certain way is recommended either on the basis of false or dubious factual representations or with no reasoning at all to justify an aversive attitude. I suggest that any theory recommending a moral aversion with no firmer basis does not succeed.

There have been more serious criticisms of utilitarianisms. For instance, it has been claimed that the very conception of a "good state of affairs" or "well-being" cannot be spelled out, or that the values of the various good things cannot be compared or measured, or that no one is in a position to estimate the effect of a given event on the well-being of other persons. Of course, these charges must be met; we have seen how the first one can be met if the claims of Chapter 2 are accepted, and there have been various proposals about how interpersonal comparisons can be made with reasonable reliability.[12] Again, it has been

---

[11] *The Philosophy of Law*, trans. W. Hastie (Edinburg: T. and T. Clark, 1887), pp. 194ff.

[12] See *A Theory of the Good and the Right* (Oxford: Oxford University Press, 1979), pp. 257–66. For various views on the topic, see Jon Elster and J. E. Roemer

claimed that at least some forms of utilitarianism fail to recognize either claims of *equality* of welfare or the difference between persons (as is allegedly shown by a willingness to sacrifice important goods for a minority group in view of a superior total benefit to a larger number). These objections probably strike a responsive chord in many people; but in Chapter 7 we shall see whether a form of utilitarian theory can accommodate the force of both of them. It is often said that the theory makes too severe demands on individuals. Must one do what will benefit many others when the cost to oneself is severe? Or should we demand at most only, as T. M. Scanlon has suggested, that people make sacrifices in deference to general rules of behavior that could not *reasonably* be rejected by *anyone*, including the person asked to make the sacrifice?[13] (I shall discuss this view in more detail in the section "An Antiutilitarian Alternative: Contractualism" later in this chapter. But one thing needed from the critic of utilitarianisms is a clear demonstration that an optimal form of utilitarianism will really suffer from these defects. And it needs to be shown how some other theory can recommend a morality that provides desirable protections and prohibitions that no utilitarianism can provide. It is possible that a utilitarian-type theory is only part of the story; but anyone who wants something more complicated must be prepared to explain how it can be recommended. I am assuming that if one can show that a certain social morality would be wanted by fully informed people, in view of its anticipated consequences, it has been recommended.

But first, we have not even sketched the detailed kind of utilitarianism to which our theory, so far, tends to lead. We must now go into this.

Must one insist that the *specific* motivations a utilitarian-type theory recommends are ones that should be universally

(eds.), *Interpersonal Comparisons of Well-being* (Cambridge: Cambridge University Press, 1991).

[13] See T. M. Scanlon, "Contractualism and utilitarianism," in A. K. Sen and Bernard Williams (eds.), *Utilitarianism and Beyond* (Cambridge: Cambridge University Press, 1982), pp. 103–28.

adopted by all societies, at least by people who are not making factual mistakes? Or may they vary from group to group? Presumably the latter. One need not question that some abstract form of utilitarian theory (as explained later) is correct for all groups. But such abstract theories do not identify specific social moralities – with guilt feelings, the disposition to reproach others, and so on. And the detailed aversions (etc.) that these theories recommend will not be uniform throughout all societies, for life conditions and institutions vary. For instance, some societies are monogamous, some polygynous, others polyandrous. Some societies live in a benign climate (Greece, Egypt), others in a harsh one (Eskimos). These variations must make a difference to morally permitted treatment of others.

I have suggested that in considering whether a given moral system can be recommended, we have to take account of its costs as well as its effects. In counting the costs, I suggest that we need to bear in mind, at least normally, the cost of keeping a standing rule in operation – mainly the effort of teaching that moral system to children (or students, say in medical schools), so as not to burden them with excessive feelings of guilt, and, of course, the costs to the individuals who must make some sacrifice in living according to the principles – not the cost involved in getting a new rule introduced in opposition to the status quo. The latter, transition costs are ephemeral, whereas the question of whether a given type of code has more costs than benefits is a long-term one. Of course, in any case, the normal costs to an individual of even a transition will be small, for an individual can't make a big change all by herself, her only cost being talking and setting an example. In some cases, however, there are complications, which involve possible modifications of the normal rules. Take racial discrimination. It might be best to have a system in which a man/woman has a right to cohabit with/marry a person of a different race or ride in the same part of a bus. But if a person tried to introduce such a system both by precept and by practice, she might occasion violence, especially against herself. The question is what is the best thing to do in such a situation. The right morality to preach/practice for now might be a gradual, peaceful movement in the direction of total non-discrimination, but so calculated as not to incite serious violence along the way. (This would be a move in deference to another rule: not to cause serious harm.) There is no reason why the "right" moral rule should not take such a complicated, progressive form in a given society and time.

So, the moral rules the (quasi) utilitarian, direct or indirect, will recommend to persons in a given society are, at least as a first approximation, the ones it would be best, compared with other possible ones – all the costs and benefits taken together – to have taught in that society (or relevant groups in it), including the costs–benefits to other societies affected, along with animals and future generations.

THE SPECIFIC CONTENT OF AN OPTIMAL MORAL SYSTEM

But what is the content of the moral conscience(s) that can be recommended as best to teach and have prevalent in a society, given all the costs and benefits?[14]

One proposal that has attracted numerous philosophers, especially in this century, is very simple: It is that the optimal conscience contains only one requirement: that one always perform that act, among the options open to one, such that the consequences of so doing are maximally beneficial (some would say: maximize happiness) for everyone affected at any time or place. Or at least one should perform that act, among those that on the evidence are available to one, that will most *probably* maximize benefits – that is, "expectable utility." Put a different way, the theory holds that the right act is the one that maximizes utility (or expectable utility), and hence that the one basic principle of an optimal morality is the requirement to do that. This view, this form of "direct" utilitarianism, is usually known as "act-utilitarianism." (On this view, we need not think of separate moralities for different groups; there is only one basic moral

---

[14] I propose to ignore the question of whether benefit might be maximized by enlarging the population, although I suggest there is such a thing as optimal population size from the point of view of total well-being.

principle, the same for all.) Since I have suggested that the code to be chosen is the one teaching and prevalence of which would (probably) maximize benefit, why not this one? Is it not at least a simpler view that one take each act individually and decide what to do on the basis of probable beneficial consequences, rather than make a large comparison between the teaching/ prevalence of somewhat different moral codes in a whole society, such as "indirect" forms of theory advocate?

Specifically what this one-principle code calls on one to do, in each case requiring a decision, is to identify the consequences affecting benefit if one act is performed compared with another, identify utilities, and estimate the probability of each consequence when a certain act is performed. Then one should perform the act the expectable utilities of which have the higher sum. This sounds complicated, but if we are taking into account only probabilities given our evidence, in many cases it will be relatively easy. The hard part will be to identify the "products" of utilities and probabilities, but most proposed normative theories face either the same problem or one very much like it. Of course, we have generalizations from all known past experience to go on – for example, how counterproductive it is to be given false directions, in unfamiliar territory, about how to get somewhere when an informant could easily give correct directions. We can use such information from past experience to guide judgments about an instant case. But the basic principle is to maximize public benefit, and although we may know that normally this is done by avoiding deceit, if in a given case we know that deceit will have the best consequences, then we know that that is the moral thing to do.

There are several problems with reliance on an act-utilitarian moral system of this sort. First, the problem to be solved can be complex enough to invite self-serving rationalization. Suppose one is considering whether to make an income tax report that dodges payment of $1,000. The benefit is partial payment of a vacation in Greece for me. What is the cost in general utility? Who will have which benefit, and who would not have it if I save money for a vacation in Greece? This would be hard to say. But the implications and benefits of specific moral *rules* being prevalent are clear, such as "Report your income honestly." Second, if a person follows this one act-utilitarian principle, it will often be relatively difficult to predict what he will do. For instance, suppose I have performed some service – mowed your lawn in response to a promise of payment of $10 for so doing. But when the service is completed, will I collect? The theory tells a person to do whatever will maximize utility by her expenditure. It seems that whether I am paid will depend on, say, your conception of the relative importance of various other purposes for which you might spend the money. When this occurs, the incentive to perform such services will be reduced, as will the incentive to make any plans that count on the predictable behavior of others.[15] Third, the theory seems to make harsh and oppressive demands on the moral agent. For instance, at the present time I am relatively certain that, come evening, all my moral obligations (except the duty to give more to needy causes) will be discharged, and indeed that I will be free to go on writing, or to read a book or watch TV, without being morally derelict. But if I really have an obligation to do what will maximize benefit, this evening I might be obligated to phone some acquaintance and find out if there is something I could do to improve the quality of his life (provided there was no reason to think he would be irritated by the interruption). Doubtless it would be better if I felt called on to do more of this, particularly for needy people, but the idea of always being morally obligated, with no area of freedom to do just what I want or to enjoy myself (except where this would maximize expectable utility), is not a recommendation to me. Nor do I want others to be so circumstanced. (This is not to say that we may not recommend self-sacrificing behavior in the service of worthwhile causes.) It will hardly be possible to recommend a moral system of this sort to thoughtful people.

The first view, however, has the virtue that it recommends/

---

[15] See John Harsanyi, "Morality and the theory of rational behavior," *Social Research* 44 (1977), 631–6; "Rule-utilitarianism and decision theory," *Erkenntnis* 11 (1977), 27–9; and "Basic moral decisions and alternative concepts of rationality," *Social Theory and Practice* 9 (1983), 231–44.

prohibits action on the ground that the action does affect the production of the really good (see Chapter 2) – for example, either pleasure/happiness or events that persons want for themselves (at least when they are not making, or are allowing for, certain "mistakes" in their desires), or some combination of the two. An action is prohibited/required because it will (probably) bring about the really good for all sentient beings. This fact is a somewhat moving recommendation both to self-interest and to empathy/sympathy.

WHAT AN INDIRECT UTILITARIANISM WILL RECOMMEND

If we are not to recommend a single moral rule always to make a maximal contribution to well-being, then what is a teacher of morality to do if he is to recommend specific moral codes essentially along utilitarian lines? Possibly he should recommend a morality somewhat similar to the commonsense morality of persons he is addressing, but revised to take more account of expectable benefits. How might he do this?

We know what he should be aiming at: to sketch a system of plural moral *motivations* (aversions, etc.) so devised that, taken with the implications of these aversions for special situations, the *teaching* and *prevalence* of them will, all costs and benefits included, probably enhance (ideally, maximally) the happiness or well-being (properly construed) of sentient beings. Such a system could be recommended both as providing protections that virtually all people will want and as appealing to the empathy/sympathy of many.

Such moral codes can be called examples of "indirect conscience-utilitarianism."[16] A central part of this theory will be that the *morally right act* is said to be the one that best incorporates (roughly, follows the strongest of) the proposed system of optimal moral motivations for instant cases. (I do not say that

---

[16] I have presented a fuller statement of this theory in "Fairness to indirect optimific theories in ethics," *Ethics* 98 (1988), 341–60, reprinted in *Morality, Utilitarianism, and Rights.*

this conception is analytic of the ordinary meaning of "morally right act," but rather than it gives a sense to this term, so that the "right act" is one that can be recommended to informed people and so that the term has a useful meaning that everyone can understand.)

In considering which moral codes to recommend to a society, we must bear in mind that the society will be composed of somewhat different groups in different morally relevant positions in relation to other persons, such as parents, physicians, lawyers, business people, and teachers. These special positions may make a difference to exactly which moral principles are socially most beneficial for them to be taught and apply, given the situation of the special group, hence the one to be recommended to their consciences. But presumably there will also be a core basic code that it is optimal to teach all adults or even children in a given society.

But which specific rules will be taught? Ideally, we should ransack both the law and commonsense morality to get a list of types of situation in which the agent needs to know what to do. Then we shall seek to instill the motivations of a proposed moral code according to the conscience-utilitarian conception of optimal moral codes. I am not about to undertake a massive investigation of that sort. What I can do here is simply list, as possible samples, prohibitions one might teach children, such as these: not to beat up smaller siblings, to pay attention to the burdens and desires of others by sharing toys and helping with household chores, and not to grab the largest piece of cake. Other rules might be taught only when the child has started to school, from the lower grades through high school. Some of these will be: not to cheat on tests, to be truthful, not to get into fights with classmates, not to steal, not to carry a gun, not to intimidate anyone by threats, to keep promises (say, to meet someone after school), to treat everyone kindly and indeed generously, irrespective of race, religion, or national origin, and not to be cruel to animals. These requirements, slightly revised, will be suitable for adult life as well. Some further requirements will generally be relevant only if the addressee is an adult: for instance, not committing bigamy and not interfering with the free actions of other people. (We can draw numerous examples from the criminal law.) One might also teach a requirement to help others in distress when one can do so at relatively low cost to oneself, perhaps to stand ready to perform community services, and perhaps to show gratitude to those who have performed a service for one. There might also be special permission for any agent to seek her own well-being with more avidity than she seeks the well-being of other persons, although probably not to give her own well-being priority over a much larger gain of welfare by others when she has a choice. And, of course, there will be special requirements governing one's relation to persons with whom one has special ties: special obligations to one's employees, or clients if one is a physician or lawyer; special care and concern for the health and well-being of one's parents, spouse, and children, and to a lesser extent other relatives and maybe friends. These special requirements may be recommended by pointing out that in the actual organization of society, satisfying them will produce a great deal of well-being. (Some of these duties are best identified by experienced teachers in the professional schools: business, law, and medicine.) Obviously, there are many principles to be taught and absorbed, but some of them only by professionals like lawyers and physicians.

In general, these suggestions, of course, are roughly embodied in contemporary commonsense morality (taken broadly, so that physicians' duties are included) but, as stated, they are only a very simplified form of part of that complex. (But they are clearly very different from the one rule of the act-utilitarian.) They are directives about how to act in specific types of situations, corresponding to *motivations* to perform or not perform certain kinds of action, the motivations being selected by the test of being the optimal ones, all the costs and benefits of people teaching and acting on them being taken into account. Ideally, such conscience motivations of a sophisticated person will come equipped (after adequate teaching and experience) with varying degrees of strength and a list of exceptions attached to each, so that in an actual situation the agent will be holistically impelled to give a certain requirement the relative strength optimally required in most types of ordinary situation.

Thus, if a promise has been made, the motivation to keep it will depend on various factors, such as the cost of keeping/failing to both parties, how serious the commitment was (it could have been a causal commitment between friends, and a casual promise can be broken for relatively trivial benefits to the promiser[17]), how long ago the promise was made, whether there was an understanding about the conditions in which it would be binding, and so on. (So, one will hardly be morally required to give up a chance for a weekend of skiing in order to keep a promise to the paper deliverer to pay her on Friday!) One might think that the force of a given promise depends, as the direct act-utilitarian would have it, only on the anticipated good/bad consequences for everyone concerned. But this is not so: The indirect utilitarian is asking, in regard to the whole complex attitude about promise keeping, whether one or another form would be more beneficial in the long term for society as a whole, including the difficulties of teaching.

As mentioned earlier in this chapter, the "rules" will be taught so as to include a system of "excuses," so that a person is not condemned for an infraction he could not well have avoided or that does not reflect on his moral motivations as a whole. To condemn him would be pointless.

Even if we had a complete list of what the normally taught specific requirements of morality should be, there is another question: Should the complex of motives best taught for most situations in the long run be followed in a particular situation where following them would have bad consequences? Just as in the law, which regards some acts prohibited by the legal code as justified when a serious public good is at stake (say, destroying another's home in order to prevent the spread of a fire), so we may say that a moral code of this sort (e.g., about promises) simple enough to be learned may have to be stretched in an emergency situation when following it would cause severe harm or prevent a great deal of good. Such a view seems to have

---

[17] See, for instance, Donald Regan, "On preferences and promises," *Ethics* 96 (1985), 56–67.

been accepted by Mill.[18] Jonathan Harrison has asked just "how bad the consequences of adhering to a rule must be, before one ought to break it."[19] To this I would reply that persons in a specific situation need to supply numbers no more than the courts, which seem to have no difficulty with the distinction.[20] For example, the use of torture (normally strongly forbidden) to extract information might be justified if the issue is an atomic bomb set to destroy New York City – provided there is probable ground to think one has the right party.

The details of a complete system will obviously be complex. And even if one has absorbed such a system, it may sometimes not be easy to decide whether one moral requirement is more weighty than another – or what a teacher should say about which is more weighty, when she considers that a decision about comparative weight must be justified by appeal to the impact of the teaching and by the prevalence of each moral requirement for the general well-being. In any case, it does appear that the outcomes of such subtle discriminations cannot be built into conscience in as salient a way as the simpler rules, like not telling a lie, so that they will manifest their comparative force motivationally when a decision has to be made. It therefore seems as if some decisions about relative weight must eventually be made by the actual agent (or an adviser) at the time of a specific decision, that is, by a *judgment* about the relative long-term benefit of teaching *alternative rules*. Now if a conscience-utilitarian morality is to this extent dependent on the specific judgment of agents at the time of decision, does this

---

18 About a page from the end of Chapter 5 of *Utilitarianism* he wrote: "Particular cases may occur in which some other social duty is so important as to overrule any one of the general maxims of justice. Thus, to save a life it may be not only allowable, but a duty, to steal or take by force the necessary food or medicine, or to kidnap and compel to officiate the only qualified medical practitioner."

19 See his "Rule-utilitarianism and cumulative-effect utilitarianism," *Canadian Journal of Philosophy* 5 (suppl. 1979), 22.

20 See Charles Black, "Mr. Justice Black, the Supreme Court and the Bill of Rights," *Harper's Magazine* (February 1961), especially pp. 67–8. See footnote 24 on a suggestion by Sanford Levy about how to avoid this difficulty.

conscience-utilitarian theory not suffer from a defect I cited against act-utilitarianism: that following it would not permit prediction of the behavior of other people, with the resulting problems for coordination and motivation based on sound expectations about the behavior of others? Would these rules, which reflect complex judgments to this extent, permit prediction of the behavior of moral persons, so as to permit coordination and reliance?

To this query about the possibly unhelpful effect of teaching/having such a moral code, we can reply, as Berkeley did, that at least the basic principles do "to right reason evidently appear to have a necessary connexion with the Universal well-being." Berkeley's view seems to be seconded by J. D. Mabbott, who raised the question of whether life would be tolerable, or a particular kind of society possible, if certain moral rules were not recognized and generally observed.[21] What this means is that at least in the case of the major prohibitions to be taught, it is manifest that their teaching and prevalence will be roughly beneficial to the relevant society, at least as compared with no such teaching – that society will be much better off if people have internalized the recommended standards, as compared with having no such standards or significantly different ones, despite some costs of teaching. It is only some more specific points, such as allowable exceptions in special circumstances or the relative weight of principles where there is conflict, that may be matters of agent judgment about which rule should have priority and of some uncertainty. This distinction may correspond roughly to what W. D. Ross had in mind when he distinguished between moral requirements that are "self-evident" and those that, at best, are matters of probable opinion, so that in complex cases we are lucky if we do the right thing.[22] Fortunately, the moral motivations that will optimally

---

[21] George Berkeley, *Passive Obedience* (1712), reprinted in *Berkeley*, ed. M. W. Calkins (New York: Charles Scribners' Sons, 1929), p. 436; J. D. Mabbott, "Moral rules," *Proceedings of the British Academy* 39 (1953), 97–117, especially 107–17.

[22] W. D. Ross, *The Right and the Good* (Oxford: Clarendon Press, 1930), pp. 30ff.

govern the main business of society will, we may think along with Berkeley, not be controversial, so that normally one person can reliably predict what another person will do in a certain situation, provided that this other person is a moral person who has absorbed the recommended motivations. Such rules of morality will be known to most members of a whole society (or perhaps a subgroup like physicians). So, a main pragmatic criticism raised against the act-utilitarian theory is applicable to the present "conscience-utilitarian" theory, but only to a minor extent. I see no reason why this amount of possible disagreement should be a pragmatic obstacle to acceptance of the general proposal.

Some philosophers have criticized the foregoing conscience-utilitarian view, comparing it unfavorably with the act-utilitarian theory. Philippa Foot, for instance, wrote that "Surely it will be irrational, we feel, to obey even the most useful rule if in a particular instance we clearly see that such obedience will not have the best results."[23] We have seen, however, that an optimal moral code will surely contain prohibitions of injury to others and an injunction to aid persons in distress. So presumably, telling people to do what fails to maximize benefit will usually occur only when any harm done is relatively small or when aid is not needed. Moreover, as we have just noted, there is a second fact that narrows the gap between a conscience-utilitarian view and such critics: that a moral system is optimal only if it permits or even enjoins behavior otherwise prohibited by the normal rules, when omission of such behavior would be significantly harmful or costly for the production of good. Presumably an agent will normally abide by the standard rules in her own conscience in many or most cases, and certainly will not always be looking around for some harm that might require her to ignore the built-in rules of conscience; it is only when the prospect of a loss (or gain) from breach is so serious that it becomes salient in her consciousness that we want to recommend that she reflect on whether the gain/loss in benefit justi-

---

[23] "Utilitarianism and the virtues," *Mind* 94 (1985), 196.

fies some breach of the rules.[24] A conscience-utilitarianism will recommend that this sort of exception be built into the basic set of moral motivations.

I think we have to admit that some of these details, although they can be presented convincingly to thoughtful persons, can hardly be expected to be incorporated into the core consciences of everyone, including children. What we should try to teach, as a moral code, will necessarily depend on the intellectual level of the recipient. Exactly which aversions one should try to inculcate in a given person must depend on the judgment of the tutor.

There is, however, still another complication. Suppose there is a certain amount of obstinate noncompliance with the standard moral code, perhaps out of selfishness. In that case, do we not need to be able to take the amount of noncompliance into account in order to know which moral requirements are optimal – just as, in the law, it is optimal to set a speed limit in view of the dispositions, difficult to change, of average drivers? I concede that for fine-tuning we may need this (although we must be careful to avoid unfeasible complexity), but we hardly need to know in advance exactly who will cooperate with the optimal requirements or even roughly how many. Suppose we do know roughly which requirements would be optimal if everyone were disposed to cooperate. How much, and how, would we need to change these rules if we had good reason to think that, say, 25 percent of the population would flout a given requirement? Even if dishonesty is frequent in business, things will manifestly work better – even economically, in terms of transaction costs – if a standard of honesty is fairly widespread and recognized as morally required. (Doubtless it makes a difference what the specific rule in question is.) It is true that, out of fairness, we should not want people to shoulder a large burden if many are unwilling to assume it; perhaps in some situations it is desirable to identify a rule deciding who must assume any burdens. And it is true that some requirement would not be

---

[24] This way of putting matters is due to a personal communication from Sanford Levy.

optimal if the compliance were so meager that compliance of the morally committed would serve no purpose. My suggestion, however, is that we know enough, in most cases, to identify an optimal rule – the motivation the teaching and prevalence of which would maximize social benefit – so that we can know which kinds of motivations to try to inculcate in recipients. Doubtless there is a limit to fine-tuning for some situations.

The conception of an optimal moral system can be applied in two contexts: first, as determining what is the right thing to do if the present institutions of society are accepted as social facts not subject to moral criticism; and second, as reforming criticism of the system of existing institutions. Thus a philosopher, in his role as reforming critic of institutions, will presumably wish to comment, at some stage, on the implications of the various moral principles he is teaching for the institutions of his society: rules about how corporations should be run in a capitalist society (e.g., how officers are selected and paid), tax laws, how public officers are selected and the powers they should have, whether marriage with all its rights and duties should be made available to couples of the same sex, and so on. In other cases, the existing institutions will serve as a background for identifying the optimal moral code.

These complications do not make trivial the difference between an optimal conscience-utilitarian moral code and the actual codes of actual societies – so that the conscience-utilitarian will by no means in all cases be an "incrementalist," in the sense of one who advocates only minor changes in a society's commonsense moral code. For there have been and are major and serious differences between the optimal and the actual moral codes of different societies – for example, some holding that it is morally permissible to exterminate Jews for the sake of the well-being of the Third Reich, or to approve vast inequalities in wealth and opportunities, as is the case with some monarchies in the Middle East (or in the United States!), or to accept barbarous forms of punishment in implementing the accepted criminal law. These actual moralities are incompatible with a conscience-utilitarian theory of morality: Their standards and practices are in direct conflict with the requirement that moral codes contribute maximally to the general well-being. In the societies where these moralities prevail, whoever teaches the code may be doing a partial job – perhaps passing the content of his own conscience on to her students, but not subjecting her prescriptions to the requirement of contribution to social benefit.

There is another complication concerning what the conscience-utilitarian theory should say about "acts of supererogation": acts that would be required by an optimal morality but for the personal costs to the agent. What should we say about the morality of a person like Mother Teresa or Albert Schweitzer, or about a soldier who throws his body on a dropped live grenade, killing himself but saving others? I suggest it may be useful for such persons to be admired and praised for what they did. But it is clear that if persons fail to do these things, their moral motivation need not be below the standard it is useful to *demand* – what we might call the level of "good character" – on pain of condemnation. It would be silly to try to make people feel guilty for failing to do these things or to condemn others who fail. So, the rational teacher of morality may want to encourage doing such things but not demand them on pain of criticism for falling below the appropriate moral level of motivations. The things these "saints" did are good, but the types of things they did are not as important for social benefit as are, in the average person who is hardly capable of more, honesty, kindness, and so on. How far a teacher of morality should go in encouraging (and perhaps to some extent teaching) saintly behavior and traits of character is difficult to determine. Such encouragement might just result in frustration for some persons and not much benefit for others. For many people, learning such saintly traits may be impossible.

The foregoing picture has included some brief examples of the kinds of conscience-utilitarian principles that can be recommended to possible agents, mostly children. But it should be clear that the conscience-utilitarian *theory* does not include a specification of moral motivations it would be best to have prevalent and taught. (The suggested examples were just that: possible examples.) The general theory is essentially a directive for *thinking* to be done: things a person must do to identify the moral codes it would be best to have prevalent and taught, all costs and benefits considered, and therefore able to be recommended in view of what people nonmorally want or care about if their desires have been carefully appraised.

If we agree to all this, how close do we come to being forced to include at least some of these specifications in an account of the ordinary *meaning* of moral statements, as was done by old hard-line naturalists? For although I say that moral statements are *expressions* of the speaker's actual moral code, I leave open that one might say that "*justifiably* thought wrong" should be taken to imply or perhaps even to *mean* something like "would be contrary to a moral code that can be widely recommended because its teaching and prevalence will maximize social benefit." How we should answer this question of meaning can be a question for the philosophy of language. However that may be, it seems that the proposal here put forward is at least a revisionist naturalism, if a naturalism at all. The whole claim is derived not from consideration of whether various moral statements are analytically entailed by the ordinary meaning of "is morally wrong" but rather from reflection on what informed, thoughtful people would expect of the attitudes expressed in moral statements, including universalizability and the necessity of some of them being recommendable over others in view of prospective social benefits.

One can hardly claim that it is impossible for two persons' conclusory appraisals/judgments, in different societies or even in the same society, to meet all these requirements and still differ in substance; in that sense, there is room for relativism. And if so, some corresponding relativistic construction of the concept of "justification" of moral statements may be called for.

Can we then say that a moral statement that meets all these conditions, possibly construed relativistically, is true? This depends on how we construe "true." Perhaps it makes little difference what we say, provided we understand the epistemological status of the claim.

THE PLACE OF MORAL RIGHTS

Thus far, nothing has been said about the concept of "moral rights." For an explication of this, we must turn to the concept basic to the indirect utilitarian theory outlined earlier: the notion of an *optimal* moral conscience, where "conscience" is construed as motivations not to do certain types of thing, plus a disposition to feel guilty if one acts contrariwise, plus a disposition to be indignant with others who do and a disposition to believe that the foregoing attitudes can be justified in some appropriate way. The outcome of this conception of an optimal conscience is that "it is morally *wrong* for X to do A" is best construed as "X doing A would be contrary to the requirements of an *optimal moral conscience* – the one it would be most socially beneficial to have taught and prevalent."

How does the conception of moral rights fit into this picture? A traditional view, espoused by various philosophers, would be the following explanation of "rights" language: "X has a moral right to Y against Z" comes, at least approximately, to "It would be seriously wrong morally for Z to prevent (or fail to promote) X's getting Y."[25]

Since I have defended an *indirect utilitarian* account of moral obligation – right and wrong actions – I am committed by this explication of moral rights to defending a roughly indirect utilitarian theory of moral rights.[26] And indeed, I do hold such a theory, although I should wish to amplify the foregoing traditional explanation of "rights" talk to some extent. First, by explaining, as I think defenders of the preceding explication of rights language all do, that when one person has a right to something, then what it is morally obligatory for others to do is enable this person to do, have, or enjoy that to which he has a

---

[25] See my "The concept of a moral right and its function," *Journal of Philosophy* (1983), 29–45, reprinted in *Morality, Utilitarianism, and Rights*, p. 184.

[26] I defend this view in "Utilitarianism and moral rights," *Canadian Journal of Philosophy* 14 (1984), 1–19. This article replies to some criticisms by David Lyons and draws a contrast with the views of R. M. Hare, reprinted in *Morality, Utilitarianism, and Rights*, pp. 196–214.

right. This is accomplished partly by noninterference but also, when needed, by cooperation in bringing about the opportunity – and all this largely because of the importance to people in the situation of the rights holder of having this noninterference and cooperation from others. But, more substantially, I would add, as some philosophers would do,[27] that the right holders are morally permitted to feel resentment of the hurt/disappointment that arises when others fail to meet this obligation, and to protest without any feeling of shame, and to take reasonable steps of protest designed to call attention to the situation and to encourage remedy of it. (This is not to say that they *must* do this – especially if they are children or animals, which cannot – but only that they morally may, and perhaps, if adults, that they are subject to a mild degree of moral criticism if they don't.) The utilitarian will emphasize this latter addition because of the historical importance of protests by right holders, like women and blacks, in support of the strength of the moral condemnation of right infringements.

One might ask why, if rights statements can be thus translated into statements about the moral obligations of others who confront right holders, it is important for there to be a concept of "moral rights" at all. The main answer is pragmatic. For one thing, rights talk focuses attention on the goods to be protected; it is simpler, and it contrasts with any listing of all the obligations people are under when a person has a moral right. (Compare "A woman has a moral right to equality of opportunity" to a listing of all the duties others may owe on this account.) This can be a rallying cry that might start a revolution; a listing of obligations owed to rights holders would not be a call to arms. For another thing, the term "rights" expresses strength; the obligations involved are strong, and rights talk naturally expresses this force without having to mention it.

Various philosophers have held that rights are "trumps," which is not quite true, since one right can conflict with another and rights have only prima facie force. Yet it is true that their force

---

[27] Roughly, W. D. Ross, David Lyons, Joel Feinberg, Richard Flathman, and Richard Wasserstrom.

is superior to that of relatively minor public benefits. How is this, and how can an indirect utilitarianism support this view? For instance, why should an indirect utilitarian give moral weight to a woman's saying "no" as a result of a momentary whim when no comparable moral force is given to a strong desire of some man to have intercourse with her, who would greatly enjoy it? A possible answer is that this capacity of hers may be an important part (maybe not if it is only a whim) of her liberty to live her life as she wants to and plans it, and this possibility would be undermined if this right were not recognized. Somewhat parallel to this is the case for the whole list of moral rights that an indirect utilitarian would seriously support. For there are many requirements for living a decent life: having health care, protection of bodily integrity, access to education, freedom of speech and associations and lifestyle, a free press, a voice in political decisions, a floor of economic welfare, and so on. Which rights exist, and which ones have superior strength in case of conflict, the indirect utilitarian will say must be settled in essentially the same way we settle any conflict of moral duties, like duties not to murder or commit perjury or sell marijuana: by weighing the severity of the impact on well-being of such offenses and, as a consequence, of the importance of a moral (or legal) code providing protection against their occurrence.

The indirect utilitarian supports a moral aversion (etc.) to offending against these rights in the same way he supports aversion to murder and rape: by pointing out that everyone – or virtually everyone – will want motivation (etc.) of this sort to exist, in view of the consequences of the states of affairs envisioned (especially consequences for the right holder), either because he wants protection of this sort for himself (or his loved ones) or from empathic altruism. So, affirmation of a set of moral rights forms a package, along with a list of moral wrongs or obligations, on the basis of a comparable set of normal human desires.

The complications that arise for an indirect utilitarian moral theory concern its theory of rights, as well as the theory in general, as we have seen in this chapter. Rights are not fixed by actual moral codes but rather by a code's being optimal. And to determine which moral code is optimal for a given society may

158

not be obvious. For an individual to know what the moral rights are, and how weighty they are in comparison with each other and with other obligations, she must do some thinking. That this thinking may be successful I hope has been made clear – and that the results will be support not for an act-utilitarian morality but for an indirect utilitarian morality of rights, as well as of the morally right and wrong generally.

AN ANTIUTILITARIAN ALTERNATIVE: CONTRACTUALISM

There are many theories about the identities of, and support for, moral principles other than the suggested utilitarian one. Kant's theory is one, although it has been contested whether his theory may not be construed as a form of utilitarianism.[28]

Various nonutilitarian theories have been labeled "contractarian." Of these, I wish to consider one, put forward by T. M. Scanlon, that has attracted favorable attention. It seems worthwhile to compare this theory with the sort of indirect conscience-utilitarianism discussed in this chapter.[29] A rather similar view is espoused by Thomas Nagel.[30]

Scanlon summarizes his theory as follows: "An act is wrong if its performance under the circumstances would be disallowed by any system of rules for the general regulation of behaviour which no one could reasonably reject as a basis for informed,

---

[28] See R. M. Hare, "Could Kant have been a utilitarian?" *Utilitas* 5 (1993), 3ff. Also see Kant, *Werke*, vol. 4 (Berlin: Cassirer, 1922), pp. 280–9.

[29] See his "Contractualism and utilitarianism" in A. Sen and B. Williams (eds.), *Utilitarianism and Beyond*, pp. 110, 120; "Value, desire, and quality of life," in A. Sen and M. Nussbaum (eds.), *The Quality of Life* (Oxford: Clarendon Press, 1993), pp. 185–200, especially pp. 196–9; and "The moral basis of interpersonal comparisons," in Elster and Roemer (eds.), *Interpersonal Comparisons of Well-being*.

In Chapter 10, I try to answer the question of whether obedience to the optimal moral rules of one's society can conflict with self-interest or at least be rational even if it does.

[30] Thomas Nagel, *The Possibility of Altruism* (Oxford University Press 1970).

unforced, general agreement."[31] Put in my terms, this means that an act is wrong if it would be condemned by every moral code (set of aversions to act-types, etc.) that no one "could reasonably reject as a basis for informed, unforced, general agreement." This seems to say, in my terms, that an "optimal" moral code is one that could be reasonably agreed to, as having moral force in the society, by *everyone*, independently of any pressure of force or a bad bargaining position. This contrasts with the utilitarian slant of my proposal: that the optimal code is the one that can be recommended because the teaching and prevalence of it would be publicly most beneficial. Scanlon postulates that everyone in fact wants to identify agreed-upon principles that no one could reasonably reject, and everyone wants this to the same degree.[32] Indeed, Scanlon thinks that the motivation to do the moral thing derives from a desire to be able to justify one's action to others on grounds they could not reasonably reject, although he does not regard this as a "natural" desire but rather one deriving from "moral education" in a broad sense.[33]

This seems to say that everyone has a veto over every proposed moral principle or social system, and that seems a disturbing right. But the veto may not be capricious. It has to be "reasonable." This fact makes it necessary to specify what is a reasonable objection. Scanlon says explicitly that he is not at-

---

[31] Scanlon, "Contractualism and utilitarianism," p. 110.

[32] Scanlon points out that his conception allows different and discrepant systems of rules to be agreed to, e.g., different rules about agreement keeping and responsibilities for the caring of others. These specific forms are fixed by conventions, and given the necessity for them, it could not be agreed to disregard such conventions. This conception "introduces a degree of cultural relativity into contractualist morality," (ibid., p. 112).

[33] Ibid., p. 117. Scanlon seems inclined to hold that animals are included in the scope of morality, since in a sense there can be "justification" to them (pp. 113–15). Here his view differs from the contractualism of David Gauthier, who concedes that morality, conceived as a mutually beneficial constraint among rational persons (based on the assumption that others can be expected to obey the same constraints), cannot be extended to animals (or fetuses, etc.), which cannot perform beneficial services for us. See his *Morals by Agreement* (Oxford: Oxford University Press, 1987), e.g., pp. 17, 268, 285.

tempting to give any definition of "reasonable," such as, say, Harsanyi's, that it is reasonable to object if and only if that is what one would do if one did not know what position one would occupy in a social system and so could not estimate a rule's specific impact on him. For some specific moral code might be beneficial for the average person but still be very bad for a given individual. For "reasonable," Scanlon says he is only trying "to describe it clearly and show how other features of morality can be understood in terms of it." To make the idea specific, consider the possibility of an economic reward and tax system that would be beneficial on the whole but that includes features very disadvantageous to some – the losers. The losers might well reject such a plan "reasonably," primarily because of its bad impact on them, but also *only if* any alternative plan, that is better for them, would not impose even greater burdens on others. In order for a person to reach a reasonable decision, she must be such (e.g., be capable of suffering) that things can go better or worse for her – that she have a "good" – and comparisons between the impact on her and on others must be possible.[34] The strength of one's complaint will be greater the worse off, comparatively, is the impact on one of a principle/system. But to justify rejection, it is not enough that one is the *worst* off under some alternative plan that would not cause others to suffer comparably to one's suffering under the initial plan. Thus there are two grounds for "reasonable rejection." First is the impact on the complainant, varying with (1) how much *worse* off (than she otherwise would be) the principle/system makes her, (2) how unfavorably her total/final position *compares* with that of others, and (3) how *bad* her final position is. But second, rejection of a principle is reasonable *only if* there are alternative plans that would be better for her but would not impose comparable or greater hardships on others. (Scanlon does not consider how to weigh the disadvantages to one person against the considerable advantages to many oth-

---

[34] The "hardships" for some must be ones in terms that are generally compelling; there must be a consensus concerning their status (Scanlon, "Value, desire, and quality of life," pp. 196–7).

ers, perhaps those nearly as badly off, of that plan.[35]) Thus, clearly, a person may reasonably reject any proposed principle that gives her own well-being *no* weight whatever. Basic to our willingness to pay attention to such "reasonable rejection" is our "sympathetic identification with the good of others," but not being moved *just* by aggregate benefit. As Scanlon puts it, the *utilitarian* is moved by a gain of a certain magnitude, "whether it is obtained by relieving the acute suffering of a few people or by bringing tiny benefits to a vast number, perhaps at the expense of moderate discomfort for a few. This is very different from sympathy of the familiar kind toward particular individuals."[36] To summarize it briefly, Scanlon's view is that a principle is immoral if it imposes severe hardships (as explained) on some, even if this is balanced by considerable benefits to a great number – a rather familiar criticism of utilitarianism.

There are some intuitive grounds for doubt of this claim that what is morally best is to minimize the worst (and very bad) condition. One is that the nature of two complaints can be such that what can be done to *relieve* the worst may achieve less *benefit* (at the same cost) than what can be done to help the slightly less badly off. Does the size of the *benefit* not count? Are we bound to confer a trivial benefit on a person badly off in contrast to a big benefit to someone slightly better off? Again, suppose there are *many* persons with a slightly lesser complaint, and they would be substantially helped by a program that would not help the worst off. Is it obvious that we should pass them by in order to help the worst off? What does seem obvious is that a great many trivial benefits are not morally as demanding as one very serious hardship; for example, buying

---

[35] This problem is discussed lucidly at length in David Brink, "The separateness of persons, distributive norms, and moral theory," in R. G. Grey and C. W. Morris (eds.), *Value, Welfare, and Morality* (Cambridge: Cambridge University Press, 1993), chap. 13. But see Scanlon, "Contractualism and utilitarianism," p. 123, on the role of aggregation in cases involving many persons.

[36] Ibid., p. 115f.

snowmobiles for many would not compensate for failing to relieve the pain of a cancer patient. But in the absence of a program for comparing help to the nearly as badly off, the simple plan of Scanlon is not very convincing.[37]

How far does Scanlon's proposal differ from my rather complicated proposal about how to light on correct moral motivations in accordance with conscience utilitarianism? Scanlon himself suggests that his contractualism may be very close to a form of rule- or motive-utilitarianism.[38] Obviously, the most likely difference will be in moral adjudication of the justice of distributions of welfare, as by the economic system, or redistributive modes of taxation. In Chapter 7, I shall explain a kind of tax/welfare program that would implement the indirect conscience-utilitarian theory, a program that may be compatible with the requirements of Scanlon's contractualist theory.

But how about the various other problems about which contractualism seems to give no special guidance, for example, where the issue is not a choice between agreeing to a system that would make one very badly off, although an alternative system would not make others equally badly or even worse off – a rather special situation? Indirect utilitarianism offers guidance about many other types of problem situation, including sexual freedom, abortion, retributivism in the criminal law, and speaking the truth. (Sexual freedom seems to raise many issues other than that of meeting the needs of the most deprived!) Indirect utilitarianism gives a clue about how to decide these and many other issues, but at least some of these issues seem to be outside the scope of the contractualist theory.

[37] These problems are fully discussed by Brink in "The separateness of persons."

[38] Scanlon, "Contractualism and utilitarianism," pp. 110, 120.

Chapter 6

Neonaturalism

In the past 20 or so years a somewhat novel type of moral philosophy has emerged. Members of this group, sometimes self-styled as "moral realists," will have none of the straight emotivist/prescriptivist analyses of moral language like those of A. J. Ayer, C. L. Stevenson, and R. M. Hare or of an error theory like that of John Mackie. For they think these views do not leave room for the concept of a "moral truth as a fact of the matter," which they want to defend. But they also reject the realistic polar opposite of expressive theories: the view that there are evaluative/moral properties essentially different from "natural" properties – for knowledge about which we must rely on self-evidence or intuitions, as defended by a line of philosophers including G. E. Moore and W. D. Ross. Their view is an attempt to be somewhere in between. At least some members of the new group think that if we make proper adjustments in our theories of knowledge and language, we can justify moral/value conclusions by an argument that is compelling in the same way as are arguments for theories in the empirical sciences. Obviously, we must look into this.

The term "moral realism" can be applied to a wide spectrum of views. I shall concentrate on a type of view I call "neonaturalism." We might be guided in defining this concept by the anthologies on moral realism, one in the *Southern Journal of Philosophy*, supplement to volume 24, and the other edited by G. Sayre-McCord, *Essays on Moral Realism* (Ithaca, N.Y.: Cornell University Press,

1988, as well as a book by David Brink, *Moral Realism and the Foundation of Ethics* (New York: Cambridge University Press, 1989). I shall have in mind writers including Nicholas Sturgeon, Peter Railton, Geoffrey Sayre-McCord, David Brink, Richard Boyd, William Lycan, David McNaughton, Richard Werner, Hilary Putnam, and, with some reservations on account of significant differences, John McDowell and David Wiggins, although others have quite similar views, and these differ markedly among themselves.[1]

These philosophers have put forward various positive theses. (1) Although there is hardly unanimity, they seem to affirm that moral/value statements connecting a moral/value term with some nonmoral predicate can be literally true or false.[2] (2) These judgments are sometimes true. (3) The moral/value properties are identical to natural properties, that is, play a role in our empirical thinking like that of the theoretical properties of science.[3] (4) Knowledge of the truth of evaluative/moral statements can be obtained through ordinary methods of reflective

---

[1] In a careful survey of metaethical theories, S. Darwall, A. Gibbard, and P. Railton classify Wiggins and McDowell as "sensibility theories," with most of the others being listed as "postpositivist reductionists," whereas Railton is listed (along with David Lewis, Gilbert Harman, and me) as a "reductionist." See "Toward *fin de siecle* ethics," *Philosophical Review* 101 (1992), 115–89. I am treating all of these (of those listed here) as "moral realists" but relegating Wiggins and McDowell mostly to footnotes, since they seem uncharacteristic in not arriving at any general ethical statements as a result of their views – much less *identifying* moral with natural properties. This is particularly true of Wiggins, who distances himself from moral realism, which he regards as a confused concept, although he seems to defend cognitivism and moral truth, at least in some sense. See his *Needs, Values, Truth* (Oxford: Blackwell, 1991), pp. 314–18 and 344–56 for brief formulations of his distinctive position, part of which seems to be what I have called "contextualism" – that in the appraisal of a moral statement, it is legitimate to rely on other moral/value beliefs, currently not in question (as also does Sturgeon). I also say little about some other figures, e.g., Hilary Putnam.

[2] See Geoffrey Sayre-McCord, "The many moral realisms," *Southern Journal of Philosophy* 24, supplement (1986), 17. Also see Sturgeon, "What difference does it make whether moral realism is true?" *Southern Journal of Philosophy* 24 (1986), 116–17.

[3] Ibid., 117.

(empirical and moral) reasoning but do not require appeal to self-evidence or any "intuitive" faculty; and we actually have at least an approximation to some such knowledge. (5) These conclusions do not derive solely from an analysis of the meaning of moral/value terms.

In what way is the neonaturalist theory different from old-fashioned naturalism – which certainly implies that there is a fact of the matter about evaluations – at least of the stripe that held that statements relating evaluative and nonevaluative properties are just *analytic,* as Hobbes did when he wrote: "Whatsoever is the object of any man's appetite or desire; that is it which he for his part calleth good: and the object of his hate, and aversion, evil."[4] The neonaturalists seem to go along with G. E. Moore's view of "good": that no statement, affirming that something is good if and only if some property definable in an empiricist language belongs to the same thing, is *analytically* true in view of the *meaning* of evaluative terms in their ordinary use and in the ordinary sense of "meaning."

But despite their agreement with Moore on this point, many of them believe that evaluative facts (properties) can be shown to be identical to "natural" facts (properties), although there are no analytic statements relating them, roughly in the same way in which we know that water is identical to H_2O, through general ethical/scientific theory.

What kinds of empirically observable properties might be thought capable of being shown to be so identical? One widely favored view is that the property we have been calling "moral rightness" is identical to the property of producing a maximal amount of good. For "good" they may propose "pleasant" or "is desired" or "would be desired on the basis of full factual information." The writers defending such views are not committed to any one theory about what these properties are; they agree only in holding that they, and their relation to moral/value terms, are empirically accessible. Some of these writers (e.g.,

---

[4] *Leviathan,* Part 1, chap. 6, in D. D. Raphael (ed.), *British Moralists* (London: Oxford University Press, 1969), vol. 1, p. 25.

possibly Sturgeon) seem to think that evaluative terms cannot be given any *reductive definition*, whereas others (e.g., Railton) say it would be "intolerably odd if moral facts were held to be sui generis."[5]

THE COHERENCE EPISTEMOLOGY

These are startlingly sweeping claims. What is their argument?

1. It would seem that the first move in an argument might well be to explain what evaluative terms *mean*. At least if it is to be said that the property F is identical to the property G, in order even to understand the claim we seem to need to know what F means. So, if it is said that "Water is H_2O," we seem to have an evaluatable claim of identifying only if we know what "water" means.[6] So, if it is said that moral rightness is identical to (or coextensive with) X natural properties, one needs to know what "moral rightness" means in the view of these writers.

Of course, it may be thought, as Moore thought, that we all use these terms and understand them, so that they need not be explained.

We can still ask, however, what they think an evaluative statement, in ordinary language, is doing. Do they think evaluative statements are doing anything at all that could not be done simply by making some naturalistic statement such as "That is pleasant"? If evaluative and natural properties are identical, may we infer that talk in traditional evaluative terminology can simply be dispensed with as adding nothing?

Some propose a sort of answer to the question of what important *function* value predicates have as follows. They say that it is

---

[5] Peter Railton, "Moral realism," *Philosophical Review* 95 (1986), 171.

[6] I assume that the ordinary meaning of "water" is something like "is a liquid that, in a more or less impure state, comprises rain, rivers . . . ; when pure, it is transparent, tasteless, freezes at 32°F, and boils at 212°F."

widely agreed that evaluative properties are "supervenient"[7] on sets of natural properties. Thus, since various somewhat different natural properties (like a society being unjust in any one of several different ways) may have the same supervenient value property (injustice), it may be helpful to have an evaluative term to affirm the supervenient property, rather than being confined to listing the disjunctive sets of natural properties on which it supervenes. (This may be useful in framing ethical generalizations.) Some think that it is sufficient to avoid the "ontological dualism" to which John Mackie objected, to say that evaluative facts are just supervenient on nonevaluative facts.[8] (But one may surely wonder what this supervenient property, such as injustice, is supposed to be like if it is different from the description of the disjunctive base set.) Some of these writers propose that when a value/moral property supervenes on some set of natural properties, that is sufficient reason to *identify* it with that set of natural properties on the ground that this is the best way to explain the supervenience relation.[9] However, some of

---

[7] Saying that a property P (of some X) supervenes on base properties QRS means that QRS does not entail P but that it is impossible for P to change without a change in QRS. To say that a moral/evaluative property supervenes on some natural properties requires some defense. This claim, although widely held, is not just trivial or obvious.

I agree that some *action* being QRS cannot have the *moral* property P but another action with the same natural property fails to be P. To deny this would be to deny that moral attitudes are directed toward *types* of action (for which I have argued in an earlier chapter). But one can accept this without holding that the properties of one state of affairs (synthetically?) necessitate some moral property. It may be true that informed persons would condemn an action of the kind QRS only because it had these properties, but this suggestion requires a lot of explanation and background conditions. For an interesting discussion, see J. C. Klagge, "Supervenience: ontological and ascriptive," *Australasian Journal of Philosophy* 66 (1988), 461–70. Also, for a much fuller discussion, see S. Blackburn, *Quasi-Realism* (Oxford: Oxford University Press, 1993), chap. 7.

[8] D. O. Brink, "Moral realism and the sceptical arguments from disagreement and queerness," *Australasian Journal of Philosophy* 62 (1984), 111–25, especially 118.

[9] This is suggested by W. G. Lycan in "Moral facts and moral knowledge," *Southern Journal of Philosophy* 24 (supplement) (1986), 84–5.

these writers think that evaluative properties are in some sense sui generis and irreducible.[10] All of this, so far, does not seem to give an agreed-upon account of the *meaning* of value predicates.

There is one possible, simple way out of this difficulty of explaining meaning for some instances. It may be that the *identification* of moral properties with natural ones is obvious for "thick"[11] moral properties like being cruel, insensitive, dishonest, treachery, and so on, granting that these are really "moral" properties.[12] (The term "just," in some uses, seems to be of the same kind, as are "decency" and "fair-mindedness".[13]) But if the analysis is confined to terms like these, the neonaturalists are not in any necessary disagreement with noncognitive ex-

---

[10] This view is also held by David McNaughten, who says moral facts are "distinctive" and irreducible: *Moral Vision* (Oxford: Blackwell, 1988), pp. 44–6. On p. 95 he says that "moral properties are not to be thought of as created by our feelings, but as real properties which can only be experienced by beings who share a whole network of emotional response with us." See also pp. 7, 13.

[11] But it is not obvious what is meant by a "thick" moral property. What I have to say may apply to only a segment of the terms someone calls thick – where the main concept is clearly descriptively analyzable. (See Crispin Wright in *Aristotelian Society*, supplement [1988], 1–26, on "sensitive".) Also see the helpful discussion by Allan Gibbard in the symposium on "Morality and thick concepts," *Aristotelian Society*, supplement (1991).

[12] Mark Platts appears to regard such terms as the basic ones in moral language: "sincere," "loyal," "honest," "prudent," "courageous." (Wiggins includes "callously cruel" in *Needs, Values, Truth* [Oxford: Blackwell, 1991], pp. 155–8.) These properties, he thinks, are supervenient on nonmoral facts but cannot be inferred from nonmoral facts; they are thus autonomous. These properties can impose conflicting obligations, so there can be genuine moral dilemmas. See his "Moral reality" in Geoffrey Sayre-McCord (ed.) *Essays on Moral Realism* (Ithaca, N.Y.: Cornell University Press, 1988), pp. 282ff. Everything turns, I believe, on whether naturalistic truth conditions can be given for these terms, essentially in the way "having an IQ over 100" can be explained, although the trait terms here considered are undoubtedly less definite. Readers of literature on personality traits will, I think, be optimistic about this and even about "insensitive."

[13] See Nicholas Sturgeon's use of these and other like terms in "Moral explanations" in D. Copp and D. Zimmerman (eds.), *Morality, Reason, and Truth* (Totowa, N.J.: Rowman & Allanheld, 1984), p. 64.

169

pressivists, who will readily propose a descriptive account of what these terms distinctively come to (e.g., dishonesty being the state of character/motivation that is identical to the source of acting dishonestly) and will not deny that statements containing them are true or faalse.[14] The expressivist will also allow that these thick terms can enter into explanations of facts like a person stealing – explained by the fact that he is dishonest. It is the "thin" terms, like "moral obligation" or "duty," "morally wrong," and "intrinsically good," that are in dispute.

I do not find any proposal generally accepted by these writers (but see Railton later) about what moral/evaluative terms *mean*, although Sturgeon (possibly along with others) seems to imply that moral terms are "theoretical terms."[15] So far, the argument seems to lack an important initial premise.[16]

---

[14] Sturgeon disagrees, saying that a "non-cognitivist, who thinks that the terms 'decency' and 'humanity' refer to nothing can hardly agree." *Southern Journal of Philosophy* 24 (1986), 122. Why should anyone affirm that these terms refer to nothing?

[15] In "Brandt's moral empiricism," *Philosophical Review* 96 (1982), 395, footnote. Sturgeon seems to imply, in his papers on moral realism, that he adopts an irreducibility theory. He seems to want to prove only that moral terms refer to *some* properties and that moral statements can be true.

[16] John McDowell appears to try to bridge the gap by appeal to names of secondary qualities like "red," which identify properties of objects but do so only in view of the appearances presented to a normal person. He considers the notion of "fearful," which is the property of something that merits fear. In the case of valuations, a person will be able to back up value attributions by showing how the evaluation is well placed. In light of the secondary-quality model, we can see how "something that is brutely there could nevertheless stand in an internal relation to some exercise of human sensibility." What one would like to see is some account that comports with what we know of the sources of valuations, as described in Chapters 2 and 3 of this volume. Is there more of a real-world foundation for desirability than someone desiring something, given full information about its factual properties and making none of the mistakes listed in Chapter 2? See McDowell, "Values and secondary qualities," in Sayre-McCord (ed.), *Essays*, pp. 176ff. and in T. Honderich, *Morality and Objectivity* (London: Routledge and Kegan Paul, 1985), pp. 110–29. For a discussion of associating moral perception with secondary qualities, see Crispin Wright, "Moral values, projection, and secondary qualities" in *Proceedings*, the Aristotelian Society, supplement (1988), 1–26.

2. But despite the absence of any thesis about the meaning of ethical terms, some of these writers offer an epistemological theory designed to show that the properties intended by value terms are identical to certain natural properties. The epistemological reasoning most widely accepted by neonaturalists seems to be that ethical *theory*,[17] presumably normative theory based on "reflective equilibrium" of moral beliefs (a conception that may lean on the conception of moral *intuitions*, which these writers wish to reject), will yield some universal statements of the type "Something is intrinsically good if and only if it is a pleasant experience" or "Some act is morally obligatory if and only if it will be – or it is reasonably thought by the agent on the basis of her available evidence to be – an act that will maximize the general good" (not necessarily just happiness). If we could somehow justify one of these generalizations of the form "X is right if and only if Y," it *might* be plausible then to go further and to accept Y as a state of affairs *identical* to the state of affairs X. But not necessarily, for such "if and only if" statements can link two properties that are not identical. Suppose an electrically charged particle is moved and an electromagnetic wave is generated; these two events are related by an "if and only if" (and lawful) relation without its being true that the motion of a charged particle is identical to the generation of an electromagnetic wave.[18] So, if moral theory can generate such statements of equivalence, it does not yet follow that the second event (state of affairs, property) is *identical* to the first, as some of these writers seem to think.[19]

---

[17] For instance, N. Sturgeon, "Moral explanations," in Copp and Zimmerman (eds.), *Morality, Reason, and Truth*, 61; and "What difference does it make whether moral realism is true?", 117. Also see W. G. Lycan, "Moral facts and moral knowledge," ibid., 84–8.

[18] This example was suggested to me by Larry Sklar.

[19] David Wiggins seems to want little truck with wide generalizations or purported identities. He suggests it "would be better [for the case of values] to . . . interest ourselves afresh in what everybody knows about – the set of concerns he actually has, their objects . . . and the prospects of purifying . . . or extending this set." We have to "appreciate and describe the working day complexity of what is experientially involved in seeing a point in liv-

Passing the question of what is shown if we prove some "if and only if" statement, there is a prior question to be answered: how moral *theory* is to support, rationally, these "if and only if" statements. Are these to be obtained inductively, and if not, then how? Are we, for instance, to look at this, that, and the other lie and *see* that they are all wrong, and then inductively conclude that lies are all wrong? Very well, but this reasoning assumes that we can know that this and that lie are wrong. How are we supposed to know this? In science, an inductive argument begins, basically, only if we know by *observation*, say, that this has the property P and similarly for that. So, if there is to be a parallel with science, it must be that we are in a position to become aware of the fact that this lie is wrong *before* being justified in believing the generalization. (The same is true if we think scientific inference is always "to the best explanation" of the data.) How is this supposed to be? Does the alleged parallel

ing." What he has in mind can be illustrated as follows: "Out of good nature a man helps his neighbour dig a drainage ditch. The soil is hard but . . . together the two of them succeed in digging the ditch. The man who offers to help sees what he is doing . . . as worthwhile. Insofar as meaning is an issue for him, he may see the episode as all of a piece with a life that has meaning. He would not see it so, and he would not have taken on the task, if it were impossible. In the case as we imagine it, the progress of the project is integral to his pleasure in it. But so equally is the fact that he likes his neighbour and enjoys working with him (provided it be on projects that it is within their joint powers to complete). . . . In truth, the embracing of the end depends on the man's feeling for the task of helping someone he likes. But his feeling for the project of helping equally depends on the existence and attainability of the end of digging the ditch." This view seems very similar to what I called the objects of "informed satisfaction" view of "a good thing" in Chapter 2. Wiggins opposes the expressivist view that the man's belief in the goodness of the project merely reflects the fact that he happens to want to participate. But it seems very different from the views of other neonaturalists. However, in *Needs, Values, Truth*, pp. 133–6, he seems to arrive at a firm conclusion that Captain Vere (in Melville's *Billy Budd*) was definitively *morally* wrong in his decision about what to do with Billy Budd, and, on p. 355 he says, "We converge in the belief that the slaughter of the innocent is wrong because, in the end, there is nothing else to think on this question." So, it seems he would accept some *general* statements about what are considerations of *moral* weight.

with science imply that we also have comparable observation in ethics? Some of these writers have said that wrongness is, in some sense, an observable property,[20] but it is not clear exactly in what sense. It is true that some writers have thought that, for example, moral requiredness is part of the "given."[21] Some of these neonaturalist writers may possibly mean, then, that evaluative reasoning begins partly on the basis of a kind of moral (or value) "sense datum," but in fact, I think, they don't seem to do this. William Lycan comes close to conceding a given, saying that we can begin with "spontaneous beliefs"[22] (among which he includes our "moral intuitions") and that these *beliefs* are our evidence.[23] Is this or is it not acceptance of a given in moral theorizing? I would think it is *not* parallel to observation in empirical science (although Lycan would deny that these beliefs are any less worthy of reliance than beliefs about sensory observations). We can, for the moment at least, leave open whether some neonaturalists think there is a given for ethics.

Some other moral realists seem to attain much the same result as affirming a given just by claiming to "know" that intuitive statements about particular cases are (at least *mostly*) true. Thus, Sturgeon believes that unless most of our moral beliefs

---

20 Richard Werner, "Ethical realism," *Ethics* 94 (1983), 635ff.; McNaughton, *Moral Visions*, pp. 39–40, 55–7; William Tolhurst, "On the epistemic value of moral experiences," *Southern Journal of Philosophy*, supplement (1990), 67–87, and "Supervenience, externalism, and moral knowledge," *Southern Journal of Philosophy* 24, supplement (1986), 43–56.

21 The psychologist Wolfgang Koehler affirmed that there is an observable "requiredness phenomenon" (*The Place of Value in a World of Fact* [New York: Liveright, 1938], pp. 329–40 and Index), and one of these writers might want to go along with that conclusion. And Rawls suggested in an early paper ("Outline of a decision procedure for ethics," *Philosophical Review* 80 [1951], 186) that when we judge that "This interest is to be given preference to that," the statement "states the felt preference." So Rawls apparently did not, at that time, dispute the view that at the basis of our moral knowledge there are some observations of the given.

22 W. G. Lycan, "Moral facts and moral knowledge," *Southern Journal of Philosophy* 24, supplement (1986), 85. For empirical science, the "spontaneous beliefs" would be those induced by sensory stimulation.

23 Ibid., 85–8.

are true, we can't formulate generalizations about moral and natural properties.[24] Does this reflection show that many or most of them *are* true? Actually, Sturgeon has a general epistemological theory that goes much further. He says, following Quine on "epistemology naturalized," that "we have in general no a priori way of knowing which strategies for forming and refining our beliefs are likely to take us closer to the truth. The only way we have of proceeding is to assume the approximate truth of what seems to us the best overall theory we already have of what we are like and what the world is like, and to decide in the light of that what strategies of research and reasoning are likely to be reliable in producing a more nearly true overall theory." But on the next page he says, "Among the beliefs in which I have enough confidence to rely on in evaluating explanations, at least at the outset, are some moral beliefs."[25] And later, "typical moral assertions have testable implications . . . so long as you include additional moral assumptions of the right sort among the background theories on which you rely in evaluating these assertions." These views seem strange in light of his repeated contention that a big problem for moral philosophy is that there seems no clear way to *settle* moral disputes.

3. But to go back to the question of how we may construct a theory of ethics based on "spontaneous beliefs," given that there are at least these beliefs, how are we to move from them to some ethical principles? Take the whole set of these, of a given person, and call them her "initial moral judgments." Perhaps what we should do is take them together, perhaps along with other data from our general knowledge, and seek a general theory. Call the result one's "reflective equilibrium" or "wide reflective equilibrium." A problem remains: How can we determine which ones, among conflicting evaluative/moral beliefs, to regard as correct? Only most of them are. Then how do we

---

[24] N. Sturgeon, "Harman on moral explanations of natural facts," in Spindel Conference, *Southern Journal of Philosophy,* supplement (1986), 73.
[25] "Moral explanations," p. 67f.

make correct judgments? Where there is conflict, one might decide to give the preference to beliefs that are firmer, stronger, or more numerous. But suppose we identify this act as a lie and think it is wrong, and that is another lie that we think is not wrong. How are we then to proceed? Do we drop the belief that is less firm? One way to avoid making the choice is to notice that lies are of different kinds or told in different circumstances; so, we refine our judgments and say that a lie of kind K is wrong, whereas one of kind K' is not wrong, thereby using both cases to support different general principles. Here we have a choice: We might say that these cases support two different but not conflicting generalizations, or we can say that one or the other must be rejected. How are we to decide which to do? If we construe apparently conflicting judgments as not really conflicting, in general, then we are not doing any weeding out at all. But if, as some of these writers think, pluralistic consequentialism is the right moral theory, it seems as if some moral judgments have been weeded out, such as retributivism.[26] As Brink has remarked, coherentism favors, to some extent, a unified moral theory like utilitarianism[27] on pain of the inability to decide between apparently conflicting principles. We might drop retributivism, as contrasted with consequentialism, on the ground that consequentialism can be used to imply – if it does – our beliefs about many moral problem cases and perhaps is thus firmer. One would like a careful account of how such choices should be made and why.[28]

It is true that sometimes existing experimental data are all compatible with two incompatible theories in science. What then does the scientist do? What I think he does is to devise a

[26] Sturgeon, "Harman on Explanations," seems to concede that his consequentialism does not fit too well with ordinary intuitions (1986), 134. For comments on Sturgeon, see S. Blackburn, *Quasi-Realism* (Oxford: Oxford University Press, 1993), chap. 11.

[27] David O. Brink, *Moral Realism and the Foundations of Ethics* (Cambridge: Camridge University Press, 1989), p. 250.

[28] For a discussion, see my "The science of man and wide reflective equilibrium," *Ethics* 100 (1990), 259–78, especially 271–2.

new experiment, the facts about which will be unassailable, which is compatible with only one of the theories. There have been many examples of this in physics.

4. So far, we seem to be left without any independently credible *data* (like a given) by which a theory could be supported; the nearest we come to this is spontaneous beliefs, and doubtless a fair collection of these.

The next move, made by some of these writers, is to argue that we do not need anything like observation as the basis for moral reflection. So they attack foundationalism in ethics and elsewhere. Thus, David Brink raises an objection to foundationalism in general.[29] His view is that the foundationalist asserts that to avoid circularity, some beliefs must be justified (at least be independently credible) independently of their logical/explanatory relations to other *beliefs*. But such justification, he claims, is never possible. For to be warranted in holding that *any* belief is credible, one must have a reason, a second-order belief to the effect that beliefs of the first-order kind in question are likely to be true. In other words, in order to be warranted in believing one is in pain, one needs to be able to show why one should think that beliefs of this sort are likely true. (Is not inspection enough?) Now surely this is implausible in general, and need it be more plausible in ethics?[30] This criticism of foun-

---

[29] Brink, *Moral Realism*, chap. 5.

[30] See the remarks in Copp's review in *Ethics* 101 (1991), 617ff.

We might agree that some epistemological theorizing is necessary to support *verbal reports* of the given (presumably in the sense of Gestalt theory), for instance, theorizing about the reliability of memory. Perhaps these writers are using observation of the given to refer to verbal reports, which do require conceptualization by language. But it is not obvious what could be meant by doubting a *belief* about the given. If it is given, must not it be presented to the mind? What kind of belief is it that could err about the given? I think belief about the given is no more than attention to the given, *readiness* to conceptualize and to be *able* to decide whether a proposed verbalization fits – but not necessarily to judge even that it is *like* certain earlier experiences. It is true that in order to know that "Here is a red appearance," one has to know what "red appearance" means. But the claim that we need an epistemological theory to justify *beliefs* about the given seems to want support.

dationalism in general seems to be a mistake. Even the fullest exposition of a coherence theory of science, by L. BonJour, concedes that experiential input is necessary for empirical science. BonJour thinks he can show how a coherence theory can admit this, but I fear he does not succeed.[31]

It is interesting to note that Quine, often cited as an opponent of any sort of foundationalism for science, once wrote: "There is thus a wide gap between our data and our knowledge of the external world, and it takes bold inference to bridge it. . . . The epistemological job is to pick out what is immediate, rather than inferred across the gap, and then critically to reconstruct the inference of external objects. . . . Surely in such a construction the rational constructor must be aware of his data. But we are not normally aware of sense data, at the level anyway of color patches; we are aware of external objects outright. The Gestalt psychologists urged something intermediate. They allowed immediate awareness of forms not so atomistic as the color patches nor yet so full-blown as bodies. . . . Gestaltism . . . takes as its standard immediate awareness. This is the right standard, and the other is a confusion, if our aim is a rational reconstruction of the external world on the basis of the subjectively given." Although Quine himself does not accept this traditional route, he says that "Naturalized epistemology faces the problem of somehow tracing empirical content through this maze of theoretical sentences." A strategy for this is to trace the process by which the language of the theory is learned. "We all had to begin by learning to talk of what is pretty directly observable around us. . . . Getting back to sense data, let me say that I am still not opposed to them in principle. . . . There does remain a vital role for Gestalt psychology."[32]

An explanation of the status of beliefs about the given, in the theory of C. I. Lewis, which seems to avoid many objections, has been given by Roderick Firth, "Lewis on the given," in P. A. Schilpp (ed.), *The Philosophy of C. I. Lewis* (LaSalle, Ill.: Open Court, 1968), pp. 345–50.

[31] For an example of recent critiques, see Susan Haack, *Evidence and Inquiry* (Oxford: Blackwell, 1993), pp. 52–60.

[32] Paper, "The natural theory of knowledge," read to a National Endowment for the Humanities seminar in Ann Arbor, Michigan, Feb. 16, 1979. This

As an alternative to a foundational "observation" (or spontaneous intuition) account, Brink holds that *any* belief is justified
if it is part of a maximally *coherent* set of *beliefs* and if this fact
partially explains one's having the belief.[33] But there are some
puzzles here. For one thing, does one not have to appeal to
direct inspection to know whether beliefs cohere, or even to
know that one has a certain spontaneous belief? Or is this again
to be certified by more coherence? Surely, to identify a maximally coherent system and a belief being part of it, there must
be an appeal to something different from coherence. Again,
what serious view are we to take of one's total system *explaining*
one's having the belief, presumably in a way that adds to its
justification? (We might turn to psychological explanations of
the sources of moral attitudes – parental teaching or example,
identification, native altruism; this may or may not help with
their justification, but a here-ignored explanation is needed.)
Perceptual beliefs about physical objects are easier to deal with;
here we do have a theory that will explain why interaction with
a physical world will result in certain perceptions. There is
nothing like this for value/moral beliefs. Moreover, the fact that
certain propositions cohere does not seem to imply that there is
any fact distinct from the fact of coherence of the beliefs; the
"wide reflective equilibrium" of a set of *beliefs* does not justify
the belief that any of them is *true*.

There is another question: whether all ideally coherent theories in morality will converge on the same result. If they do not,
is not the realistic construction of morality somewhat im-
pugned?[34]

Thus, it seems that coherence with a set of beliefs is an indi-
cation of truth at best only if at least some members of the set

paper was not offered for publication because Quine thought its basic ideas
had been frequently stated elsewhere in his writings. He has, however,
approved my quoting him.

[33] Brink, *Moral Realism*, p. 103.

[34] For a useful discussion of the problems, see Mark Timmons, "On the epistemic status of considered moral judgments," *Southern Journal of Philosophy*
29, supplement (1990), 100–10.

are known to be prima facie warranted independently of logical relations to other beliefs. Brink thinks this condition is met for ethical judgments, but their status is very different from that of empirical science, by which observations are accepted because they are manifestly prima facie warranted (and, incidentally, supported by a great deal of folk knowledge on the reliability of judgments of observation).

At any rate, Brink's argument about the needlessness of a given seems to bring him into agreement with Sturgeon's (and Lycan's) view that we may suppose that *most* of our considered ethical beliefs are reliable. But there is no way in which either view supports a serious parallel with the epistemology of empirical science.

5. Nevertheless, Brink and Lycan claim that justification in ethics is not really different from justification in empirical science and is equally successful. Moral reasoning is really no different from the reasoning that takes place in empirical science, and it can arrive at sound, objective facts just as science can.[35] Sometimes it is said that scientific thinking involves value judgments about what is the "best" theory and how heavily to weigh simplicity in theory choice.[36] Doesn't this fact make scientific theorizing very similar to moral reflection? We must concede that there is some historical truth in this, although I suggest that what is decisive for preference for a scientific theory is simply that it is part of a system that most accurately explains the whole set of data of observation (enlarged by memory and records). Sometimes it is said that although it may be true that our spontaneous *moral* beliefs cannot be said seriously to report observations alone, observations in science are also theory laden; they are not reports just of something given. But this view that moral reasoning is no different from scientific reasoning, I suggest, is worlds apart from the truth. Consider the

---

[35] Richard N. Boyd, "How to be a moral realist," in Sayre-McCord (ed.), *Essays*, pp. 199–200. See comments by Blackburn in *Quasi-Realism*, pp. 180–1.
[36] See Railton, "Moral realism," 167. Also G. Sayre-McCord, "Moral theory and explanatory impotence," in G. Sayre-McCord (ed.), *Essays*, p. 277.

experiment in which the mass of an electron was determined; do we find the remotest similarity between that and ethical reasoning? It is said that science, and this experiment, make use of background beliefs, and that all observations are theory laden. It is true that the determination of the mass of an electron relied on a previous discovery to determine its charge – the discovery that there are small particles with a certain charge. But this experiment involved observations, for example, about the acceleration of oil drops possibly carrying one or more charged small particles by an electric field of known strength and the rate at which oil drops not in an electric field fall in a near-vacuum.[37] True, the significance of a scientific observation is determined by a lot of previous theory. But straight observation comes in at every stage. Scientific reasoning seems to be not at all like finding reflective equilibrium or coherence of *beliefs*, especially theory-laden ones. It is a close-knit explanatory system, almost all parts of which are supported by observation in one way or another. So, the charge that scientific reasoning is theory laden, and hence is not really different from moral reasoning, is far from being justified.[38]

6. Anyway, some of our writers use an independent argument to show that moral properties are real properties. Sturgeon thinks that moral reasoning – apparently, reliance on reflective equilibrium – leads to a pluralistic consequentialism as a general normative moral theory. (He apparently does not construe this as leading to a reductive definition of moral terms.) But he has a separate argument to show that moral properties are real properties, since they are relied upon in various accepted scientific explanations. Thus, he thinks that moral properties have the same explanatory standing as the concept of an electron, and that therefore there is as good reason for believing there are objective moral properties as there is

---

[37] See the comments by A. Gibbard, *Wise Choices, Apt Feelings* (Cambridge, Mass.: Harvard University Press, 1990), p. 121.

[38] For an account of how scientific reasoning really works, see R. I. G. Hughes, "The Bohr atom, models, and realism," *Philosophical Topics* 18 (1990), 71–84.

for believing there are electrons. As evidence for this, he offers the following cases: (1) Hitler's moral "depravity" explains many things that he did; (2) a criminal's sentence was reduced because of the judge's "decency"[39]; (3) antislavery sentiment in the United States increased because of the "oppressiveness" of that institution; and (4) children's dousing a cat with gasoline and then igniting it coming to be believed wrong by observers shows that wrongness is an explanatory fact.[40] One would have thought not: that the behavior of Hitler (and similarly, mutatis mutandis, for cases two and three) is explained by his non-morally describable character traits; and our reaction to the burning of the cat is owing to our empathy/sympathy or moral aversions (possibly a result of past tutoring), not to the alleged extra fact of wrongness. Sturgeon, however, is dissatisfied with this; he thinks that "if a particular assumption [here of the wrongness of an act] is completely irrelevant to the explanation of a certain fact [the *belief* that it is wrong], then the fact [belief of wrongness] would have obtained, and we could have explained it just as well, even if the assumption had been false." So, if children are burning a cat, if the (assumed) wrongness of this act is causally irrelevant to observers' belief that what they are doing is wrong, then the fact that children are burning the cat, plus the empathy and/or moral attitudes of the observers, cannot explain the belief; for that, we need to take into account the act's wrongness. Why so? We know enough about the psychology of moral disapproval of actions (impact on sympathy or tutored moral attitudes) to see that observation of the treatment of the cat is sufficient to produce the disapproval, say, in this observer or most observers. Moreover, it is logically possible that for some reason this treatment of the cat was *not* wrong; perhaps it was part of an important experiment or perhaps the children were so stupid as to be beyond moral criticism. Whether or not this was the case is causally irrelevant to production of the belief. Essentially this point has been made by Gilbert

---

[39] Sturgeon, "Moral explanations," p. 64. See David Copp, "Explanation and justification in ethics," *Ethics* 100 (1990), 237–58.

[40] Sturgeon, ibid., pp. 63–6.

Harman.[41] It is true that the nonmoral state of affairs, on which the "moral fact" is thought (by realists) to be supervenient, will play an important role in the explanation of moral beliefs, taken with the observer's empathy and moral aversions. It does not follow from this that the alleged moral wrongness plays an explanatory role. So, Sturgeon has not shown that the alleged wrongness of acts plays an explanatory role in the belief that an act was wrong, and therefore has not shown that wrongness is scientifically as well certified as belief in electrons; it is not a necessary part of the best explanatory theory of the belief. So, the argument does not show that there are moral *facts*.[42]

---

[41] Gilbert Harman, in "Moral explanations of natural facts," in N. Gillespie (ed.), *Moral Realism*, supplementary issue of *The Southern Journal of Philosophy* 24 (1986), 63ff.

[42] Sturgeon's criticism of Harman is essentially seconded by David Wiggins in "Truth as predicated of moral judgments," *Needs, Values, Truth*, 155ff. His argument depends on the view that the moral condemnation essentially involves, or is identical to, a perception of the act as "callously cruel." I think we can do fairly well with a purely psychological analysis of a *callously cruel* personality; and although I agree that we shall not like such a person, this argument trades on the already discussed confusions about thick concepts. (Wiggins, *Needs, Values, Truth*, p. 158, says that "there is still room for plain truth.") So, my argument in the text still stands. Wiggins thinks the psychological explanation in terms of tutored attitudes overlooks the fact that this tutoring is itself "a response to something that is simply *there* (thereto be found by anyone, or by anyone who is sufficiently attuned to what bears upon the matter.)" He goes on to question "whether one can imagine a psychological theorist's dispensing entirely with value-properties not just in the case of non-standard reactions but in every case . . . and whether one can imagine him dispensing altogether with predicates that possess non-accidentally the same extension as his subjects' evaluative predicates do." Wiggins agrees that we can expect convergence in such judgments only by "people of a certain culture who have what it takes to understand a certain sort of judgment" (p. 160).

This understanding will also produce convergence in attitude. "Suppose that I find myelf in the midst of a social morality . . . that I have already been caught up in the shared sentiments and responses that are presupposed to my having grasped the sense of the moral and political language that my membership in the social morality commits me to learn to express myself in. Then, presumptively but only presumptively, the link must already be in place between the affirmation of a judgement and some determination of

When we look over the reasoning designed to show that moral/value properties are identical to (or even coextensive with) natural properties, it appears to break down at every point. So I have to conclude that we have not advanced over where we were 15 years ago.[43]

So much for a major portion of moral realists' explanation and defense of the positive parts of their reasoning. But they also defend it by attacking what they take to be the main opposition – noncognitivism.

CRITICISM OF ANTIREALIST POSITIONS

Neonaturalists often support their view by pointing to various (alleged) difficulties for pure expressive theories, not necessarily my theory.[44]

1. It has been said that the expressive view cannot explain why moral properties seem to be out there in the real world; nor can it explain the authority of moral judgments. To these points one should reply that it is far from clear in what sense moral facts do seem to be "out there." (Do we really think our moral opinions are somehow cosmic truths?) Nor is it clear why the "authority" of moral judgments cannot be analyzed as the aversion to infringing them and the expectation of guilt feelings and disapproval by others if one does, plus (for less purely expressivist theories) the belief that these attitudes are appropriately justified.

---

the will. Otherwise I could not have grasped the sense of the distinctively moral and political language that sustains the practices in which I participate." In John Haldane and Crispin Wright, *Reality, Representation, and Projection* (New York: Oxford University Press, 1993), p. 307f.

[43] David Wiggins has a general discussion of the meaning of "true in L" that may throw light on how he can view moral statements as true. See his *Needs, Values, Truth*, pp. 147ff.

[44] Some of the following points are drawn from Sturgeon, "What difference does it make whether moral realism is true?" *Southern Journal of Philosophy* 24, supplement (1986), 120ff.

One should note that these criticisms, if valid at all, may not apply to the theory proposed in the foregoing chapters.

2. It is sometimes said that the expressive theory cannot explain the possibility of the amoralist.[45] But what is an "amoralist"? If an amoralist is just someone who is only mildly moti-vated to do what he thinks he morally ought to do, there is no difficulty. The expressive theory need not hold that moral evaluations are always of overriding weight – overriding all considerations of self-interest, temptation, and so on. But an amoralist might be defined as someone who uses moral language in its ordinary sense but has no motivation whatever to do what he says he morally ought to do. The realist says that we can readily *imagine* that a person uses moral language in its ordinary sense but has *no* motivation (etc.) whatever to avoid what he thinks wrong. The problem for the argument, then, is to show that there really *are* amoralists – persons who use "wrong" in its *ordinary sense* but completely lack the syndrome of moral motivations (etc.) – unless, for instance, they are taken to mean by "wrong" just "what most other people call wrong," which is not using "wrong" in its ordinary sense. Is there reason to believe that anyone states firmly that some act would be wrong without having *some* aversion (etc.) to it – even Nixon in his famous statement "It would be wrong but . . ."? Might a sophisticated hearer think that possibly he was not expressing a moral attitude? (True, one might think the speaker had no idea of how his attitude could be *justified*.) It is, of course, a logical possibility that people should so use moral language that it does not (necessarily) express any motivation; but the serious question is whether this is in fact the case with uses in the ordinary sense. Why should an expressivist theory of the actual use of moral language be concerned about the *logical possibility* of moral *words* ("morally wrong") being (incorrectly) used in the absence of all motivation?

3. It is alleged that the expressivist cannot allow that there are "moral mistakes," provided that persons have gotten all the

---

[45] D. O. Brink makes a good deal of this thesis in his "Externalist moral realism," *Southern Journal of Philosophy* 24, supplement (1986), 23–42; see also his *Moral Realism and the Foundations of Ethics* (Cambridge: Cambridge University Press, 1989), pp. 45–60.

nonmoral facts straight, whereas a realist can concede facts such as deficiency in "sensitivity."[46] The expressivist can, however, explain differences in sensitivity by pointing to someone's deficiency in empathy or sympathy, or deficiency in parental explanation of moral rules, or deficiency in the ability to bring one's moral stance in all its complexity to bear on a case at hand – or even lack of subtlety in appreciating the various facets of a problem situation. Such facts can amount to a lack of sensitivity. (She can also express her own disapproval of such deficiencies.) Given the type of moral theory I have been supporting, as well as various other ones, we do not have to suppose that moral facts are somehow out there, unrelated to human psychology and past personal history, which can be perceived more or less dimly, depending on one's sensitivity to them. (Given my own theory, it is quite possible that a person might wonder if her own moral attitudes may not reflect defects of some sort, not being ones that could be recommended to informed people.)

4. It has been said that the noncognitivist cannot make sense of our belief that a person should not be held responsible for his crime if he did not know it was wrong – and the expressivist cannot admit any such *knowledge* that something is wrong, so that a miscreant is always legally blameless.[47] (Actually, the law is ambiguous about whether it is "criminality" or "wrongness" that is supposed to be known.) But what the law can be construed to suppose is that there are widespread standards of conduct, serious departures from which are prohibited by criminal law. If an accused person can show that he was (nonculpably) unfamiliar with these standards, or the fact that the law condemns them, he will be excused on the ground that, for all we know, his moral aversions or "principles" may be perfectly all right.[48] (It is true that unfamiliarity with some standards could hardly be nonculpable – for instance, the standard forbidding murder.) Part of the reason for punishment is to bring offenders' standards closer to the widely accepted ones, and this purpose is not served if the person is not known to have

---

[46] See Sturgeon, "What difference . . . ?" 127ff.   [47] Ibid., 126f.
[48] See Chapter 9.

defective standards. Another aim of punishment is to warn potential offenders against deliberate breach of the law, but this aim is not thwarted if a person is not punished when it is known that there was no deliberate infringement of law. I concede that these explanations depend on a utilitarian theory of the justification of the law, which a moral realist may not accept; but then it is not clear what justification of the cited view the moral realist can put forward – except perhaps that the point is intuitively clear!

5. It is sometimes said that an expressive theory cannot explain moral "conversions" when there has been no change in factual information. For instance, a person who had not condemned slavery might change her mind as a result of viewing *Roots*.[49] It is suggested that the reason for the change is that, as a result of seeing this film, she *observes* that slavery is wrong. But in fact, psychology opens the way to alternative accounts: that the series just made vivid what it is like for a person to be treated as a slave or that it strengthens identification with such persons. Why such events occur is a complex topic and in no way requires observation of a moral fact as the only explanation.

6. Noncognitivism is said to be unable to explain why moral statements are made in fact-stating form, why we debate and seriously reflect on moral issues, and why we should have any intention to communicate feelings. We need not indulge in linguistics to explain why moral attitudes are expressed in indicative form, although presumably there is some historical story to be told. But *orders* can perfectly well be put in indicative form, for example, "Cadets will appear for exercise at 5:30 A.M." (Of course, various difficulties have been raised by Peter Geach, which I think have been adequately dealt with by Simon Blackburn and Allan Gibbard, in discussions sufficiently well known – but complicated – that I ignore the issue here.)[50] If we take our

---

[49] See Richard Werner, "Ethical realism," *Ethics* 93 (1983), 657ff.

[50] But see especially Simon Blackburn, "Attitudes and contents," *Ethics* 98 (1988), 501–17, reprinted in *Essays in Quasi-Realism* (New York: Oxford University Press, 1993), chap. 10. Also, for comments on various others of these charges, see his "Rule following and moral realism" in S. H. Holtzman and

evaluative appraisals seriously, why should we not want to adjust them so as to conform with nonmoral facts or meet other implied conditions for moral appraisals? Is this not enough to account for debate and serious reflection? As to the claim that we do not experience any intention to communicate feelings (attitudes) when we make moral statements, we may reply that sometimes we do want others to know where we stand on some issue and hence wish to express our attitudes (not necessarily with the intention of getting others to change their own attitudes).

Are there any facts that it is difficult for the *neonaturalist* theory to accommodate? Yes. One derives directly from the basic affirmation by neonaturalists that evaluative/moral properties can be known to be, or be identical to (or at least coextensive with), natural properties, just as the property of being water is identical to the property of being H_2O, and by normal forms of reasoning. For then, if this is so, the truth of value/moral propositions can presumably be known essentially in the same way the truth of propositions in empirical science can be known. And in this case, we should expect there to be agreement among factually informed, intelligent people in relevantly similar situations just to the degree that there is about the affirmations of empirical science, although, of course, it can be urged that the moral/value issues are more complicated, as indeed they are. Consider, for example, the view that what is morally wrong is to be found by considering whether the act does the most good – pluralistic consequentialism. How will this fact comport with the widespread support of retributivism in the justification of punishment or the variety of views about suicide? Sturgeon agrees that this fact is the major obstacle to accepting a moral realist view.[51]

In contrast, however, there seems to be great diversity of valuations of moral judgments around the world (or between

C. M. Leich (eds.), *Wittgenstein: To Follow a Rule* (London: Routledge and Kegan Paul, 1981), pp. 175ff.; and his *Essays in Quasi-Realism*, Part II.

[51] Sturgeon, "Moral explanations," 49, 73.

you and your next-door neighbor, say on the subjects of abortion, euthanasia, and capital punishment). And it seems we must concede that moral/value standards have not converged historically, around the world, to the same extent as have scientific beliefs. What might the neonaturalists say in reply to this? Earlier, I stated that much moral disagreement can be explained by the different living conditions of disagreeing groups – or, if not the actual living conditions, then differences in opinion about the facts, for example, beliefs about what is forbidden by the gods. So, the problem may mostly boil down to a rather difficult decision on whether or not there are "basic" disagreements – ones that remain when there is no disagreement about the relevant nonmoral facts. But in Chapter 2 I suggested that societies differ even in the value they place on having friends, being approved of by others, achievement or prestige, order in the household, or having knowledge; no one has shown that these derive from difference in the life conditions of the various societies.[52] The perdurance of such standards among the individuals of various groups (e.g., the Hopi) is doubtless to be explained by familiarity with the valuations standard in the society, identification with one's parents, and so on. Somewhat the same holds for *moral* standards that seem to vary around the world, possibly for reasons such as diversity of life situations or beliefs about them.[53] But again, it seems as if we know some-

[52] One might reply that the Hopi deemphasis of the values of achievement/power does have an explanation: The political/economic structure of their society is such that achievement can bring no significant reward, since political office is determined very much by blood relationships; the same is true of property rights (except for ownership of sheep and cattle).

[53] It is hard to deny real basic differences. For instance, when talking with a Hopi (in 1945), I asked if "there are sometimes fights between men on the reservation." The answer was: "Oh, yes, I remember there was one in *1916.*" The Hopi are strongly opposed to any sort of violence, including fist fights. (In Chapter 2 I expressed a doubt about whether this is a specifically moral aversion, although my guess is that it probably is. I suggest that the Hopi would take a very different view of the Navahos if they do not observe the custom of matrilocal residence, as compared with their reaction to a Navaho being violent.) Possibly we don't think well of college students who

thing about processes of cultural change (e.g., intergroup contact), in-group dynamisms (e.g., the influence of the pill), and the processes of moral development in the individual (by identification with parents or other models) to think that divergences in moral opinion are often to be explained by these factors rather than by diverging factual beliefs, say about whether the behavior appraised is likely to maximize happiness, as the moral realist might have it. Or how about the evidence that guilt feelings may be a residue of parental punishments, for example, the threat of loss of love? Or the evidence that a person's condemnation of a particular form of behavior is dependent on parents showing that this sort of behavior is harmful? The moral realists seem to make no effort to accommodate their theory to this mass of evidence.

NEONATURALISM BASED ON PSYCHOLOGY AND SOCIAL HISTORY

The main preceding types of argument for the view that there can be knowledge of the truth of value and moral statements were essentially the claims (1) that (some kind of) reliance on a coherent system of evaluative beliefs is a satisfactory method of theory formation and (2) that such reliance on a coherent system of beliefs is essentially no different from scientific theory building. Thus, it is concluded that there is as good reason for affirming that the right act is one that conforms, say, to pluralistic consequentialism as there is for believing that there are electrons.

But there is a different way of arriving at the same result: showing that evaluative *language* should be "construed" in a

fight physically, but is there strong condemnation? To this Wiggins replies that there is doubt whether there are real moral disagreements. "What matters . . . is only that the judgment should represent an answer to a question asked with respect to a given place and time, that the question should have a sense held fixed by reference to the historical context and circumstances of that place and time, and that the answer should be better than all competing answers to that question, so understood." *Needs, Values, Truth*, p. 162. Does this resolve the problem?

naturalistic way – some kind of "revisionist" construction of evaluative language. (We have seen that most neonaturalist writers apparently offer no account of the *meaning* of moral/value terms at all.) There are various ways in which such a construal might be supported. But the outcome can be that evaluative terms ("intrinsically good" and "morally right") are concluded to be identical in function and force to naturalistic expressions (formulatable in an empiricist language). If this move is made, the identification of evaluative *properties* and natural ones may not need to be argued further.

This general conception is not a novelty introduced by some of the contemporary neonaturalists. It was presented, for instance, years ago in a series of books and articles by R. B. Perry.[54] I myself urged (in 1979) revisionary naturalistic constructions of "good" and "morally wrong." Earlier, I suggested that various other contemporary writers, whom I have classified somewhat loosely as "revisionary,"[55] include John Rawls, Elizabeth Anscombe, and Philippa Foot. And I speculated that some passages in both J. S. Mill and Kant can also be construed in such a revisionary way.

In light of these reflections, it is useful to turn to some arguments produced by Peter Railton,[56] who styles himself as belonging to the "neorealist" camp but who, unlike at least most of the others in the group, makes assertions about the semantic *function* of value and moral predicates and offers proposals about the truth of evaluative and moral beliefs that, unlike the argument discussed earlier, do not depend on inferences from

---

[54] *Realms of Value* (Cambridge, Mass.: Harvard University Press, 1954), pp. 2, 13, 87.

[55] In Chapter 1, Part 2.

[56] In "Moral realism," *Philosophical Review* 95 (1986), 163–207; "Facts and values," *Philosophical Topics* 14 (1986). "Naturalism and prescriptivity," *Social Philosophy and Policy* 7 (1989), 151–74; "Nonfactualism about normative discourse," *Philosophy and Phenomenological Research*; and "What the noncognitivist helps us to see the naturalist must help us to explain" and "A reply to David Wiggins" in John Haldane and Crispin Wright (eds.), *Reality, Representation and Projection* (New York: Oxford University Press, 1993), chaps. 12 and 14.

reflective equilibrium of moral beliefs or on alleged parallels between ethical and scientific reasoning. But nor does Railton claim that his proposals about the properties moral/value predicates designate are analytic of the ordinary meaning of these terms, in the simple sense in which "is an unmarried male" might be thought to be analytic of "is a bachelor." What Railton wants to show is that there are reasons for understanding moral/evaluative terms in a certain way – the same sorts of reasons there are for construing "scientific *explanation*" roughly in the way Hempel did, as permitting an understanding of this conception in its actual use in empirical science. I do not suggest that Railton thinks there is an exact correspondence between the status of an explication of "scientific explanation" and his revisionist explication of value/moral language. But Railton's implication seems to be that terms like "nonmorally good" and "morally right" can be construed so as to throw light, if we adopt his proposed revisions perhaps, on such facts as how evaluations are made or how moral conceptions are adjusted as a result of empirical facts. Thus, he is a reductionist about the analysis of ethical language.

More specifically, Railton thinks that there are two main desiderata for selection of these "revisionary definitions." One is to choose them so that there is an appropriate connection between evaluative statements so (naturalistically) construed and *commending* or *prescriptive* force. Such a choice of definition would have the effect that, on the suggested understanding, these terms would do what the emotive/expressive theory claims that ordinary value/moral language does – express a favoring or prescriptive attitude – thereby having (if the theory is correct) the motivational force of ordinary evaluative/moral statements. The second desideratum is that the properties involved in a naturalistic construction of evaluative concepts play an *explanatory* role in an account both of the development of values in the individual (for nonmoral value statements) and of the development of a certain kind of morality in societies (for the case of moral values). So, he proposes an understanding of nonmoral value statements (and, mutatis mutandis, much the same for moral judgments) as part of "a good explanatory ac-

191

count of what is going on in evaluative practices involving claims about a person's own good."[57]

Railton's most fully sketched outline of his view is presented in "Noncognitivism about rationality: benefits, costs, and an alternative," second part, currently only partly published, the first part published as part of a symposium on Gibbard's *Wise Choices, Apt Feelings* in *Philosophy and Phenomenological Research* 52 (1992), 961–8. His proposal for framing a naturalistic definition (here of "rationality") is to develop a "job description" of the many roles a term plays in discourse, deliberation, and regulation of affect and action. We then form a definition something like this: Rightness is "whatever unified (or almost unified) property plays all (or most) of these roles (or the most central among them) fully (or most fully)." So, about a given definition one might ask: "Does it capture the paradigm cases? Does it preserve all (or most) of the truisms? Can it fit into a framework for the explanation and understanding of behavior? Does it enable us to understand the assumed normative or motivational pull?"

This kind of program leads Railton to suggest, as a model, an analysis of "the non-morally intrinsically valuable" as just "pleasant" or "happiness-producing." (Actually, he prefers another analysis, in terms of being the object of a person's "informed desires" or of being what is in one's "objective interest" – which he explains and defends in other papers – but I shall discuss the simpler view because the reasoning strikes me as sharper and as having wider scope.)[58] The construction of the

---

[57] Peter Railton, "Naturalism and prescriptivity," *Social Philosophy and Policy* 7 (1989), 151–74. By "evaluative practices" I believe he means the process of a person's forming and changing his values.

[58] Railton, "Moral realism," and "Facts and values." These papers seem to me to have narrower scope, his first example concerning negative reinforcement of drinking milk when in a physical condition strongly antagonistic to milk consumption, and the second concerning negative reinforcement of an ambition to write arising from failures stemming from lack of talent for writing. On this view, preference goes to the better-informed aspiration or desire, namely, the one that remains after fuller experience (with consequent positive or negative reinforcement). The "pleasure" proposal, although perhaps

"nonmorally valuable" as referring to a property identical to pleasure-happiness he regards as a tentative one, which could be modified on the basis of empirical discoveries, just as can the ordinary identification of water as being H_2O. The proposal, he thinks, like any defensible one, must also account for various truisms about nonmoral value – such as Mill's view that the preferences of experienced people are indicative of what is desirable.

How might one argue that pleasure/happiness *explains* our norms about what is good? Railton suggests that according to influential psychological theory, pleasure (or displeasure) is the primary reinforcer of desires; what we now want is fixed by our experiences with the now desired sort of thing as having been pleasant in the past. Railton concedes, of course, that it is obvious that people want other things besides happiness. But he points out that these goods – and variation about them from person to person and place to place – covary with conditions in which happiness is normally produced. In these various conditions, experiences of happiness reinforce the desire for the ends that tend, in those conditions, to produce happiness. Thus, happiness can enter into an explanatory theory of the individual's desires (and presumably nonmoral values), and therefore this proposal meets one of the criteria for a satisfactory revision.

But like many straightforward, clear proposals, this one can be reasonably queried. An initial query about it is that if we explain "nonmorally good" as being just "pleasant," it would seem that pleasure must be the only thing intrinsically good, which seems doubtful. Moreover, that conclusion seems not to follow from the psychological theory used to support the identification. Why might not, as he concedes, reinforcement by pleasure produce a strong desire for knowledge in me, a desire so strong that I regularly set aside pleasures in order to gain more knowledge? The critic might go on to point out that if you asked

not very different, seems to me simpler and clearer. On the other hand, if there are natural positive/negative reinforcers other than pleasure/displeasure (as possibly has been contended by McClelland), Railton's preference for reinforcement theory may have an advantage.

Freud, during his last illness, whether he preferred happiness or more knowledge, he would have said "knowledge"; and so, pleasure is not always the goal with superior normative force. Thus, it is not clear, from pleasure having primacy in a psychological explanation, that it always has superior normative force. The argument to the hedonist's analysis of the nonmorally good, then, basically only shows that the connection of happiness with motivation is very deeply rooted.

Moreover, the argument seems to be open to question on factual grounds. It appears to assume what L. T. Troland called "psychological hedonism of the past," that is, that the motivation to produce a certain state of affairs is a function of the number and intensity of pleasures from such states of affairs in the past – a controversial thesis that appears to ignore various complications,[59] as well as the influence on values of parental teaching and example.

Railton also suggests that such a hedonistic account might explain why different values occur in different cultures through the fact that in different cultures there is corresponding variation in the conditions in which happiness is normally produced. This claim, however, although interesting, seems at best speculative: One would like to know which such variations explain the strong distaste for violence and concern about criticism among the Hopi compared with the Ifugao desire for wealth and status and their consequent indulgence in head hunting. The proposal, however intriguing, is not obviously supported by facts.

Second, Railton points out that this hedonist suggestion can account for the *normative force* of judgments of nonmoral value, for it is impossible for a person to have the experience (and recollection) of happiness and not be drawn to the prospect of it; so, "pleasant" must have normative force, just as do "good" and "valuable." So, Railton's point that a "pleasure" analysis would give nonmoral value judgments some of the commend-

---

[59] I have discussed these problems in *A Theory of the Good and the Right*, pp. 135ff.

ing force they seem to have appears well taken, although hardly conclusive.

In another paper[60] Railton pursues much the same strategy with the term "morally right." He proposes that a preferable understanding of an act as being "morally right" is its being *"rational* (in the instrumental sense) not from the point of view of any particular individual, but from what might be called a 'social point of view,' in the presence of full and vivid information, treating the objective interests of everyone equally."[61] As thus stated, this view *seems* to (but doubtless is not intended to) underwrite act-utilitarianism as the criterion of right actions. The proposal is more convincing if taken as a thesis about *social* actions like adoption of a law or a declaration of war.

This conception, Railton thinks, permits the notion of the moral good to be explanatory, to play an important role in the understanding of social history. For societies in which the interests of some are favored, in contrast to institutions and policies that are rational from the social point of view, have a potential for dissatisfaction and unrest, alienation, loss of morale, and decline in the effectiveness of authority. Such a potential produces feedback that "promotes the development of norms that better approximate social rationality."[62] The same pressures have led to the broadening of the concept of "society" to include all other peoples. (It is not clear that this movement has fully succeeded.) The same applies to movement in the direction of attaching important moral requirements to the conditions for well-being, for satisfying human interests. These pressures occur because persons whose interests are denied "are led to form common values, and make common cause along lines of shared interest, thereby placing pressure on social practices to approximate more closely to social rationality." Social history can give us information about which social structures best satisfy this ideal of social rationality.

One may, however, question whether these reflections show that a set of practices/institutions is morally justified if and only

[60] Railton, "Moral realism," especially 189ff.   [61] Ibid., 190.   [62] Ibid., 193.

if they satisfy an ideal of "social rationality." Why should an explanatory function – the fact that disparity from the ideal causes disfavored groups to initiate changes – tell us what is justified?[63] Moreover, although the proposal is in line roughly with a broad indirect-utilitarian view of morality, a good deal more needs to be said – about the possible complexity of such a system, or about the costs of teaching it, or about its relation to empathic sympathy. But these are only details. One might also question whether this explanation justifies acceptable views about the status of animals and future generations. (Possibly the proposal could be broadened to include these items in its scope; the problem is a difficult one for most theories.) Actually, if some kind of indirect utilitarianism like that defended in the preceding chapter is the view we think justified, there is no reason why something *closer* to Railton's proposal should not be accepted as a possible empiricist "revision" of "optimal morali-ty." However, the broad sweep of Railton's supporting explana-tory account seems to require it to ignore the details of how moral changes are brought about in historical cultures – for instance, by missionary activities, or the acceptance of Christian standards by tribal chieftains, or the increase of polygyny and reduction of killing of the aged brought about by the introduc-tion of domesticated reindeer among the Asian Chukchi, or the changes in standards of sexual behavior brought about by intro-duction of the pill (although possibly these changes could be squeezed in in some way). The explanatory power of Railton's ideal of social rationality comports best only with a broad, rath-er undetailed look at history. I believe Railton would not contest this.

Railton thinks that his revisionist conception of moral right-

---

[63] One might concede that this property may well explain why certain things *are* widely valued morally, but one might not be convinced that people are *justified* in valuing them or why *we* should endorse them. I believe Railton's response to this is that to draw this inference is to rely solely on the explana-tory function as a clue to what is justified. "Right" also carries normative implications in addition to its explanatory function. When one takes into account these other functions of "right," one might wind up with an accept-able view.

ness also explains the normativity (*motivation* for decision making about *actions*) of moral statements, for, so construed, moral statements will appeal to considerations that are moving to persons concerned with human well-being, who are aware of the importance of certain moral standards for maximizing the well-being of sentient creatures, and who are "willing to submit themselves to relevant sorts of scrutiny." The conception, however, may go only partway; for a fuller account of the normativity of judgments of right and wrong we may have to bring in further considerations, conceivably associations of moral terms acquired in the process of teaching by parents.

Railton concedes that these are, to some extent, revisionist proposals for the interpretation of evaluative terms. How far should we accept this kind of "reductionism"? Is this neonaturalist view of the nonmoral good superior to the earlier proposal in this book: that something is intrinsically good (for a person) if and only if it is something he would want for itself if he were factually fully informed about it and had not made any of the mistakes listed in the final section of Chapter 2? And is the proposal about "morally wrong" to be preferred to the one offered earlier: that it is a property of an action, of being the target of a person's moral aversions (etc.) given that he is factually informed about relevant matters, and that his aversions coincide with those of a social moral code that can be recommended as optimal to fully informed persons (including himself) who are familiar with the alternatives and expect to live in the relevant society? Both of my analyses seem to me to carry moving force, just as do the value/moral terms in ordinary use. Whether these conceptions explain nonmoral values is a question. As to standards of the morally right, I am content to say that the history of moralities in the world is a complicated business that I am prepared to leave to psychologists, historians, anthropologists, and sociobiologists; but I think the conception of an optimal moral code that I have outlined would be moving to thoughtful, factually informed persons if they thought about it carefully.

So, novel, intriguing, appealing as straightforward and clear, and helpful as Railton's proposals and arguments are in providing a definite proposal about the meaning of moral terms (which other neonaturalist proposals fail to do) and in not rely-ing on lame comparisons (as other neonaturalists do) of the logic of evaluative thinking with that of the natural sciences, I am still unmoved by them and prefer the ones offered in the earlier chapters of this book. Of course, I think my own pro-posals can properly be classified as a form of moral realism, construed a bit more broadly than in terms of the five theses I have attributed to the neonaturalists.

Chapter 7

Utilitarianism and distributive justice

There are at least two reasons for discussing the implications of a conscience-utilitarian theory of optimal morality for distributive justice. The first is to find out whether such a theory has definite implications for this controversial issue. The second is that many people are not at all clear what system of income/tax allocation or other income-affecting regulations they should support on moral grounds and would like to know.

But, first, let us consider the *concept* of "distributive justice."

There is a large problem concerned with material income and personal well-being that has traditionally been called the "problem of distributive justice."[1] This problem is how to evaluate morally the whole set of institutions that affect income and well-being, including compensation for work performed (or interest paid for use of one's money), taxes imposed, welfare grants made by the state, provision of public education up to some level, and other regulations such as those concerning affirmative action.

It is sometimes suggested that following the conscience-utilitarian theory about optimal morality might be a good or even the best proposal about how to distribute material goods

---

[1] For a useful discussion of possible differences between the claims of charity and those of distributive justice, see Allan Buchanan, "Justice and charity," *Ethics* 97 (1987), 550–75.

(etc.), but it need not be *just*.[2] Various other principles of just distribution have been advocated: that productivity of a worker, effort expended, compensation for hazardous or unpleasant work, "minimax relative concession" (Gauthier[3]), or moral virtue be the basis of at least major economic rewards, provided that persons have had an equal opportunity to develop the relevant characteristics.[4] Other egalitarian principles have also been advocated.[5]

Here there is obviously a conceptual problem of some interest. What we have been trying to do is to find a satisfactory theory of which actions are morally right. Is this endeavor partially misguided in that what we should be looking for is (also) a theory of which acts are *just*?

The term "just" is, however, rather vague and is sometimes used so broadly as to cover paying debts or respecting the property of others as "duties of justice." There is a question of whether we might not do well to just drop the term "distributive justice," although it does have a peculiar rhetorical force. "Unjust" does seem intuitively to imply "prima facie wrong," but not conversely; an act (e.g., incest) might be prima facie wrong but not unjust. Or we might suggest that "is unjust," applied to some distributions of goods, could sensibly be construed to mean "is prima facie wrong because it allows too much inequality of welfare (or resources)" or "is prima facie wrong because it fails to recognize adequately the rewards to which a person is entitled by his services (or perhaps by his fine moral character)," and so on (where the "prima facie wrong" clauses need not be viewed as *basic* moral principles and need at least some theoretical justification). Such principles might conceivably be supported by a conscience-utilitarian moral theory –

---

[2] See W. K. Frankena, *Ethics* (Englewood Cliffs, N.J.: Prentice-Hall, 1973) pp. 43–52.

[3] David Gauthier in *Morals by Agreement* (Oxford: Oxford University Press, 1987).

[4] See, for instance, the discussion in Robert Young, "Egalitarianism and personal desert," *Ethics* 102 (1992), 319–41; also see Allan Buchanan, *Ethics, Efficiency and the Market* (Totowa, N.J.: Prentice-Hall, 1959), chap. 16.

[5] See Frankena, *Ethics*.

might, insofar as they are definite and sound, be derivable, as rules with prima facie force, from a conscience-utilitarian theory. Thus, productivity might be a prima facie ground for reward because the optimal system may need to provide an incentive to produce, and so will pay favorable attention to one's productivity. Much the same holds for effort and for compensation for unpleasant or dangerous work: Without such compensation, it might be difficult to hire people for such jobs, and there is a somewhat moving appeal to equality of treatment when the payment is proportional to the discomfort or risk of the work. Some meritarian principles are too vague to be of use in guidance: The proposal that economic reward be based partly on the degree of a person's moral virtue involves as a standard something that is very hard to pin down: How much more should *A* be paid if he is somewhat more virtuous than *B*? How do we identify different whole levels of virtue? Somewhat the same holds for equal opportunity: Should one person be paid more than another if he does better work, but not if his achievement is a result of the work ethic learned in his family or because of his gene-based skills or native intelligence and hence because of opportunity that is more than equal? Such questions are very difficult to answer. Doubtless much more needs to be said in criticism of the various proposed alternative standards.

We must not forget that if one claims there is some principle of morally justified distribution of income other than the conscience-utilitarian one, one needs to explain the justification of this principle – and surely do more than expect one's intuitions to be shared. I have argued that a conscience-utilitarian moral system can be recommended to persons who want protection against injuries and frustrated interests (etc.) and to persons with empathic, altruistic motivation. I have argued that a morality that can be thus recommended is a form of utilitarian morality – that is, the set of aversions (etc.) to act-types the prevalence and teaching of which aversions (etc.) would maximize the benefit to sentient creatures. It seems to follow that justified moral attitudes toward wages, taxes, and so on will be ones that support laws/regulations the prevalence of which will be maximally beneficial publicly. On the assumption that principles of distribution different from those recommended by an indirect-conscience-utilitarian theory have not been justified, it seems that identifying optimal rules for wages, taxes, and other regulations, as the conscience-utilitarian theory proposes, is a project that may not fall short of identifying principles of distributive justice.

One might wonder if it is necessary to have any specific principles of conscience at all in this area comparable to the justified aversions (etc.) to deceit or breach of promise. Perhaps the average person encounters problems of distribution rarely enough that no conscientious aversions are called for. But this view is too simple. Some principles are needed in the family: in deciding what is a fair distribution of the household chores, whether the children should have equal allowances, and whether the children should be provided with some or equal means for higher education. Or, if one is in business, one has to decide about wage levels for one's employees, what is a fair contract with the union, and whether to offer especially favorable consideration in hiring to women or the disabled. And as a citizen, one must decide whether to vote for more taxation to provide more parks, improve the streets, or raise the level of education in the schools. And so on. Thus many principles about distributions of welfare are needed in practice, and some theoretical basis for them seems called for. But I am not suggesting that a special moral principle (with a disposition to feel guilty or condemn others for infractions) should be built into *conscience* specific to each of these various types of problem. What is needed for conscience is some broader principle, or a list of considerations considered to be relevant and weighed, in reflection about the more specific problems. I am also not proposing that the principles I shall adduce relevant to income/tax distributions will be adequate to resolve all the types of moral problems just listed.

Is there any simple, basic principle that the conscience-utilitarian might be said to espouse for laws/regulations/practices (etc.) governing distributions of all sorts, provided that it is not excessively costly for some reason (such as administrative problems or problems of teaching)? One might think that one basic goal is to reduce the disparity between some persons having a high level of well-being and others having a lower level of well-being (other things being equal), where "well-being" is construed either as happiness or as the satisfaction of "rational," subjective preferences. Taken by itself, this proposal faces awkward difficulties. For instance, should we disfavor a person who has a higher level of well-being just because she has a cheerful disposition (or favor one with a lower level just because she is naturally gloomy)? To take another example, one person might be naturally better off because she is happy to drink beer (and so needs to spend less in order to be happy), whereas another is worse off because she is unhappy unless she drinks champagne (and so needs to spend more), although some would advocate ignoring such differences because such preferences are a matter of autonomous choice – which they may or may not be. But such differences are relatively trivial and, incidentally, such disparities are easily faked (or at least the claim that the person is unable to change them); hence a social order need not take them seriously. Moreover, it would be absurd to ignore the situation of the ill-fed on the ground that they would not mind being ill-fed if only they had a more cheerful disposition! So, if we are to identify a "simple principle" that the conscience-utilitarian might support as a way of optimizing general well-being, perhaps we should subscribe to the principle of reducing disparities (roughly following Sen on the subject of identifying a standard of living) in *capacities* or *opportunities* that are known normally to lead to disparities in well-being[6] when these can be identified reasonably by public officials charged with administering relevant rules. Such capacities/opportunities will usually be closely related to economic income, but they may also involve preferences in hiring, provision of training, medical care, and so on. Why would the

---

[6] See the discussions by A. K. Sen, "Capability and well-being," in A. Sen and M. Nussbaum (eds.), *The Quality of Life* (Oxford: Clarendon Press, 1993), pp. 30–52; "Equality of what?" in S. M. McMurrin (ed.), *Tanner Lectures on Human Values* (Salt Lake City: University of Utah Press, 1980); and *Resources, Values, and Development* (Cambridge, Mass.: Harvard University Press, 1984).

conscience-utilitarian support such principles? Because in the long run it will enhance the total social well-being. We shall see how this works out specifically for the case of economic income, which is the major focus of my discussion.

An initial question to be considered is what we are to take for granted as the background assumption of our proposal for laws/regulations/practices relevant to economic income. For instance, are we to assume that there is an institution of private property or even, beyond ownership of land, housing, and other things for private consumption, private ownership of the means of production? The answer to this question I am going to assume is that whereas the Marxist view of public ownership of all productive resources and central planning of the economy is an interesting and attractive proposal, its practical problems are so great that it is no longer a serious competitor of private ownership of the means of production and a market system of exchange roughly as these exist in the United States and Western Europe. (This contrast ignores democratic and worker-controlled systems such as those that existed in the former Yugoslavia; if one decided to favor such a system, the proposals to be offered would have to be modified.[7])

This being the case, what is the need for government intervention in the market, with laws and institutions concerning taxes and other regulations? The answer has various parts. First, the market does not (although it could) provide public goods like lighthouses, emergency services (fire and health), traffic controls, protection against invasion by foreign powers, protection against externalities (businesses spewing poisonous fumes in an area, for which cost they do not have to pay), and so on. A government can do these things. But it can also support policies that foster economic growth (ideally involving full employment) and stability. All of these activities have to be paid for. All of these presumably every rational person would want, from the point of view of his own long-run well-being and any

[7] See R. G. Peffer, *Marxism, Morality, and Social Justice* (Princeton, N.J.: Princeton University Press, 1990).

concern he may have for the public good. There are also further possible goals, which we shall want to appraise, such as transfers to the poor from the rich, or preventing discrimination against groups like women or the handicapped, or insurance protection against illness.

An argument directed against any progressive feature of income taxes is that it reduces the incentive to work or at least work well. And it is, of course, true that a person will perform arduous work only if he expects a personal reward (this may include welfare for children or others with whom he identifies) or at least the satisfaction of some desires (e.g., to fund an art gallery), and we do not expect sheer altruism to be the exclusive motive of long-term economic contribution. So far, the competitive capitalist economic system has support. But it does not follow from this that incentive must be regarded as a decisive consideration in setting *income-tax rates*. Owners of corporate common stock will notice the frequency of requests to vote for increasing the number of shares of common stock of a company on the ground that this is needed to provide stock rights for the compensation of executives whose services are important for the company. And it is true that high salaries and stock rights may be needed to retain employees from the grasp of competing companies; but it does not follow that a high tax on *all* highly paid persons would reduce the work incentive generally. As Joseph Pechman has observed,[8] "Work habits are not easily changed, and for most people in a modern industrial society there is little opportunity to vary their hours of work or the intensity of their efforts in response to changes in tax rates." Baseball players will hardly drop fly balls, or prize fighters lose interest in winning, or academics slack off in productive work, or business executives lose interest in keeping their company in the black just because of an increased tax rate. Moreover, a favorable tax rate has relatively little effect on the actual supply of labor; as Pechman observes further, "The 1969 reduction of

---

[8] In *Federal Tax Policy* (Washington, D.C.: The Brookings Institution, 1987), pp. 76–7.

maximum marginal tax rate from 70 to 50 percent was justified on incentive grounds, but there is no evidence that it had a significant effect on labor supply. . . . The reduction in tax rates resulting from the tax reform legislation of 1986 may increase total labor supply by about 1 percent." But one must concede that the relative unimportance of tax rates for some groups of individuals does not at all imply that it is unimportant for everyone, including contractors, owners of small businesses, farmers, housewives (who might take an outside job if the tax rate did not render it practically worthless), or physicians (or other professionals) who might enter some other occupation that did not require so long and expensive an education. There we must concede that a lower net income after taxation might make a noticeable difference in incentive. So much for the incentive argument against high taxation of large incomes.

There are various points at which the economic-related policies of the U.S. government are open to criticism – for instance, the vastly inflated military budget. Even when all reasonable military reductions have been made, however, the budget of the federal (and also the state/local) government will be huge and, in order to avoid a painful and enduring federal budget deficit, some taxes will almost certainly have to be raised (as of 1994). So we face the question: What sorts of principles for this will be recommended by a conscience-utilitarian morality?

How might the goal of maximizing social well-being of conscience-utilitarianism support some specific principles of taxation? We must go into this. To identify the proper principles of taxation, we need to take into account the (slightly controversial) economic principle of the "declining marginal utility of money." Let us consider this principle. With the advent of a money economy that permits saving, a person will normally give priority in purchases to the things she wants most (will do her the most good in the long run, in her judgment, or will most promote the projects in which she is interested). So the things to the purchase of which she will assign priority (in the long run – she may decide not to purchase until she has the money to buy expensive, highly desired items) will be those of most benefit (as she thinks) to her or her projects, which means that the items with lower priority will, as she thinks, have less benefit to her. So, the more income a person has, the larger proportion she will, over the long term, spend on less preferred items. This means that she gets less benefit, relatively, from successive increments to her income (above what she pays for necessities). This reasoning supports the thesis of the declining marginal utility of money.

There have been criticisms of this theory, but on the whole it is sensible and a cautious use of it is beyond reproach.[9]

In view of the declining marginal utility of money, it might seem that the optimal way for a conscience-utilitarianism–supported government policy to allocate the monetary benefits of national production, other things being equal, would involve dividing the total economic value of national production equally. But this hardly follows, in view of the absence of a precise method for making interpersonal comparisons of utility, since an equal division might ignore the inequality of benefits. Nevertheless, some utilitarian-type principle of *equal* income allocation can be justified by appeal to the principle of the declining marginal utility of money. For, as many economists (e.g., A. P. Lerner) have argued effectively, in view of our relative ignorance of the comparable utilities of events for different people, an equal distribution is the way at least to get a *probably* maximal sum of utility.[10] That is something to be taken seriously into account.

---

[9] See M. S. Stein, "Diminishing marginal utility of income and progressive taxation," *Northern Illinois University Law Review* 12 (1992), 373–97; Joel Slemrod, "Optimal taxation and optimal tax systems," *Journal of Economic Perspectives* 4 (1990); J. Bankman and T. Griffith, "Social welfare and the rate structure: A new look at progressive taxation," 75 *California Law Review* (1987); and William Shaw, "Welfare, equality, and distribution," in Bradford Hooker (ed.), *Rationality, Rules and Utility* (Boulder, Colo.: Westview Press, 1993), chap. 11.

[10] See A. P. Lerner, *The Economics of Control* (New York: Macmillan, 1944); also see Allen Buchanan, *Ethics, Efficiency, and the Market* (Totowa, N.J.: Rowman and Allanheld, 1985), pp. 58ff.

Such a policy, however, taken by itself, would manifestly be counterproductive. In the first place, it ignores incentive effects. Second, we shall see that some (the ill or handicapped) need more than the average income to bring the utility of a (marginal) dollar in income up to that of the normal person. To question this, on the ground that it presupposes that it is possible to compare exactly the benefits of different individuals, is to carry skepticism much too far, as I have explained elsewhere. Is it too much to assume that we know that a person who has come in from an hour's tennis on a hot day enjoys a cold Coke more than does his companion a glass of warm water, given the expected behavioral responses of each?[11] And if we can know that the enjoyment reactions of different people to certain physical stimuli are much the same, we can go on to use this knowledge as a basis for further comparisons based on the judgments of the individuals about how much they prefer various other experiences to these reactions to physical stimuli. This is not to say that such comparisons are easy but only that they can be made, with care and to a limited extent. Surely it would be a bit much to suggest that we do not know that we shall be adding more to utility by providing a hungry family with the money necessary for basic food than by providing the same sum to a well-off family for caviar. It follows that, given that other things are equal, we maximize benefit by equalizing incomes, to some extent, among comparable groups. A conscience-utilitarian will, accordingly, favor governmental policies that, other things being equal, *tend* to maximize equality of income units in the society and conscientious attitudes that support these policies. This is not to say exactly how egalitarian the institutions ought to be; we shall come to this later. The benefits from equal slices of a pie must be compared with those of everyone having a fair piece of a larger pie.

Some philosophers take a very dim view of the moral acceptability of any scheme of income division that any kind of utilitarianism would call for. Bernard Williams, for instance, says: "In this light, utilitarianism does emerge as absurdly primitive. . . .

---

[11] See my *A Theory of the Good and the Right* (Oxford: Oxford University Press, 1979), pp. 257–64.

On the criterion of maximizing average utility, there is nothing to choose between any two states of society which involve the same number of people sharing in the same aggregate amount of utility, even if in one of them it is relatively evenly distributed, while in the other a very small number have a great deal of it; and it is just silly to say that in fact there is nothing to choose here."[12] This statement ignores the fact that a utilitarian will pay attention to the declining marginal utility of money. Whether such criticisms are fair to other features of a sophisticated conscience-utilitarian theory of distribution we shall have to consider.

One might ask whether traditional utilitarianism has recognized the importance of government policies favoring equality. Here it is of modest interest to note the views of J. S. Mill. Mill certainly did not overlook the importance of equality: he wrote that "I look upon inequality as in itself always an evil,"[13] and said that everyone has an equal claim to "all the means of happiness" except where the general interest excludes it. But he seems to have thought that equality is good primarily as a means: He believed that rough equality is a prerequisite for social cohesion, and that inequality demoralizes the worst-off group and at the same time corrupts those in power. He went on to conclude that the "true idea of distributive justice consists . . . in redressing the inequalities and wrongs of nature." One must admit that he seems to pay relatively little attention to this in his practical recommendations. For although he conceded the decline of the marginal utility of money income and thought taxes should be levied on the basis of "least sacrifice," he objected to a progressive tax rate on the ground that the marginal utility of a given income is not capable of being identified with certainty and that "to tax the larger incomes at a higher percentage than the small is to lay a tax on industry and

---

[12] In J. J. C. Smart and Bernard Williams, *Utilitarianism: For and Against* (Cambridge: Cambridge University Press, 1973), pp. 142–3.

[13] "The Later Letters," *Collected Works* 10, p. 421, cited by F. R. Berger in *Happiness, Justice and Freedom* (Berkeley: University of California Press, 1984), p. 164.

economy."[14] (One wonders if larger incomes do derive mostly from industry and economy; how about wealthy parents, education, intelligence, a good marriage, or pure luck?) He did favor steep inheritance taxes, since the beneficiary has not earned his advantage; unearned income may be subject to heavy taxes. He did, moreover, advocate exemption from taxation for persons who need every penny for the "requisites of life and health" and as "protection against habitual bodily suffering," hence a £50 deductible. He also wrote that "Since no one is responsible for having been born, no pecuniary sacrifice is too great to be made by those who have more than enough, for the purpose of securing enough to all persons already in existence." His concept of what is "enough," however, seems far from generous.

What might a contemporary conscience-utilitarian propose, with the intention of combining incentives for production with the degree of equality called for by the fact of the declining marginal utility of money income (and other factors such as illness or handicaps), in an optimal mix? For this purpose, we may assume that the main feasible method for equalizing income is (along with a system of providing remunerative *work* for those needing assistance) a tax system possibly including a negative tax (instead of food stamps and other transfers of the sort already obtaining in the United States). Then the basic question is how to set optimal tax rates so as to make incomes more equal, in view of the declining marginal utility of money, compatibly with sufficient incentive to work and work well. (We have noted reasons to doubt a universally serious impact of tax rates on work incentive, but I propose to take this possibility theoretically into account due to its effects on small entrepreneurs, farmers, housewives, etc.) How might the conscience-utilitarian identify the optimal mix?

Making use of statistics, a reformer might consider various tax programs (including a negative tax) and then ask economists to assess how production (GNP) would be affected by changes to each new system of tax allocations (both positive and

14 J. S. Mill, *Principles of Political Economy,* (1948), pp. 806–8.

negative), taking into account incentive effects. (I have suggested that the answer might be no effects on production at all, but one must not forget that substantial income differences have the beneficial effect of placing persons with superior managerial talents or ingenuity or technological training in positions of influence, a situation the utilitarian reformer will want.) Admittedly, this would require a good deal of research (and some speculation). Assuming the economists have done a good job, we then have information about differing totals of national product, depending on which tax system is adopted. We then have a picture of the total economic pie to be divided corresponding to different kinds of welfare grant/taxation. (The figures are bound to be rough, possibly depending on the state of the economy at a given time.)

With this information in hand, we need to determine the *utility* optimum of the various tax systems, weighing the effects of greater (or less) production in some cases with the utility benefits deriving from greater equality in view of the declining marginal utility of money. I shall come to this.

But there is a preliminary question: whether there should not be a government-mandated minimum income. The census statistics show that 3.6 percent of the *individuals* reporting income in 1990 had an income below $5,000, 5.8 percent between $5,000 and $10,000, and 7.5 percent between $10,000 and $15,000; among *families*, 14.9 percent had incomes below $10,000, and 9.5 percent between $10,000 and $15,000.[15] So, then, what might be the average income among families in the bottom 10 percent? Perhaps $7,500? (We should remember that many people have no income at all and do not file tax returns – with no place to sleep and obtaining food by either raiding garbage cans or asking for handouts.) It would seem that many of these people are very badly off and, according to the Scanlon criterion (see Chapter 5), entitled to complain. One wonders just how low an income should thus entitle a person to complain. Is it enough, to entitle one to complain about the justice of the sys-

---

[15] For 1990: *Statistical Abstracts of the United States* and *The National Data Book*, 1992.

tem, if her income falls below the official poverty line of $13,924 for a family of four or $6,392 for a single person?[16] In 1991 14.3 percent of the population was living on an income below this line, according to a Census Bureau report cited in the *Ann Arbor News* of September 3, 1992. (The poverty line itself provides only for quite spartan living. It works out at roughly $1,150 per month for a family of four or $550 a month for a single person. In Ann Arbor, Michigan, this figure for a single person barely covers the rent of a studio apartment! Whether all these people qualify as being very badly off by Scanlon's criterion, they are manifestly *worse off* than those with larger incomes.)

Should we then, on grounds of justice, set a lowest limit on incomes to be guaranteed by government, say *at least* $10,000 for a *family* of four and a bit less for a single individual with the capacity to work? Should the government establish such an income floor? Obviously, barring bad repercussions on the national economy of such a policy, the position of the worst off would be improved somewhat, and it would seem that a conscience-utilitarian thesis about just tax/welfare would favor it. But to follow the previously cited Scanlon criterion a bit further, we must ask whether such a policy would make the position of those who have to pay for it even worse off. In other words, we might ask whether the welfare gain of those benefiting from the guarantee would be more than the welfare loss from the additional tax on those who have to pay for the guarantee.

One way of answering this question is by an intuitive comparison. Suppose that a family in the lowest income group gains $1,000 in income from the guarantee. If this gain meant only

---

[16] The identification of a poverty line is a judgment of the U.S. Department of Labor about an adequate standard of living, based on the amounts actually spent for a modest but adequate diet multiplied by a certain factor, reflecting the percentage of income people actually spend on food. What would count as poverty in India could be something very different. In underdeveloped societies we might define poverty as an income level inadequate to avoid starvation and morbidity. See A. K. Sen, *Inequality Re-examined* (Cambridge, Mass.: Harvard University Press, 1992), chap. 7.

the ability to buy a new car every fourth year rather than every eighth year, that is one thing; but it is another if the extra $1,000 meant that the typical family could now heat its home to 70°F rather than 50°F and enjoy a diet richer than rice and oatmeal. Correspondingly, we can ask what the person at the upper income level, say, over $200,000, would have to sacrifice in order to pay the $1,000 guarantee. It is hard to say what this might be. Put in these terms, it seems obvious that the transfer from the rich to the poor would bring a gain in well-being. Of course, for purposes of decision making, we need a clearer picture of both the gains at the bottom end and the losses at the top end across a wide spectrum. This line of thinking obviously makes use of interpersonal comparisons of well-being. It may be that this requires us to decide whether *everyone* would prefer the gain of $1,000 if he were in the position of the low-income person to the loss of $1,000 if he were in the position of the high-income person. What we might assume is that if the details of the gains (by the poor) and the losses (by the rich) are fully specified, everyone will agree that the gains will exceed the losses. Of course, it is possible that there will not be agreement when reflections cover the whole list of gains and losses that would be involved in a major change in tax laws. So far, I concede there is an element of speculation in my suggested conclusion.

How would this work out for the assessment of taxes? Suppose that a given tax rate would reduce the income of an individual from $500,000 to $200,000 – a fairly extreme level of taxation. Well, this tax rate might reduce the total *well-being* of the wealthy person by only one point, whereas the funds made available would be adequate to pay a $10,000 guarantee for 30 families at the bottom level, raising them from perhaps a utility level of 5 to 10, and a further increase to $15,000 might push the utility level up six points more. Figures about actual incomes of families with an income of $75,000 or more vary from 6.5 to 12.3 percent. If we think there are 40 million families in the United States, so perhaps 3.2 million (using an 8 percent figure for the number with income over $75,000) with a *taxable* income (after

213

deductions) of perhaps $50,000 each, then a straight, rather vicious 50 percent tax on the whole $50,000 or more, the entire group would be paying $80 billion plus 50 percent of their total earnings beyond $75,000. This would not cover the entire national budget, depending on how much income was earned beyond the $75,000, but it would go a long way. Would such a tax rate upset the entire economic system?

Of course, we need details before making predictions about how this whole system of setting tax rates would work. It is clear, however, that the employment of relative utility levels of various incomes in determining tax rates must have a major effect on making incomes more equal (since higher incomes will not correspond to utility gains, so that reduction of after-tax income at the higher levels will count for less) and therefore responding to the fact of the declining marginal utility of money.

I do not see why a rough conclusion something like this about the total utility of a given tax/welfare scheme, supported by economists and statisticians, could not, at least if a serious attempt were made to set aside political biases temporarily, be reached by a legislative body such as Congress. (I concede the political problems would be great, but I see no more difficulty in the application of this proposal than in the legislative enactment of Rawls's theory, say, the difference principle.) The result of this scheme would be that the bottom 10 percent would receive the largest part of any cash negative income tax, with the top segment of the group that still benefits from any negative tax having a somewhat larger total income, in view of its members' position in the capitalist system, on account of the market economy and the benefit of incentives. Beyond a certain point (say, $14,000, but this figure might be revised depending on the whole picture), members of higher income groups would (roughly) pay taxes and get no welfare grants. One must recognize that this kind of plan would probably imply rather large tax increases for the relatively wealthy when we reflect that 55 percent of the total income tax is now paid by persons in the 15 percent bracket. The suggestion is that those now paying the top 45 percent of taxes above the 15 percent level, especially the top 5 percent of the income units, would have steep increases.

(In 1990 the top 20 percent of the population had 46.4 percent of the income.)[17]

A word on how the negative income tax might be framed: a tax to replace food stamps, aid for dependent children, supplemental security income, and so on – grants that now do not help families headed by an able-bodied male who, for some reason, cannot compete effectively and so is unemployed. More important, there could be a work *requirement* for receiving government assistance – indeed, ideally, a job available or even required for *all* adults, an arrangement that would doubtless involve government Works Progress Administration (WPA)–type employment in times of less than full employment.[18] (There could be problems with the work *requirement:* For instance, if a 15-year-old girl with a baby has *no* income, it would seem some cash subsidy would be in order, since she could hardly be required to work.) But we might decide that a family of four is to be helped, *to some extent*, if its total wage/investment income – counting the employment furnished if necessary by the government – falls below the poverty level of roughly $14,000, where this figure itself would be set as a result of calculations about the distribution that would be maximally beneficial. We might then set a total income of $14,000 as the point at which no government contribution is due and also no positive federal tax on the wage earner. It is the breakeven point.[19] We might then decide – as suggested earlier – that the maximal government contribution for a family of four with *no* income whatever from the economy would be $10,000. How then might the negative tax be reckoned for persons who work, with an income from wage/investment but less than $14,000?

---

[17] See Tables 707 and 731, *National Data Book, 1992*.

[18] If a person were paid, say, only $4 an hour – a small sum, encouraging the worker to move into the private sector – he would receive $160 for a 40-hour week, or $8,000 for 50 weeks. This would greatly reduce the need for cash assistance – obviously if two or more persons in a family were working. If the wage rate were higher, the family would need no cash subsidy at all.

[19] For a helpful discussion, see J. Pechman, *Federal Tax Policy* (Washington, D.C.: The Brookings Institution), pp. 86–91.

The answer might be that from this total wage income would be deducted all state and local taxes and contributions to charity (etc.) – all the deductions currently recognized by the federal income tax law. Suppose, then, that the taxpayer finds that her *net*, after all deductions, is zero. Then she would receive the full allowance of $10,000 from the government. (This family does slightly better than a family with no wage income because the various deductions from income, including charity, have already been paid.) But suppose that a family has *net* income from wage employment (possibly from WPA-type government jobs) or investment, say $5,000 after subtracting all deductions? There is then a question of how much it should receive from the government. One possibility is that the government contribution be only $5,000. Or the rule might be that the individual could keep, say, 50 percent of the $5,000, so that only 50 percent of her net earnings (after all deductions) would be deducted from the $10,000. So the net receipt from the government would be $7,500 plus the earned net of $5,000, for a total of $12,500. There are, of course, possible variations – for instance, ones specifying a different basic allowance – but a negative tax might work in somewhat this way. Evidently the details should be debated, but I would think that all decisions within this general range would be compatible with the requirements of a conscience-utilitarian morality.

Whether some comparable system could be devised for state, local, and other taxes is a question. The very issue is daunting. To some extent, some of these taxes are already somewhat (desirably) progressive.

One might ask how, on this conception, income would be distributed to the sick, the handicapped, and the mentally defective. These situations, of course, are somewhat different. I would think relief from pain and the long-term benefits of medical care are so productive of utility (by reducing pain/inactivity and returning to productive life in minimal time) that the ill have a prior claim for medical care. I suggest, therefore, that there should be a universal health service plan funded out of taxes, including possibly a special tax on employers. (I spare myself the problem of recommending whether a person absent from work on account of illness should be paid for his lost time as if it had not been lost.) The handicapped should benefit, in the same way, by a provision funding them so as to enable them to get around and function in a fairly normal way. (Conceivably, "normal" could be so construed as to be prohibitively expensive.) There is much to be said for an affirmative action program supporting the *employment* of the handicapped, which might mean an additional expense of providing employers with special equipment.[20] Beyond that point, I see no reason to think their utility curves will differ from those of the rest of us; and therefore, they will be treated exactly the same way as others in the job market. If they are unable to do any productive work, they might receive the basic $10,000 family-of-four income allowance of the negative income tax, plus the suggested supplement to enable them to move about more or less normally. For persons suffering from native mental disability or an early life deficiency in training, the treatment might be the same as for the physically disabled, except that training of skills (etc.) could take the place of the help to the physically disabled. (There might well need to be an expansion of the program of sheltered shops.)

The question remains of how to treat a normal person capable of working who simply refuses to take a job and prefers to go fishing. I do not know how utility would be maximized. If performing a job (or attending a training school) is compulsory, presumably at the least, a serious cut in the negative income tax allowance would be in order. Such persons might be helped just enough to subsist at a marginal level.

There are various complex problems to be worked out – for instance, the size of a family. Current income tax law allows for this, but if significant negative income grants (or even relatively low tax rates) are to come into play, we should be careful not to encourage large families as a means to increase family income. Presumably the number would drop off sharply after two chil-

[20] See G. S. Kavka, "Disability and the right to work," in E. F. Paul, F. D. Miller, and J. Paul (eds.), *Economic Rights* (Cambridge: Cambridge University Press, 1992), pp. 262–90.

dren. (To people who want many children, having a child is a consumer good for which they should be willing to make some sacrifice.) There is also the question of whether both husband and wife should work as a precondition for receiving a government subsidy. I should think the answer is yes, partly because of the personal benefits of being employed for wages and partly because of the productivity of useful additions to the labor force (a consideration that may not hold for the handicapped, so that the claim for an affirmative action program for them is a bit more tenuous), but with liberty to make *substantial* adjustments for purposes of child care and a special postnatal holiday. Presumably, to make the whole system work, we need to guarantee a job to everyone able and willing to work effectively – government employment being offered where necessary, but at a lower rate to encourage movement into the private sector.

One might ask whether a cash subsidy for the worst-off group might not undermine their incentive to work. I suggest it would not: Surely at this level there is motivation to have more money and to work to earn it.

Utilitarian theories are often accused (e.g., by Williams) of ignoring the difference between persons, of "person merging." And it is true that the preceding proposal is dominated by the conception that the goal is total utility maximization. But the individual is not lost: She is assigned an income class on the basis roughly of her wages in the capitalist/free-market system (presumably a function of productivity, ability, and effort), the size of her family, and whether anyone is handicapped. I think the total dollar incomes of the lower groups would be far more equal to those of other groups than they are at present; people with an earned income of over $200,000 would pay *very* heavy taxes. How might further differentiations be justified?

Let us consider how the anti-utilitarian contractualism of T. M. Scanlon would respond to this proposal. His view, as we have seen in Chapter 5, is that a wage taxation scheme is morally in the clear only if no one could reasonably object to it, where a person can reasonably object only if he is in the worst-off – and also very badly off – group, and provided that there are no alternative schemes (which would ameliorate its position) that would not make others even worse off. Who would be the worst-off group on the proposed scheme, assuming that the ill and handicapped are provided for? Presumably those whose incomes would be at the bottom because their skills and abilities are not sought by the capitalist market system. What we can ask such persons is: "What are the realistic options?" There could, of course, be a flat-out equal-income form of socialism, which experience – insofar as there has been any – seems to show does not work well, brings about abysmal production and distribution, and is apt to encourage a bureaucracy, so that power rights, at least, are very unequal. I concede, however, that some persons might prefer to go for equal incomes even if this meant that nearly everyone would be worse off. One cannot but wonder if they have considered the costs carefully, and I doubt whether many persons at the bottom of the proposed income scale would really raise this objection. The formula "From each according to his capacities to each according to his needs" is not easy to apply. I find it difficult to believe that Scanlon would wish to underwrite so complete a departure from a capitalist market, since such a departure would presumably imply a significant reduction in the size of the economic pie available for distribution. There is a further fact Scanlon would have to recognize: that the result of the proposed system of tax rates would vastly diminish the differences between the after-tax incomes of almost everyone. It could well turn out that the lowest after-tax income of a family of four would be $25,000 and that the highest after-tax income of a family of four would be only $55,000 (with adjustments for illness, handicaps, etc.).

The most vocal objection to the proposed system would doubtless come from those presently in the top 10 percent income bracket, who would have to make considerable sacrifices from their present position in terms of dollar net after-tax income, if not in utility. Hence, again, the system might be charged with injustice. This query is formulated by Thomas Nagel in a recent volume.[21] These people might ask, "Why

---

[21] Thomas Nagel, *Equality and Partiality* (New York: Oxford University Press, 1991), p. 70.

should I have to take this big loss just in order to make a lot of other people better off?" Even persons in the middle income group, like members of labor unions, might be expected to raise this cry. (But Nagel has suggested that no one should overlook the fact that everyone has *some* motivating egalitarian concern.[22]) To the upper-income objectors the reply should be that the proposed system does take into account the contribution able and industrious people make to the economy, by recognizing that many higher incomes are justified by the contribution the relevant persons (occupying the positions they have in the system) make to the GNP. And if they think that their contribution to economic efficiency/productivity is not the justification of their higher reward (justified because what they do adds to the size of the economic pie), then one can retort to them: "Why should you receive a very high income for no good reason at all?" – at least, no good reason beyond the fact that their present incomes are part of the status quo. (I confess to being somewhat appalled by the number of executives of even rocky companies who receive a salary of over $1 million. I am prepared to admit that there may be more to be said on their behalf, but I would like to know what it is. Many of these people seem merely to be lucky beneficiaries of a traditional system.) So I suggest that any contractarian-type objection to the justice of the kind of proposal I have sketched, as a conscience-utilitarian proposal, needs to be spelled out in more detail if it is to have force. It has not been shown that the proposed system is one to which anyone could reasonably object, as allowing some people to be rather badly off when other possible systems would not make others still worse off.

My tax proposal is doubtless complex and needs detailed development, but it does seem to be what a reasonable conscience-utilitarian would propose. We should note that, in all probability, if such a system were instituted and people became accustomed to it, any objections would very probably be less determined.

There are various important inequalities that the foregoing

22 Ibid., 70, footnote.

system would not remove: the advantages of native talent or good health, or of being born and reared in a family with wealth and a high level of education and culture, strongly motivated to pass on its own advantages to its children. Even the effort an individual puts forth in her work capacity will have been influenced by her family's tradition. Such advantages cannot be removed by any rule against nepotism, and they are advantages that I see no way to justify. But I doubt if there is any feasible way to estimate precisely the scope of such advantages, much less compensate for them.

The kind of economic system a conscience-utilitarian can advocate, then, is something of a compromise: taking into account, on the one hand, the fact that real people will often or mostly need some economic incentive for ideally productive work/investment, and, on the other hand, that it is necessary to reduce disparity of incomes in order to obtain maximal utility in view of the declining marginal utility of income, as far as the preceding condition permits. An individual can claim it as a moral right that he be treated as this optimal system requires, just because this system is, overall, optimal. I do not find this objectionable.

Chapter 8

Morally required charitable giving?

Most (affluent) readers of this book, having just learned that in my opinion an optimal (justified) morality would require them to support an increase in their taxes, may be in no mood to learn that in my opinion a justified morality would require them to be prepared to spend more, this time in the form of giving to charity. Let us see what is to be said.

We want to identify the implications of the optimal morality – conscience-utilitarianism – for "charitable" giving, which a dictionary defines as "private or public relief of unfortunate or needy persons." (Kant said that an act of charity is only one to "alleviate the extreme necessities of life."[1]) This definition excludes voluntary giving in support of art galleries (etc.), however federal tax law classifies it. I shall follow suit. Gifts to charity are for support of the truly needy.

It is a familiar fact that advocates of the here rejected act-utilitarian theory of morality hold that there is a *moral duty* to give to charity (in this defined sense), and further, that a given individual should give of his own income so much that if he gives more, the benefit to the (optimal) recipient will be less, or at least no more, than the benefit to him of not giving more. Many writers reject this implication as being far too demanding and in fact, for better or worse, are disposed to reject act-

---

[1] *Lectures on Ethics*, trans. Louis Infield (New York: Harper & Row, 1963), p. 235.

utilitarianism as a justified theory because this implication of it is sharply divergent from considered moral intuitions.

If, however, we reject the demanding act-utilitarian view for the possibly less demanding conscience-utilitarian theory, we can still ask whether, according to this rule theory, there is a moral duty to give to charity, and if so how much, and also whether we may say (what is often denied) that some persons have a *moral right* to receive such charity. We might recall, incidentally, that Rawls held that there is a moral duty to give to charity, but less demanding than the act-utilitarian theory, saying that there is a "natural duty" to "help another when he is in need or jeopardy, provided that one can do so *without excessive risk or loss* to oneself."[2] Kant too, may have thought that the duty to give to charity is less demanding than the act-utilitarian theory, holding that there is a duty to help others in need, "according to one's means." (Kant also thought that charitable giving is a matter of justice, since divine Providence and nature provide enough for all and, but for human injustice, there would be no poor to be objects of charity.)[3]

How should a proponent of a conscience-utilitarian theory decide how much an individual should give to a certain charity? Of course, the basic idea is that one is morally required to give to the extent to which an optimal – the teaching and prevalence of which would be benefit maximizing – morality would demand. But how much will this be? We have seen that such a utilitarian theory might well involve relatively *simple* rules (on account of the problems of teaching) and, of course, the traditional requirement to tithe (10 percent of *total* income?) at least meets this condition. But this rule might well be too simple: At least it is possible that a tenth of total income could be too much for a person at the poverty level or below (the widow may have been thoughtless in giving her mite), or could be too little for a business executive with an income in the millions. It seems

[2] John Rawls, *A Theory of Justice* (Cambridge, Mass.: Harvard University Press, 1971), p. 114.

[3] *Lectures on Ethics*, pp. 192–4; and *Metaphysical Principles of Virtue*. trans. J. Ellington (Indianapolis: Bobbs-Merrill, 1964), p. 118. See also footnote 5.

obvious that an optimal system of morality will require a well-off person, who can do so without excessive cost to herself, to make *some* charitable contribution to the truly needy. The question is, how much?

A highly relevant question is whether we may assume that the proposals of the preceding chapter about tax/government grants have already been adopted into law. As of the time of writing, they have not, although some form of universal health insurance remains a (distant) possibility. Some government grants to the severely poverty-stricken are available, but not on the scale suggested in the preceding chapter. The most hopeful prospect – and hardly a likely one at present – is the possibility of a government guarantee of work for all adults, which would solve most of the problem of poverty in the United States. If the recommendations of the preceding chapter became law, there would be no severe poverty in the United States and the moral demand to help the very poor would arise mostly in connection with the position of the very badly off in the developing countries or perhaps in some of the strife-torn countries in Europe. But given the law at present, the scope of the problem includes the poor in the United States.

Perhaps the best way to approach the problem of how much to give to charity (in the narrow sense of helping the truly needy) is by considering the computations required for calculating one's federal income tax. Presumably we begin with a person's income, net above essential costs (casualty losses, professional expenses, capital losses), as with one's tax return. Following the federal return, we also make a deduction of a modest allowance for living expenses, taking account of the number of persons whom one must support, and their ages and possible handicaps such as blindness. We then also deduct what the individual has already paid in his federal income tax. But one should then add, for purposes of determining the total amount available for real charities, disbursements already made for charities to the truly needy. (Should we deduct amounts given to charities but not for the truly needy?) The balance is what is (was) available for charitable giving in my narrow sense. There are some remaining questions. Should a person who wants to know what she should give to charity set aside what the government allows as deductible living expenses for self and family, as perhaps being too little (or too much)? There is, however, another adjustment that may be called for. Should part of what a person already pays in taxes be viewed as essentially charitable? Suppose a certain portion of one's local tax payment is used to provide low-cost housing. And consider that part of the national budget that is expended for food stamps or Supplementary Security Income for the poor, Medicaid, or gifts to underprivileged nations for food and medicine or improvement of their economy or educational system. It would seem reasonable to count the proportion of one's taxes spent for these purposes as essentially charitable giving in my narrow sense. So, we can count this sum as a contribution to real charity as already made.

Of course, sums contributed for charity are already tax-deductible; so, the question for a person who wants to know what he should contribute is what he should contribute beyond what is returned to him in the form of tax deductions.

The sum available for gifts to the truly needy is net income (excluding business expenses and casualty/capital losses, as well as some modest amount for family living expenses) *after* all taxes. Then the remaining question is the proper rate of *further* giving from this available sum, taking into account such contributions already made, directly or indirectly, and in view of tax savings from further giving.

The proper rate for further giving will presumably vary both with the size of the net available and with the magnitude of the need.

One would hope that justifiable requirements for charitable giving would not be such as to absorb the total amount available after taxes. There is a reason for this. If everyone thought that the total amount of her net income after taxes would be totally absorbed in morally required charitable giving, there might be little if any incentive to use effort, ingenuity, and so on to increase one's available income for various purposes, such as vacations, entertainment, luxuries, normal personal gifts (e.g., to family members), and giving for preferred charitable purposes such as art galleries. Moreover, human motivation being what it is, so large a moral requirement for charitable giving might well reduce the motivation to do what is morally required, as we can infer from the disinclination of philosophers to take seriously the requirements of act-utilitarianism. At least, such a requirement would make the corresponding morality more difficult to teach.

So, one thing it would be helpful to know is the total amount of giving required to alleviate *severe* suffering and poverty either near us or around the world, a goal that most of us think has a considerable moral claim. This is perhaps all a teachable morality of charity can aspire to.

One might, of course, ask why charitable giving should be viewed as morally required at all. The answer is at least relatively clear for a person who is already a committed conscience-utilitarian: Incorporation of some rule about this into the aversions of conscience (provided people respond to this demand of conscience), and dispositions to disapprove or praise in the attitudes of possible observers, would avoid a great deal of suffering. (It would be very unwieldy to embody any requirement for charitable giving into the law.) But why should people generally want a *moral code* that requires avoiding suffering on the part of the worst off? The inclusion of *some* rules of conscience in the *social* morality of one's society, such as for avoiding injury to others, keeping promises, and the like, can be defended by appeal to selfish desires for protection of one's own person or interests. But such support for a rule about charitable giving in social morality is less easily available, although many persons might well want this (as Kant affirmed) because they might conceivably need such assistance themselves.[4] Certainly some

---

[4] Kant makes a distinction between "perfect" and "imperfect" duties, the former arising from the impossibility of making some maxims universal laws, the latter arising from the impossibility of *willing* that they be made universal laws. The latter duties are less precise and allow exceptions; the duty of benevolence does not prescribe how often or to what extent one should help the needy. See Keith Ward, *The Development of Kant's View of Ethics* (Oxford: Blackwell, 1972), pp. 103–7. See *Kant's Critique of Practical Reason and Other Works*, trans. T. K. Abbott (London: Longman's Green, 1909), pp. 39ff.

standard for charitable giving is one that can count on the reasonable approval of the dispossessed in society, but also on the support of persons who at least do not feel completely secure about their own financial future. Still, it seems that the most serious support for a social conscience-utilitarian rule about *charitable* giving must be the force of empathic altruism, which may be weak in some people but is widespread, so that knowledge that there is such a social rule and that it is being respected will leave almost all of us feeling more comfortable.

I suppose the main reason for subscribing to a conscience-utilitarian attitude to charitable giving, then, is some residual personal concern about the financial future, plus the important fact that we do care about the plight of the very poor and would feel uncomfortable about living lavishly in the presence of need and poverty.

How much of a contribution do we have in mind when we talk of giving to charity to an extent needed to alleviate extreme poverty *around the world?* It is alleged that "in 1990 individual Americans contributed $101.8 billion [perhaps averaging $500 per person or $2,000 per economic unit?] to nonprofit charitable organizations"[5] (but it is not clear how "charitable" is being defined, and hence how much of this ended up helping the "really needy"). But let us turn to the magnitude of the worldwide problem and ask what would be needed to bring all the severely poverty-stricken persons in the world up to the standard of living at the poverty line in the United States – that is, on an income (in 1991) of approximately $14,000 for a family of four, giving everywhere the food, clothing, medicine, and other necessities included in the Department of Labor's calculation of what quality of life this sum provides.[6] Presumably a sum

---

[5] J. Bourque, "The cautious Samaritan," in *Modern Maturity* (December 1991), p. 66.

[6] The Department of Labor figures were arrived at by taking the least generous of four estimates of the cost of "nutritionally adequate" food and tripling this amount on the basis of a survey showing that poor families spend about one-third of their income on food. These figures are slightly increased for single men, to $6,652 (if over 65 years, $6,268). These seem to me surely poverty-

somewhat smaller than $14,000 would be needed to bring a family of four in India up to this level. Then let us take the total sum *available* for charitable giving among all the nations in the world (ideally, the poor nations as well as the rich) and determine what proportion of this sum everywhere would be sufficient to bring the poverty-stricken up to this standard level. This rough proportion would give us the needed rate of average giving (to bring the poor up to the poverty line). Payment at this rate on the sum available for charitable giving would be what everyone ought to give at least for the basic purpose of relieving distress and poverty everywhere in the world, providing, of course, that everyone else does his share. (Persons already below the poverty line would not be morally required to give anything.) This would be at least an installment on what we ought to give.

It should be noted that unlike a negative income tax in the United States, raising the economic status of the poor around the world would generally not consist of direct grants in aid. The grants would presumably be made to governments, say, to improve methods of agriculture and manufacture, to improve sewage treatment and the water supply, to make medical treatment available especially to young children, to reduce the population by providing methods of birth control (rural families now often have seven or more offspring), and to encourage elementary education. The effects of such aid will require time, but the situation of the underdeveloped countries has been improving,[7] so that grants in aid will presumably not be necessary indefinitely and such charitable giving could be phased out – although there will probably always remain the worse off, even if not very badly off. (In the developing countries between 1965 and 1985, life expectancy increased from 51 to 62 years.) Many

line figures. For a single man the figure works out to about $550 a month. If one estimates what one has to pay for rent (at least in Ann Arbor, Michigan), much of the $550 has already been spent on housing.

[7] See the World Bank, *World Development Report* (New York: Oxford University Press, 1990), discussion of progress in the developing nations.

of the developing countries are helping themselves by not wasting funds on military establishments and so on. And there are various things they can do within their power.[8] In a full account, some story must be told of conditions the right holder must satisfy in order to be entitled to the right, such as the condition that officials of the recipient governments do not pocket the receipts but rather adopt thoughtful, long-range plans for use of the income to improve their society's standard of living.

Let us recall that the conscience-utilitarian proposal is that an act is required morally if and only if it is called for by the set of rules of conscience (aversions, etc.) that it would be maximally beneficial, all costs and benefits included, to build into the consciences of persons in *one's society*. It should be noted that the theory calls for rules to be built into the conscience of the agent's society, not just in view of the costs and benefits to this one society but also in view of the benefits (and costs) to *everyone* affected. The costs should be limited mostly to the costs of maintaining such a morality in the conscience in the society *of the agent*, but including the costs to agents of following the rules. So, the theory calls for setting the rules of conscience about charitable giving roughly in view of consequences of *worldwide* scope, along with the costs of building in and following the prescribed conscience.

There are two interrelated problems here: first, what the rate of giving capable of meeting the needs would have to be and, second, whether this is much more than can seriously be recommended as being realistically teachable in a strongly capitalist country like the United States.

As to the first point, I draw figures from reports of the facts in Brad Hooker's *Mind* paper of 1991.[9] According to his figures, the annual GNP of the better-off nations is approximately $10

---

[8] See J. Dreze and A. Sen, *Hunger and Public Action* (Oxford: Clarendon Press, 1989), p. 270 and chaps. 11 and 12.

[9] Brad Hooker, "Rule-consequentialism and demandingness: a reply to Carson," *Mind* 100 (1991), 269–76.

trillion. The number of persons living in "extreme poverty" is between 1 and 1.5 billion.[10] Hooker's suggestion is that a *per person* $400 annual average contribution ($1,600 from a family of four?) from the well-off persons in affluent nations, on behalf of those in extreme poverty, would be adequate. Would it? On the basis of figures about those below the poverty line and about the incomes of the well off of the wealthy nations, it seems that an annual contribution of $600 would be enough ($533 for each of 1.125 billion persons), compared with a $10 trillion GNP of the wealthy nations, or the $8 trillion income of the richest 60 percent of these nations,[11] or only 1.33 percent of their *total* GNP. (This ignores possible contributions from the wealthier members of the poorer nations.) This percentage may seem rather small, but we must recall that the huge total of the GNP of the wealthy nations is by no means identical to the sum available for charitable giving. (It is also not clear that the equivalent of $533 would bring families up to the U.S. Department of Labor's conception of the poverty line.)

The figures of the World Bank are somewhat different. Its 1990 report affirms that "the aggregate poverty gap – the transfer needed to lift everybody above the poverty-line – was only 3 percent of *developing countries'* total consumption. The transfer needed to lift everybody out of *extreme* poverty was, of course, even smaller – just 1 percent of *developing countries'* consumption."[12] Unfortunately, these figures do not give a total dollar value for rescue of the developing countries or any estimate of what is needed to lift *everyone* (in all countries) up to the poverty

---

[10] *Living Conditions in Developing Countries in the Mid-1980s: Supplement to the 1985 Report on the World Social Situation* (New York: United Nations Publications, 1986). Among the developing countries covered in its 1990 report, 33 percent, or 1,115,000,000 people were listed as living below the poverty line (World Bank, *World Development Report* [New York: Oxford University Press, 1990], p. 28). This estimate, of course, does not include the number of the very poor in other than developing countries, e.g., the United States.

[11] World Bank, *World Development Report*, p. 237.

[12] Italics mine. World Bank, ibid., p. 28. "Extreme poverty" is defined in terms of income below $275 in 1985 dollars; 33% of the population of the developing countries is below the $370 poverty line.

line. Moreover, it chooses a "poverty line" (the higher of two) of only $370 *per capita* in 1985 dollars, which, if we take into account the 32 percent inflation in the United States from 1985 to 1992, means at least $488 today. For a family of four, this would be $1,950 (compared with the U.S. poverty line of about $14,000). Hooker's figure of a total annual need of $600 billion, divided among 1.25 billion persons, works out to about $480 per person (or $1,920 for a family of four), and thus is close to the World Bank's estimate of the upper poverty line of $370 (or $488). (I suggest this would be *very* spartan living, although many persons obviously survive on less.) So, Hooker's estimate of a $400 per year (per capita?) average contribution of persons in the wealthy nations might nearly do the job for this low estimate of the poverty line and for the developing countries alone.

These figures give an idea of what an average rate of giving in the United States (among the better-off individuals or families) would have to be to remove the worst poverty among the developing countries. I assume that other well-off nations are willing to do their fair share, so that a disproportionate contribution would not be required from the United States. (According to the World Bank, the United States gives only 0.2 percent of its GNP to assist developing nations compared with 0.5 percent for Canada, 0.6 percent for Finland, 0.7 percent for France, and 1.1 percent for Norway; and of the U.S. grants, most go to Israel and Egypt [for political reasons?] – although the benefit of the U.S. contribution is reduced by import duties imposed to protect national interests.)[13] If we consider only 65 percent of families in the United States (those families with an income of at least $25,000 per year), or 130 million people, the result is that an *average* contribution of $488 *per capita* (or $1,952 for a family of four) would come to roughly $63,440,000,000. So, if the *average* family (among the upper 65 percent) had an available-to-charity income of $40,000, that would be an average gift of $1,952, or 4.9 percent as the U.S. individual's share in bringing everyone in the developing world up to the poverty line. (It is possible that some

13 Ibid., p. 129.

time would be required for such support to have its full effect, for instance, by reducing the size of families. In India, better-off families have only about two children, in contrast to large families at the poverty level.) However, as noted previously, the requirement given here is only temporary and will become less as matters improve, as they have been doing in recent years. My percentage figure for the present situation is at least definite, although optimistic, as we shall see. (I have not specified what the broad built-in conscientious moral aversions, etc., should be, of which the suggested percentage would be a variant.)

The figure given is optimistic because it does not take into account the vast range in incomes of the top 65 percent of the U.S. population. Nor does it take into account the general moral principle of progressivity, giving with equal sacrifice. It gives only what the *average* contribution by the top 65 percent should be to get the job done.[14] Should there not be a higher *rate* for the wealthier, just as there is (and should be) for both the actual and optimal income taxes? Why not take the total amount of income available for charitable giving at all levels above the bottom 35 percent (say, with incomes over $25,000 per family) and divide it up in proportion to *optimal* income tax rates for these levels of income? Since identification of optimal income tax rates savors a bit of the distant future, a conscientious person might make a thoughtful guess at what his appropriate rate of charitable giving might be. This is the direction in which a consistent conscience-utilitarianism seems to go. So, 4.9 percent may be a fair *average* percentage of income for contributions, say, of those in the top 65 percent income levels in the United States, but averaged over a range, some below and some considerably above this figure.

The second question is whether a *morality* requiring such a rate of giving would be extremely difficult or even impossible to teach to a degree that nearly everyone is at least somewhat

---

[14] According to the World Bank report, in 1988 the successive quintiles of income in the United States were 4.7 percent, 11.0 percent, 17.4 percent, 28 percent, and 41.9 percent (p. 237), or 69.9 percent over $60,000. Other sources differ substantially. See the *National Data Book*, 1992.

(ideally, strongly) motivated to conform with it, at least in a society like ours. We must remember that, according to figures cited earlier, the average American already contributes about $500 to charity ($2,000 for a family of four?), so that perhaps the previously suggested figure for raising everyone from poverty would generally involve merely selecting one's charities so as to aim at relief of the truly needy. However, in any case the extra $1,952 would be tax-deductible, so the net cost, at a 31 percent tax rate, would be only about $1,347.[15] To me it seems hard to believe that it would be impossible to induce well-off people to give that average amount of their income available for charity (but more for the wealthy if the suggested progressivity principle is adopted) if they clearly understood the real condition of the persons whom they were helping and how much benefit the gift would bring about – and also that this level of giving is only temporary. It is probably a fact that Americans are not accustomed to giving to the truly needy on this scale. (Perhaps not if we include the United Fund, American Friends Service, Care, etc.) I do not despair of the possibility of counting on *most* people's being willing to do their fair share, in view of the basis for a conscience-utilitarian morality generally, when the needs are graphically presented and persons have received a reasonable amount of moral education. Doubtless many will not, but this is no more reason for discarding the conscience-utilitarian view of an optimal morality than the fact that many people deceive, cheat, and steal is a reason to abandon its view of standards for honesty.[16] There might also be, and should be,

---

[15] Of course, if all these tax deductions were taken, on a wide scale, the U.S. budgetary problem would be exacerbated by that amount.

[16] For the force of altruism, witness the size of blood donations (two-thirds unpaid in the United States and all unpaid in the United Kingdom). See Richard Titmuss, *The Gift Relationship: From Human Blood to Social Policy* (London: George Allen and Unwin, 1971); and Kenneth J. Arrow, "Gifts and exchanges," *Philosophy and Public Affairs* 1 (1974), 343–62, reprinted in Edmund Phelps (ed.), *Altruism, Morality and Economic Theory* (New York: Russell Sage Foundation, 1975), especially p. 18. See also R. N. McKean, "Economics of trust, altruism, and corporate responsibility," in Phelps, ibid., pp. 29ff.

disapproval of failure to do one's share of charitable giving on the part of others who know.

A question may be raised about the proposed form of conscience-utilitarianism. The preceding proposal gives us what might be the optimal *tax rate* for available charitable contributions by everyone around the world, or what would be required if everyone did her share in complying with the optimal rules. But suppose what we were looking for was a serious proposal on how much *we* ought to give, assuming that not everyone will give her share – especially among U.S. citizens. How shall we arrive at a more realistic rate for charitable giving for the morally committed? And what are the implications specifically of conscience-utilitarianism for this question? One suggestion is very close to the one proposed: that a person's obligation to give to worldwide poverty relief is the amount that would be required if there were full compliance, that is, if everyone gave her fair share.[17] (I believe this proposal needs to be amended to take account of the willingness of various persons to give with equal sacrifice.) Another possibility is to follow suggestions by Don Regan and Roy Harrod,[18] and estimate *how many* persons are, say, like (an ideal) you and me, motivated to do whatever is morally required, and then fix an optimal rate of giving by *these* persons that would (when added to what lesser altruists can be expected to do) remove extreme poverty around the world. This would probably be much more demanding; I have no idea what such an optimal contribution would be – perhaps triple the suggested figures. Some might object that this conception is too idealistic and makes moral demands that we cannot expect normal people to meet.

Of course, the suggested contributions would only bring the very poor up to the poverty line and would leave a great deal of inequality. Possibly moral people should be giving much more to charity than I have suggested. In Chapter 7 I sketched a

---

[17] By Liam B. Murphy, "The demands of beneficence," *Philosophy and Public Affairs* 22 (1993), 267–92.

[18] Donald Regan, *Utilitarianism and Cooperation*, (Oxford: Clarendon Press, 1980), and R. F. Harrod, "Utilitarianism revised," *Mind* 45 (1937), 137–56.

conscience-utilitarian morality of distributive justice. If we want to be real utopians, we could look forward to a system of world government in which there is a worldwide tax system rather like the one outlined earlier for the United States, which might achieve distributive justice worldwide. But at the present time, such a worldwide government/program is politically unfeasible, although I believe it is an ideal with serious claims from the point of view of an optimal morality and the conceptions used to support it – although the changes needed to realize it would be monumental. I suggest that however unrealistic this possibility is for now, it is something for everyone to reflect on, considering that the billions of people in the developing world are, after all, people essentially like us, who can suffer or be happy just as we can.

Ideally, the previously suggested charitable contributions are best added to one's tax burden. This would avoid dealing with people who do not want to give their share and would ensure simplicity of collection. If this were done, we would no longer need to view charitable giving as an implication of a conscience-utilitarian *morality*. But one could point out that most of the requirements of the criminal law are also requirements of a conscience-utilitarian morality. Is there any special reason why this moral requirement should not be embodied in the law? If people in our society did what they ought to do and supported enactment, the moral requirements would be enacted into law. This would surely be the most effective way of ensuring that everyone gives to charity what he should.

One might ask whether the recipients of charity from the wealthier nations can be said to have a "moral right" to what they receive. The answer seems to be "yes." For what it is for a person to have a moral right to something is for some other person(s) to have a relatively strong moral obligation to enable her to do, have, or enjoy certain things in order to avoid some harm or deprivation for her.[19] (To have a "*strong* moral obliga-

---

[19] R. B. Brandt, "The concept of a moral right and its function," *Journal of Philosophy* (1983), 29–45, reprinted in Richard Brandt, *Morality, Utilitarianism, and Rights* (New York: Cambridge University Press, 1992).

tion," be it noted, is for it to be optimal, all costs and benefits taken into account, to build into people in the society a strong motivation to act in this way, feel very guilty if they don't, and disapprove strongly of others who do not so act.) In the present case, what the needy individual is to do or have is to be provided with the material means to bring her up at least to a quality of life identified by some group (the Labor Department, the World Bank) as at the poverty line. So, something definite is to be done; it is to be done for *every* individual who falls below the poverty line; and the class of persons obligated – everybody who is in a position to give – is specified. The basic reason is to avoid severe deprivation for the poor individual and secondarily to increase the total net well-being. So, there *is* a *moral right*.

So much for the demands of a conscience-utilitarian theory of charitable giving, or at least that part of it that concerns worldwide conditions of poverty.

Chapter 9

Conscience-utilitarianism and the criminal law

If we are favorably disposed toward conscience-utilitarianism as a normative theory of the morally right and wrong (and of moral rights), the question arises of what a conscience-utilitarian appraisal of the morality of law would be like – "the law" in the narrow sense of the statutory code and judge-made rulings of the criminal law. A conscience-utilitarian normative theory seems to have implications for what these things and their enforcement ought to be, that is, what form can be morally *justified*.[1]

Law and morality have various features in common. Both condemn various types of action, and condemn them with different degrees of strength: Morality justifiably condemns certain acts more strongly, with different degrees of disapproval for different actions. Criminal law provides very different punishments for convictions of different offenses – for example, long sentences for murder and much shorter ones for perjury. Again, morality does (or should) make exceptions to its condemnation of types of action when following the normal moral code would be harmful, and it excuses nonconformity when the

---

[1] The following discussion is focused primarily on the case of U.S. criminal law and its application in the current cultural situation in the United States, namely, the heterogeneity of society, the law-abiding tradition or lack of it, the types of individuals who commit crimes, etc. It is not intended to apply equally to Japan, Sweden, Australia, Germany, Great Britain, etc.

specific circumstances are such that the sanctions of public dis-approval or personal guilt feelings would be pointless. Similarly the law, although it condemns certain types of behavior as of-fenses and provides punishment for them, allows "justifica-tions" when it would be harmful not to commit an offense and allows "excuses" for unjustified offenses when, in context, it would be senseless to punish a given offense.

But there are obviously important differences between law and morality, and consequent differences between the ways the two institutions function in relation to the public good. (1) The law, as we know it, activates its sanctions only after public pro-cedures, and the sanctions – fines or imprisonment (etc.) pri-marily – are rather severe. This is unlike the moral sanctions of guilt feelings and disapproval, which are relatively mild and psychologically fairly automatic. So, morality can concern itself with minor forms of defective behavior – failure of human-itarian decency, telling lies, or failure to give charity to the needy. The law cannot do this, although in some states there are "good Samaritan" laws requiring a motorist to stop and give aid in case of emergencies. Why does this difference exist? Mainly because of the legal role of statutes and procedures and severe sanctions. (2) It is part of morality in the broad sense that some acts give the agent satisfaction and are admired/praised by the agent's society – "superrogatory" acts, which are viewed as desirable but not morally required, although they probably would be required but for the cost to the agent. The criminal law has no department of praise; it is limited to condemnation and penalties. (3) A person cannot be penalized for an offense if the law prohibiting that kind of action has not been publicized in advance. In contrast, morality assumes that every adult knows (roughly) the difference between right and wrong. Many ac-tions may be illegal when the normal law-abiding person does not know about the fact. For example, in a famous case, Los Angeles law required anyone convicted of a felony in another state to register with the Los Angeles police within a week after arrival. How could new arrivals be expected to know of this law? Since legal penalties are relatively severe, it seems that an agent should have a fair chance of avoiding the penalty by engaging in law-abiding behavior; he cannot do so if he does not know the law. The Los Angeles law was declared unconstitutional.[2] (4) The law gives very little scope to individual reflection in determining what he is legally required to do. Morality does: If an individual thinks through his principles and concludes that he ought to do so and so, it is thought that this is what he morally ought, or at least may, do (although a person's thinking may diverge so far from how we think a decent person would reflect that we would not underwrite his conclusion).

It is clear that morality *must* allow a place for personal reflection: acting morally means primarily conforming to inner aversions to act types (not just the desire to avoid known sanctions), and the aversions society can build saliently into conscience are not optimally precise. We can build in an aversion (etc.) to telling lies, stealing, and so on, but these rules may conflict and an agent must have some way to resolve the conflict. In such a situation, it seems an agent must, at least sometimes, think what would be an optimal rule that would cover the case in question, and although her conclusion may remain more or less permanently as a part of her personal conception of morality, it may not become a salient part of her thought. By contrast, an individual's opinion about what is or ought to be the law is not dispositive for what is the law, that is, for what she legally ought to do. We should not make this distinction too sharp, however. The law does allow some scope for individual judgment. For instance, in the law on self-defense, much scope is given to a person's judgment about what is necessary to protect her life; and in general, scope is given to judgment about whether conforming to a given law would do more harm than good. The law also pays attention to scruples about serving in the armed forces in time of war.[3]

These are contrasts between law and morality that the legal system, operating to enforce a publicized, democratically approved list of offenses by sanctions, cannot avoid. What moral-

---

[2] See *Lambert* v. *California*, U.S. Supreme Court, 355 U.S. 225 (1957).

[3] See, e.g., Kent Greenawalt, *Conflicts of Law and Morality* (New York: Oxford University Press, 1987).

ity permits and what the law permits can manifestly be different.

I have argued that a morality is *justified* if and only if its teaching is about act-types and if the level of aversion to an act-type (with guilt feelings or disapproval of others for infractions) would be wanted/approved by (almost all) fully informed persons who expected that they and their children would live a lifetime in the society. And I have argued that the substantive moral code that would satisfy this condition is one the *teaching and prevalence* of which would expectably maximize the public well-being. So, this view is a utilitarianism about justified moralities.

In contrast, criminal law, at least in a democratic society, comprises in part various statutes declaring certain acts "offenses," as determined by an elected legislature or (roughly) individuals delegated by them – along with precedents set by judges – that fix punishments by fines, imprisonment, and so on for persons who do prohibited things. (It also provides rules about justifications and excuses so that behavior contrary to the statutes may not be punished.) How far would the optimal morality of a society approve of society doing these things? We must remember the mentioned differences between law and morality. So, an optimal morality might require some kinds of behavior as advancing public well-being, whereas the severe sanctions of the law would often be out of place, so that a legal requirement of these sorts of actions would not be socially beneficial. Again, the sanctions of morality (such as disapproval by others) would doubtless not affect many potential criminals whom we might like the law to deter. So, if we want to appraise morally a criminal statute or the imposition of a criminal punishment, we have to take this larger picture into account.

Thus, if we say that a given part of the criminal law is "immoral," we must claim that a justified morality would condemn it, taking into account the special restrictions of a legal system. What I want to do here is consider whether the U.S. criminal law would be approved by a justified, substantive moral system. Of course, it is not merely the list of offenses and their

punishment that calls for appraisal, but also the system of justifications and excuses.

Should we say, then, that a system of criminal law is morally
in the clear if and only if, taking into account the restrictions
imposed by its being a system of law, it is framed – in parallel
with the optimal morality – so as to maximize benefits to sentient creatures, all costs and benefits taken into account? This
kind of utilitarianism about the criminal law seems to be an
implication, for the law, of the type of utilitarianism about morality that I am supporting.

However, not everyone agrees that only such a legal system
that maximizes well-being is morally in the clear.

The dissidents include the philosopher G. E. Moore, who
thought that addition of punishment to crime is in itself better
than crime unpunished, just as a matter of intrinsic goodness
and independently of the effect of preventing the harm of
crimes.[4] And W. D. Ross held that it is better for the virtuous to
be happy and the vicious unhappy (although this falls short of
advocating punishing persons for specific acts, the proposal
concerning only the total moral life score of agents); and in any
case, he thought it not the state's business to bring about such a
situation.[5] So, both Moore and Ross accept a "retributive" theory of punishment in a very weak sense; at any rate, they do not
justify a system of punishment by appeal to the (supposed) fact
that it benefits the public primarily by decreasing the harm of
crime at the lowest possible human cost.

Another, more distinctively retributivist critic of the utilitari-

---

[4] G. E. Moore, *Principia Ethica* (Cambridge: Cambridge University Press, 1903),
p. 214. "The infliction of pain on a person whose state of mind is bad may, if
the pain be not too intense, create a state of things that is better on the whole
than if the evil state of mind had existed unpunished." On this view, punishment increases intrinsic value but not the intrinsic value of the states of
sentient beings in the sense of being states they like or prefer (or would
prefer if informed).

[5] W. D. Ross, *The Right and the Good* (Oxford: Oxford University Press, 1930),
pp. 57–61.

an deterrence justification of the criminal law was Kant,[6] who said that punishment "can never be used merely as a means to promote some other good for the criminal himself or for civil society [as the utilitarian would have it], but . . . must in all cases be imposed on him only on the ground that he has committed a crime." He went on to say that the "standard of public justice" is "the principle of equality. . . . Thus, whatever undeserved evil you inflict on another person, you inflict on yourself. . . . The equalization of punishment with offense is possible only through the rule of retribution . . . as is manifest from the fact that only then is sentence pronounced proportionate to internal wickedness. . . . If a person has committed murder, he must die." This is roughly the principle of "an eye for an eye."[7] This "standard" has problems of application: to rapists, prostitutes, arsonists, torturers, hijackers, and deaths brought about by accident or negligence, and scarcely makes allowances for duress and provocation. There is the further question of how the principle is to be defended, since it is manifestly not an analytic truth.[8]

Other retributivist contemporary writers think that general obedience to law is for the public benefit and that obedience requires a sacrifice on the part of those who set personal de-

---

[6] See J. G. Cottingham, "Varieties of retribution," *Philosophical Quarterly* 29 (1979), 238–46.

[7] *The Metaphysical Elements of Justice*, trans. J. Ladd (Indianapolis: Bobbs-Merrill, 1965), pp. 100ff. *Gesammelte Werke* (Berlin: Cassirer, 1992), vol. VII, pp. 138–40. See J. A. Corlett, "Foundations of a Kantian theory of punishment," *Southern Journal of Philosophy* 31 (1993), 263–84. R. M. Hare holds that this view is inconsistent with the general thrust of Kant's theory in "Could Kant have been a utilitarian?" *Utilitas* 5 (1993), 1–16. See Stephen Nathanson, *An Eye for an Eye?* (Lanham, Md.: Rowman and Littlefield, 1987), pp. 74–93.

[8] J. L. Mackie has argued that although retributive principles cannot be defended as objective truths, retributive attitudes can be readily understood as sentiments that have grown up and been sustained through biological (and partly sociological) processes; but this is not to say that rational, informed persons would *want*, on an overall view, retributive principles in the law. See, "Retributivism: a test case for ethical objectivity," in J. Feinberg and H. Gross (eds.), *Philosophy of Law* (Belmont, Calif.: Wadsworth, 1986), pp. 622–9.

sires aside to conform with the law; those who break the law therefore arrogate to themselves an advantage compared with law-abiding citizens and must, in fairness, be punished in order to rectify this disparity.[9] Mackie (footnote 8) calls this the "fair play" theory. But this theory has puzzling consequences. Does it imply that mere attempts to commit a crime should not be punished at all, since the agent has not succeeded in taking any advantage? (One might reply that he has allowed himself to take a risk.) And is not the criminal punished for the particular kind of *harm* he has done, not the *advantage* he may have gained over the law-abiding, who allegedly restrained their own desire (if any) to do the same – for example, murder or rape? Do law-abiding persons suffer from not permitting themselves to commit murder or rape? Is there an advantage to the criminal just in having broken the law? Or if the fault of the criminal is just his having broken the law, should not all crimes be punished equally, since all equally break the law? A somewhat similar but perhaps more convincing theory is that a criminal has harmed society by contributing to necessitating the institution of means to protect citizens from offenses like his, and can provide restitution for this harm by submitting to

---

[9] Herbert Morris, "Persons and punishment," *Monist* 52 (1968), and *On Guilt and Innocence* (1976), pp. 33–4; and various others, e.g., Herbert Fingarette, "Punishment and suffering," *Proceedings of the American Philosophical Association* (1977); George Sher, *Desert* (Princeton, N.J.: Princeton University Press, 1987); M. Davis, "How to make the punishment fit the crime," *Ethics* 93 (1983), 726–52, "The relative independence of punishment theory," *Law and Philosophy* 7 (1988–9), 321–50, and "Harm and retribution," *Philosophy and Public Affairs* 15 (1986), 236–66; George Klosko, *The Principle of Fairness and Political Obligation* (Lanham, Md.: Rowman and Littlefield, 1992); and Richard Dagger, "Playing fair with punishment," *Ethics* 103 (1993), 473–88. A somewhat similar view was put forward by Jean Hampton in "The retributive idea" in J. Murphy and J. Hampton, *Forgiveness and Mercy* (Cambridge: Cambridge University Press, 1988).

For a critique see R. Wasserstrom, in *Philosophy and Social Issues*, (1980), 139–46; Hyman Gross, "Unfair advantage and the price of crime," *Wayne Law Review* 38 (1987), 1395–1411; and David Dolinko, "Some thoughts about retributivism," *Ethics* 101 (1991), 537–59.

the penalties of the protective legal system.[10] Both theories, however, must contend with the fact that not all criminals have been fairly dealt with by society, some having been raised in poverty (etc.), and we must ask if the system of public law has benefitted them equally.[11]

It may be thought, however, that these theories give some kind of explanation of society's right to punish (since it does not advocate punishing one person just to promote the good of others), even if much more must be said about the amount of punishment for various offenses. But the theories offer no way to recommend acceptance of specific punishments.

A quite different view, also contrary to the view that a moral system is justified only if it can be recommended to rational, informed persons and as such must be shown to be the one that would most benefit society, includes the thought that a system of criminal law should require conforming with the *actual moral standards* of the community. Sir Patrick Devlin, for instance, has argued that some action is contrary to the morality of a community if a "reasonable" person (the man on the Clapham omnibus) would find it reprehensible or disgusting beyond the limits of toleration. Such "immoral" offenses are damaging to society: "There is disintegration when no common morality is observed and history shows that the loosening of moral bonds is often the first stage of disintegration,"[12] so that society is as justified in penalizing this as it is in penalizing treason. Devlin writes: "The criminal law as we know it is based upon moral principle. In a number of crimes its function is simply to enforce a moral principle and nothing else. . . . If the criminal law were to be reformed so as to eliminate [this] . . . , it would also end a number of specific crimes [. . .], the killing of another at his own request, suicide, attempted suicide and suicide pacts, du-

---

10 See Margaret Holmgren, "Punishment as restitution: the rights of the community," in *Criminal Justice Ethics* (1983), 36–49.

11 See David Lyons, *Ethics and the Rule of Law* (Cambridge: Cambridge University Press, 1984), chap. 5; see also chap. 3.

12 Patrick Devlin, *The Enforcement of Morals* (Oxford: Oxford University Press, 1965), p. 13. See also pp. 15–17.

elling, abortion, incest between brother and sister . . . ,"[13] as well as prostitution, homosexuality, and bigamy. His argument thus depends on an empirical premise about the importance of a morality for the survival of a society, and on the view that what is strongly disapproved of by the average Englishman is to be taken as the kind of immorality important for the survival of British society. He concedes that the morality of a society is subject to significant shifts with time.

This view need not conflict with the thesis that the criminal law can be justified only if it benefits society maximally, all costs and benefits taken into account. Where Devlin differs is in the willingness to take the prevailing morality of a society, and punishments needed to support it, as overriding benefits to society (and in comparing the right to punish breaches of law with society's right to punish treason). This surely is something that needs to be established.

However, at least part of the utilitarian criterion of maximizing community well-being (by its effects in reducing the harm of crime) for an optimal legal system has a long history, going back at least to the time of Socrates, as attested to by a speech that Plato puts into the mouth of Protagoras: "In punishing wrong-doers, no one concentrates on the fact that a man has done wrong in the past, or punishing him on that account, unless taking vengeance like a beast. No, punishment is not inflicted by a rational man for the sake of the crime that has been committed – after all one cannot undo the past – but for the sake of the future, to prevent either the same man or, by the spectacle of his punishment, someone else, from doing wrong again. . . . Punishment is inflicted as a deterrent."[14] Evidently a philosopher is here represented as thinking that an optimal system of criminal law operates to benefit society by punishing so as to deter harmful behavior generally and prevent the agent from repeating it.

Suppose we follow this line. If we do, we must face the fact that estimating whether a given sanction by the law would be the best thing for a society may not be easy. We have to decide

---

[13] Ibid., p. 7.   [14] Plato, *Protagoras*, 324.

what are intrinsically good/bad states of sentient beings. (Here I shall follow the somewhat open-ended results given in Chapter 2.) Prosecution of a suspect is expensive; imposition of penalties has adverse effects on the criminal and her family; successful enforcement techniques are often intrusive; when the public is not opposed to a crime (e.g., possession of marijuana), enforcement is not possible and its failure brings the law into disrepute. Presumably we should like to follow Bentham's advice to punish only to the degree that the gain in prevention of harm to society, less the cost of punishment to the criminal and her family (etc.) and society (cost of the system), would be maximal. So, weighing the pros and cons of specific legal sanctions is a complex business.[15]

This fact raises a moral question if a person thinks that the criminal law is probably, in some cases, not the one that would best serve the general well-being. Is such a person *morally* free to ignore the supposedly deficient statutes? Or is everyone, for some reason, morally bound to obey the laws enacted by a democratically elected legislature as interpreted by the courts? I think it would be agreed that legislatures are not perfectly wise and often vote to criminalize conduct (e.g., homosexuality, birth control, or physician-assisted suicides) that it does not serve the public well-being to criminalize. So, if a person thinks, after careful reflection, that a given statute cannot be justified as good law, is she *morally* bound to obey it? If we follow the results of Chapter 5, we will very likely conclude that it is best to build into the consciences of the community *some* sense of obligation to obey every law enacted by the legislature and supported by the judiciary, on the ground that it would be too costly (and chaotic) if everyone felt free to disobey *any* law that she thought could not be properly defended, and that at least most criminal laws do serve their intended purpose of preventing harm or promoting public good to some extent. But this

[15] See Jeremy Bentham, *Introduction to the Principles of Morals and Legislation* (Oxford: Clarendon Press, 1876), chaps 13 and 14. For a critique of the utilitarian approach, see David Lyons, *Ethics and the Rule of Law* (Cambridge: Cambridge University Press, 1984), chap. 5.

sense of obligation need not be a morally overriding one: It may be maximally beneficial for persons to refuse to obey laws that, after careful reflection, they think pointless or mistaken, partly because this may result in bad laws being changed, not to mention the educational benefits of controversy of this sort. So, it seems that refusal of such individuals to obey the law may be at least *morally* excused or possibly morally justified, although this is not to say that every person who disobeys the law on such grounds should escape punishment; if everyone did, then the legally binding law would be whatever the person thinks it morally ought to be. But *how much* deference is morally due the requirements of the law in a democratic society, in view of its having been enacted by elected representatives and criticized by persons versed in the traditions of the law, with the thought that the system as a whole serves the public good, partly by providing a cooperative scheme for producing the good?[16] It is not easy to say. If my preceding arguments (Chapter 5) have been correct, an individual will have to decide what rule about priorities is one the teaching and prevalence of which will maximize social benefit.[17]

THE STATUTES ON CRIME AND PUNISHMENT

What can be said of the substance of the various departments of the criminal law in the United States in terms of their being justified in light of their public benefit? Take first the *system of statutory punishments* for conviction of various offenses, ranging

---

[16] See M. E. B. Smith, "Is there a prima facie obligation to obey the law?" *Yale Law Journal* 82 (1973), and Donald Regan, "Law's halo," *Social Philosophy and Policy* 4, 15–30; E. van den Haag, "Can any legal punishments of the guilty be unjust to them?" *Wayne Law Review* 33 (1987), 1416; George Fletcher, *Rethinking the Criminal Law* (Boston: Little, Brown, 1978), p. 806; Symposium: "Law and obedience," *Virginia Law Review* 67 (1981), papers by A. D. Woozley, J. Raz, A. Simmons, David Lyons, J. G. Murphy, and J. L. Mackie.

[17] For a full discussion, see Kent Greenawalt, *Conflicts of Law and Morality* (New York: Oxford University Press, 1987).

from a minimal fine (e.g., a parking ticket) to a prison sentence going from probation to a sentence of many years. (Discussion of the rules of justifications and excuses will follow.) Probably the most plausible defense of this gradation is that different offenses are more or less harmful, the more harmful being the ones it is most beneficial to prevent by a fine or incarceration of an offender and by steps (e.g., educational or therapeutic) to reduce the likelihood of repetition (and public awareness of these), as well as public censure expressed by punishment (possibly shaping attitudes by conditioning).[18] It would be widely but not unanimously agreed that this general conception is sensible where its factual assumptions are correct. But its application requires a correct estimate of how harmful a given offense is, relatively, and how effective it is to fine or imprison (or at least place on probation, with provisions hopefully to rehabilitate) a given offender. We also need evidence to think that *potential* criminals are deterred by the prospect of punishment.[19] We need to know the effects, both deterrent and reformative, of a prison term of 6 months versus one of 20 years, compared with a fine or one of many alternatives, such as community service. How much do we know about any of these things?

In order to consider an influential contemporary sample of the law, let us look at the *Federal Sentencing Guidelines*, formu-

[18] See E. M. Wise, "The concept of desert," *Wayne Law Review* 33 (1987), 1348f. For some far-reaching criticisms, see John Braithwaite, *Crime, Shame, and Reintegration* (Cambridge: Cambridge University Press, 1989), pp. 35ff., 78.
[19] For critical discussion, see P. W. Low, J. C. Jeffries, and R. J. Bonnie, *Criminal Law* (Mineola, N.Y.: Foundation Press, 1982), pp. 14–30; S. H. Kadish, S. J. Schulhofer, and M. G. Paulsen, *Criminal Law and Its Processes* (Boston: Little, Brown, 1983), pp. 195ff.; J. Andenaes, "The morality of deterrence," *University of Chicago Law Review* 37 (1970), 649–64, and "The general preventive effects of punishment," *University of Pennsylvania Law Review*, (1966), 960–70; National Research Council, *Deterrence and Incapacitation*, ed. D. Nagin, 1978; A. von Hirsch, *Past or Future Crimes* (New Brunswick, N.J.: Rutgers University Press, 1985) and "Commensurability and crime prevention," *Journal of Criminal Law and Criminology* 74 (1983), 209–48; M. Bayles, *Principles of Law* (Dordrecht: Reidel, 1987), pp. 282–5; J. D. Larson, "Cognitive-behavioral group therapy with delinquent adolescents," *Journal of Offender Rehabilitation* 16 (1990), 47–64.

lated by the United States Sentencing Commission (effective November 1, 1987, with amendments of November 1, 1989). (The Model Penal Code[20] is an alternative.) This federal code was a response to a congressional mandate asking for a proposal of determinate sentences that would reflect the seriousness of the offense, give adequate deterrence, protect the public from further crimes of the defendant, and give needed educational or vocational training. The resulting *Federal Sentencing Guidelines* presents a conservative proposal, the penalties being almost exclusively prison terms with no indeterminate sentences, with time off at the discretion of parole boards and probation (and alternative penalties) only if the standard sentence is no more than six months. Thus, it contrasts with the guidelines provided by the sentencing commissions of several states (e.g., Minnesota), as well as with those of European countries and the proposals of contemporary writers on the law (e.g., Norval Morris).[21]

What are the provisions of the *Federal Sentencing Guidelines?* Its program lists 43 "offense levels" with prison terms varying from nothing to life. A selection of the more interesting basic offense levels follows, beginning with the more severe sentences. (The judge may vary the sentence slightly, up or down – and justifiably to take account of mitigating and aggravating circumstances – see the later discussion – but justification must be given if there is more than minor departure.) The sentences listed are for a person with no previous criminal history; for one with previous convictions, the sentences increase sharply. I omit specifically federal offenses such as espionage and aircraft piracy.

1. Homicide: deliberate killing, life imprisonment; unpremeditated manslaughter, 10 years; involuntary (negligent) manslaughter (e.g., a death caused by drunk driving), 6 to 15 months.

---

20 Of the American Law Institute, official draft, 1962.
21 Norval Morris and Michael Tonry, *Between Prison and Probation* (New York and Oxford: Oxford University Press, 1990). See also John Braithwaite, *Crime, Shame, and Reintegration.*

2. Rape involving force or threat, 6 years; statutory rape, 1 1/2 years (assumed age difference of 4 years), increased if victim was under 12 years or under the authority of the agent.
3. Kidnapping, 3 1/2 years, increased if a weapon was used or the victim was seriously injured.
4. Assault: intended bodily harm, 3+ years, increased to 4 or 5 years if a firearm was used or there was serious bodily injury; minor assault, 0 years.
5. Robbery (threatened bodily harm in the course of a theft), 2+ years, with an increase to 4+ years for large sums taken or for injuries to persons.
6. Burglary of a residence, 2 years, increased up to 4 years, depending on the value of the property taken.
7. Perjury, 1 year.
8. Larceny or embezzlement, 0 months but with increases up to 2 years if the sum involved rises to $5 million.
9. Receiving stolen property, 0 to 1 year or, if the person was in this business, increased up to 2 1/2 years.
10. Bribery of a witness, 1 year.
11. Force or threats used to suppress civil rights, 8 months to 1 1/2 years.
12. Possessing a small quantity of marijuana, 0 to 2 months; but distributing drugs (except less than 5 grams of marijuana) to persons under 21 years of age, pregnant women, or within 1,000 feet of a school or college, no less than 1 year.
13. Lesser offenses: blackmail with no threat of violence, 4 months; bribery (e.g., in obtaining a bank loan), 2 months, increased according to the involved amount; insider trading, 2 months, increased depending on the amount of money involved; fraud, such as soliciting for a nonexistent charitable cause, 0 years; mailing or phoning obscene material, 0 months.

All *attempts:* the same as for the basic offense, but less if the agent had not completed all acts necessary for the basic crime.[22]

---

[22] See the Model Penal Code, Section 5.05; however, it permits a reduced penalty for attempted murder. The Model Penal Code, commentaries on Section 5.01, Attempts, justifies this hard line by saying that it would be

This hard line is not universal, and there are complications about how to define an "attempt."[23] In common law an unsuccessful attempt was only a misdemeanor; Roman law roughly corresponded. In California the maximum term is one-half of the maximum sentence for the completed offense; in New York the classification of an attempt is one level below that of the completed offense. The German code, however, seems to identify the wrongness of an act with the volition, so there is no mitigation for an attempt alone. Among writers, Adam Smith pointed out that human sentiments will make allowance if the crime was not complete; see his discussion of a sleeping sen-

---

inequitable not to punish when an attempt was unsuccessful only because of fortuitous circumstances and in order to give police a justification for intervening in the early stages of a crime, the agent being clearly a dangerous person. It could add that punishment of attempts adds deterrent force because the agent knows he will be punished whether or not his crime succeeds. (How far these considerations justify the tough line on attempts the reader may judge.) See David Schmidtz, "Deterrence and criminal attempts," *Canadian Journal of Philosophy* 17 (1987), 615–24. However, knowledge of the law will reduce an agent's desire to discontinue his efforts if he at first fails. The Model Penal Code also wants to abolish all the frivolous talk of "impossible" offenses; even impotence is no defense against a charge of attempted rape. For a discussion, see Hyman Gross, *A Theory of Criminal Justice* (New York: Oxford University Press, 1979), pp. 423ff.; Fletcher, *Rethinking the Criminal Law*, pp. 131–97, 482; B. Burkhardt, "Is there a rational justification for punishing accomplished crime more severely than an attempted crime?" *Brigham Young University Law Review*, (1986) 533–71; Michael Davis, "Why attempts deserve less punishment than complete crimes," *Law and Philosophy* 5 (1986), 1–32; G. R. Douglas, "Criminal attempts," *Solicitor's Journal* 132 (1988), 552–3; Larry Alexander, "Inculpatory and exculpatory mistakes, and the fact/law distinction," *Law and Philosophy* 12 (1993), 33–70.

23 The Comments in the Model Penal Code recognize the problem of distinguishing between a true "attempt" and "mere preparation," saying that an attempt must be a "substantial step" toward a crime, that is, behavior "strongly corroborative" of criminal intent. It is thus limited to purposive conduct, but even if the behavior is only reckless or negligent, it is enough for an attempt that the agent believed his behavior would be unlawful. Abandonment of a crime is a defense if uninfluenced by outside events such as the appearance of a policeman; this rule recognizes the reduced dangerousness of such persons and also provides a motive for desisting.

tinel.[24] George Fletcher thought that we feel remorse if we cause harm, not if we merely risk it, and believed that the law should go along partway.

These various views need to be supported by argument, ideally including statistical evidence.

Recidivism. The federal code increases the penalties significantly the greater the number of previous offenses (approximately by one-third for each previous felony conviction), apparently because the individuals are thought to be more dangerous and because, being more inclined to crime than the average person, more punishment is needed to deter them; or at least, it is useful to render them harmless by keeping them in jail longer.[25] This principle can run wild, as is shown by a Texas sentence of life imprisonment for a third offender whose three crimes, of obtaining money under false pretenses, totaled $230; the Supreme Court upheld the sentence as not contrary to the Eighth Amendment.[26] One might wonder how recent support for life imprisonment after three crimes at least of violence, but sometimes only for drug-related offenses, can be shown to benefit the public.

Probation. If the minimum sentence is not more than six months, the federal court may substitute a term of probation not to exceed five years, the terms of probation requiring, at discretion, for example, not committing any other crime, not leaving the district, reporting to the probation officer, working in a lawful occupation unless in school, supporting dependents, not associating with persons engaged in criminal activity, possibly being required to live at home or to perform community services, and so on. Here there is similarity to the Minnesota guidelines, except that Minnesota mandates *two years* instead of

[24] Adam Smith, *The Theory of Moral Sentiments*, 11, ii,3.
[25] R. A. Posner, "An economic theory of the criminal law," *Columbia Law Review* 85 (1985), 1216.
[26] *Rummel v. Estelle*, 445 U.S. 263, 281–4 (1980).

252

six months and may require enrollment in a drug program or in therapy in the case of sex offenses.

The Model Penal Code discusses and classifies certain other offenses, not mentioned earlier presumably because they are not federal crimes. For instance, "causing" [= what?] a suicide by aiding or soliciting it is a felony in the second degree (with 1 to 3 years' minimum sentence up to 10 years maximum).[27]

The Minnesota guidelines[28] do not call for prison sentences (unless there have been at least three previous convictions) for the following offenses: second-degree sexual assault, residential burglary and simple robbery, nonresidential burglary and theft of over $2,500, minor thefts, aggravated forgery ($250 to $2,500), possession of marijuana, and unauthorized use of a motor vehicle. Crimes that call for prison terms are aggravated robbery (attempting to cause serious bodily injury in the course of theft), aggravated sexual assault (which causes injury or does not involve a social companion), first-degree assault (which attempts to cause serious injury), and murder. These are roughly similar to the first five offenses of the federal code.

A philosopher wishing to assess the justification of these criminal codes must ask, first, what is the principle behind this *ordering* of penalties? Is it supposed to represent the relative harmfulness of typical instances of the offenses? If so, we need an explanation of what it is to "harm" an individual. For this, it seems we must say that "harm" consists of either physical or psychological pain (e.g., disappointment, fear, anxiety, general distress), in contrast to "benefit," which roughly is an addition to a person's pleasure or happiness. (Alternatively, we might define loss in terms of the strength of a person's aversion to an event and a benefit in terms of the strength of his desire for it – or, we might add, what his aversion or desire would be if he

---

27 It is unclear what the "harm" is supposed to be if the victim consents and why such an "offense" is the business of the state. See H. T. Inglehardt, "Death by free choice," in Baruch Brody (ed.), *Suicide and Euthanasia* (Dordrecht: Kluwer, 1989), pp. 251–80.
28 A. von Hirsch et al. (eds.), *The Sentencing Commission and Its Guidelines* (Boston: Northwestern University Press, 1987).

were fully informed.[29]) So defined, and without attempting to choose between the two views of "harm," we might say that the law, from a utilitarian point of view, should attempt to prevent conduct that causes a person or persons (or society as a whole, say, through failure to pay taxes) loss or deprivation of benefit. Presumably an economic loss normally implies loss of the foregoing sorts, depending on the financial status of the victim.

We should note, however, that most of the foregoing legal statutes do not pay much attention to the amount of actual harm done by a type of action. Some do, taking cognizance of the physical damage done by an assault, or the amount of money stolen or obtained by bribery or insider trading. (Nor, of course, do sentences pay attention to whether the victim of robbery is a wealthy man who will hardly suffer.) This lacuna, however, is largely unavoidable in a schedule of crimes and punishments; this will necessarily be a list of *types* of offense if it is to be known to prospective criminals for deterrent purposes. So, penalties must be listed for types of offense that are roughly *equivalent* in causing harm. (Realistically, equivalence of *penalty* is hard to achieve, partly because a sentence to be served in one prison is very different from a sentence in another and for example, because of the different hardships for a person of age 30 compared with one of age 70.)

---

[29] Should we count it as harm if one person is embarrassed or upset by the behavior of another, say, his masturbating on a bus or defecating in public? Joel Feinberg (*Offense to Others* [Oxford: Oxford University Press, 1985]) lists some criteria the law should attend to in deciding how seriously to take such reactions, e.g., the importance to the agent of his activity, its social value, the availability of alternative occasions, whether the motivation was malicious, the universality of a negative reaction to the behavior, etc. There is also the question of whether shock at the mere knowledge that some activities are occurring, even if not viewed by the observers, is sufficient to justify legal prohibition. Doubtless most such types of behavior mentioned as illustrations by writers on the law are ones almost no one is apt to indulge in (masturbation on a bus!) and in any case have such trivial impact that it would be uneconomic for the law to criminalize them. Causing fear is one thing; being shocked is another. For a full discussion, see Feinberg, *Offense to Others*.

Are all crimes normally at least somewhat harmful to someone in the sense explained? Probably most of them are to some
extent. The Model Penal Code takes the view that any consen-
sual sexual behavior between adults does not cause harm justifying criminalization; therefore, it advocates not criminalizing
either sodomy or incest. Again, is counseling or, say, a physician aiding in suicide so harmful as to deserve a second-degree
felony sentence – minimum 1 to 3 years, maximum 10 years, as
the Model Penal Code proposes? (Urging a person to commit
suicide in the hope of gaining an inheritance is another matter.)
In fact, the person may be better off if allowed to commit suicide, and the world may be better off without her. We should
recall that an intelligent person hardly commits suicide with no
good reason. So, no harm is done to anybody.[30]

Assuming that some harm is done in the case of most offenses, we may ask whether the ordering of penalties conforms
to the order of harm. We might take a public opinion poll and
invite rankings of harms. John Braithwaite (footnote 21) reports
surprising agreement in response to queries. Doubtless homicide should be at the top of the list, but it is not obvious why
some forms of severely penalized (nonstatutory) rape are far
more harmful than kidnapping or aggravated assault, although
it is true that rape may cause long-term psychological damage.[31]
Robbery and burglary (especially if large sums are involved)

---

[30] If a person is in poor condition and cannot live a good life, Plato would
forbid treating him medically at all (*Republic* III, 405a–410a). Justice Comp-
ton, in concurring in *Bouvia* v. *L.A. County*, Superior Ct., 2nd Crv. No.
B019134, April 16, 1986: "The right to die is an integral part of our right to
control our own destinies, so long as the rights of others are not affected.
That right should, in my opinion, include the ability to enlist assistance from
others, including the medical profession, in making death as painless and
quick as possible. That ability should not be hampered by the state's threat
to impose penal sanctions on those who might be disposed to lend assistance" (pp. 2–3).

[31] See M. Davis, "Setting penalties: what does rape deserve?" *Law and Philosophy* 3 (1984), 61–110. Rather harshly, the law on self-defense holds that the
victim may use a lethal weapon to prevent this.

doubtless are at least next in order, but thereafter the order seems very difficult to defend (but in the case of the minor penalties less important to defend).

Even if these offenses are properly listed in terms of *order* of *harm* caused, we have to look further to find the cardinal numbers – how much penalty to assign to the worst offenses and how much to the least, and so on. If we assume that loss of life is properly put at the top, this doesn't tell us whether life imprisonment is the proper response, or 10 years for manslaughter, or much less. Is the severity of the sentence justified by its deterrent effect? It is true that we do not want such things to be done. But what sorts of people do these things and for what reasons? Jeremy Bentham had an interesting suggestion about the lower limit for a punishment: It should be severe enough so that it is to no one's advantage to commit the crime even if he receives the punishment – or better if the loss from punishment, multiplied by the probability of its actually being imposed, is at least as great as the gain to the offender. This makes sense for some crimes, such as murder by a racketeer, done for personal gain, when the individual may calculate the risks of the penalty against the gain from the offense. It is also true for robbery, insider trading, fraud, and forgery. In those cases an increase in penalty, depending on the anticipated gain, makes some sense. But given that we are justified in aiming to deter such crimes, do we have evidence that a given sentence is either necessary or sufficient to do so? A report of the National Research Council[32] states that available statistical evidence suggests some correlation between law *enforcement* and negative crime rates, with the increased *severity* of legal punishment being less important than its probability.

---

[32] "Deterrence and incapacitation: estimating the effects of criminal sanctions on crime rates," reported in S. H. Kadish, S. J. Schulhofer, and M. G. Paulsen, *Criminal Law and Its Processes* (Boston: Little, Brown, 1983), pp. 197–201. See also J. Andenaes, "The morality of deterrence," reprinted in H. Gross and A. von Hirsch (eds.), *Sentencing* (New York: Oxford University Press, 1981), pp. 191–202.

Some (or most?) of the federal guidelines for sentencing are very harsh. Even one year is a large part of one's life, although many potential offenders may not realize how long one year really is. The mental state of a judge or legislator who airily thinks of five years as a relatively small penalty is impossible to comprehend. Not only are many sentences harsh, but what good are they supposed to do? The late Judge Charles Wyzanski once told this writer that of the 200 or so persons he had sentenced for embezzlement in his years as senior judge of the federal court in Boston, he had given every one a suspended sentence; he believed that the effects on a career of known embezzlement were deterrence enough for them. So, do we need a prison sentence at all for this offense? (Perhaps some would not be deterred if they knew no criminal sentence would be imposed.) In answer to the question of whether he would have done the same for murder, his reply was roughly affirmative. He said that 80 percent of murders are unconnected with a life of crime, and are committed by persons who are uneducated or who act from passion and will never murder again. What good is done by putting them in jail for years, either for them or to deter others?[33] (Again, perhaps no good is done for them, but probably the known threat will deter others.) It is different if a murder is committed as part of a life of crime. I would think that for most ordinary citizens, deterrence from committing a crime is already maximal if one thinks one may be discovered, tried, and one's offense publicized in the media, even if any actual penalty imposed is minor – a view seconded by John Braithwaite (footnote 21). (This depends, of course, on one's status in the community.) The deterrent effect, of course,

[33] See Anna Quindlen, "Marking time," *New York Times*, March 11, 1992, p. A–16. Hugo Bedau found that in 12 states from 1900 to 1976, of 21,646 persons convicted of murder and subsequently released, only 16 were returned during the first year for a subsequent criminal homicide. A later nationwide study showed that between 1965 and 1974, of 11,404 persons convicted of willful homicide and then released, only 34 were returned during the next year for a subsequent homicide. Reported in Hugo Bedau (ed.), *The Death Penalty in America*, 3rd ed. (New York: Oxford University Press, 1982), p. 175.

is through knowledge that *types* of behavior are legally penalized, not through knowledge of the individual sentences given to previous offenders – although it is true that habitual drug dealers know quite well how tough the sentences are in a certain jurisdiction.

We should note, as a fact of life, that 90 percent of prison inmates are men, mostly between the ages of 15 and 25, unmarried, living in cities, in areas of high residential mobility, who have done poorly in school, have friendships with criminals, and are at the bottom of the socioeconomic ladder – and, if already convicted offenders, stigmatized as such.[34] Some of these data suggest important ways in which to reduce crime.

If the aim is to maximize the general well-being, it seems that the thrust of the law, at least for offenders not committed to a life of crime, should be (aside from adjustments of penalties for offenses that hardly cause harm)[35] to reduce drastically prison sentences and to make further use of nonprison sentences, particularly following successful European practices and the schedules of recent sentencing commissions like those in Minnesota. Methods should include using fines, the size depending partly on the ability of the offender to pay, or this in addition to or replaced by various restrictions on the person's behavior. Such restrictions could include a commitment to remain at home (house arrest, perhaps with electronic monitoring) most hours of the day, or intermittent incarceration (say, on weekends), intensive supervision, extensive community service (say, 30

---

[34] Braithwaite, *Crime, Shame, and Reintegration*, pp. 44ff. He also points out that an offender in the United States is 20 times as likely to be penalized as such a person in Japan. Yet the Japanese crime rate is far lower (p. 62f).

[35] For a sustained critique of the criminal law, especially for drug-related offenses, see D. B. Kopel, "Prison blues: how America's foolish sentencing policies endanger public safety," in the Cato Institute, *Policy Analysis*, No. 208, May 1994. Also see Wendy Kaminer, "Federal offense," *Atlantic Monthly*, June 1994, pp. 102–14, on the excessive concern about drug-related offenses. David Anderson, "The crime funnel," *New York Times*, June 12, 1994, p. 58, has pointed out the importance of government spending for drug *treatment*.

hours of service in place of a month in prison), enrollment in a drug program, or therapy in the case of some sex offenses, with some training to prepare for a job and assistance in finding one, and perhaps a bit of education about the point of morality and the law. All this and more has recently been advocated by Norval Morris and Michael Tonry.[36] This may also be less expensive than prison sentences. There is a widespread feeling that not even an enlightened form of imprisonment promotes reform in terms of reducing recidivism rates (prison being a great place to form close contacts with other criminals), but anyone who reads the psychological reports of educational programs of reform in prisons cannot but be convinced that they, at least, do a great deal of good.[37] Expenditure to train more police officers makes sense,[38] but it appears that the recently advocated program "Three strikes and you're out" may need evidence (should a "strike" be a felony only?) to support a claim of being maximally publicly beneficial.

At any rate, it seems fairly obvious that this part of the criminal law needs more research and hard thinking, however sound the general principles about deterrence and crime's cost to well-being. I believe that an unimpassioned second look, based on full knowledge of the facts, is strongly called for. If the U.S. system of education or health care needs reform, how about its criminal law?

LEGAL JUSTIFICATIONS

Other departments of the criminal law seem to be less open to criticism: the legal provisions governing whether conduct forbidden by law is (legally) justified in some cases, and hence not

---

[36] *Between Prison and Probation* (New York: Oxford University Press, 1990). See also Hyman Gross and A. von Hirsch, *Sentencing* (New York: Oxford University Press, 1981).

[37] For example, see J. D. Larson, "Cognitive-behavioral group therapy with delinquent adolescents," *Journal of Offender Rehabilitation* 10 (1990), 47–64; W. L. Marshall and H. E. Barbaree, "An outpatient treatment program for child molesters," *Behavioral Psychotherapy* 19 (1991), 54–79.

[38] Anderson, "The criminal funnel," *The New York Times*, June 12, 1994, p. 58.

a criminal offense, and those governing whether conduct forbidden by law may be excused on various grounds, although not legally justified.

First, justification.[39] I have already noted that an optimal morality (see Chapter 5) will prescribe ignoring the basic first-order requirements (like not stealing or lying) when following these rules of conscience would probably cause great harm. In such cases, I suggested that what the individual has to do is think about what would be a novel rule suitable for the type of case – one that it would be best to incorporate in the primary rules of conscience insofar as that is feasible. Roughly the same line of conscience-utilitarian thinking is recognized in the law. In some cases of breach of law, it is clear that it is *better* that people do infringe the statutes (e.g., by actions to promote public goods), such as burning down another's house when necessary to prevent a general conflagration or running a red light to rush a seriously ill patient to a hospital. Call this a "defense of *necessity*." Thus, the Model Penal Code (Section 3.02) states roughly that "Conduct which the actor believes to be necessary to avoid a harm or evil to himself or to another is justifiable, provided that: (a) the harm or evil sought to be avoided by such conduct is greater than that sought to be prevented by the law defining the offense charged." It should be noted that the question of whether one evil is greater than another is not settled by the opinion of the agent but is left to the court or jury, which, for example, may count the avoidance of an arrest as a considerable evil. Moreover, if a person has a choice between her own death or that of another, the principle of necessity does not authorize her killing the other, since the life of the other presumably has

[39] There is controversy about how "justification" should be defined. See, e.g., Kent Greenawalt, "The perplexing borders of justification and excuse," *Columbia Law Review*, 84 (1984), 1897–1927; also *Law and Contemporary Problems* 49 (1986). For a helpful discussion see B. Sharon Byrd, "Wrongdoing and attribution: implications beyond the justification–excuse distinction," *Wayne Law Review* 33 (1987), 1289–1342.

equal value.[40] But the justification, of necessity, does not imply a straight act-utilitarian adjudication of criminal cases. A thief cannot justify her stealing on the ground that what is stolen is more important to her than to the owner. If she could, legal protection of property would not be possible. So, there is a conscience-utilitarian slant to the law, that a condition of justification is that general recognition of the permissibility of a given *type* of decision would be socially beneficial. The law, as stated in the Model Penal Code, is perhaps more act-utilitarian than is justified.[41]

An important implication of this provision is the right to self-defense. Thus, the Penal Code (3.04) states that the use of force toward "another person is justifiable"[42] when the actor "believes that such force is immediately necessary for the purpose of protecting himself against the use of *unlawful* [my italics] force by such other person on the present occasion," except that deadly force may not be used unless "the agent believes that such force is necessary to protect himself against death, serious bodily harm, kidnapping or sexual intercourse compelled by force or threat." (Where the use of force is not necessary for self-protection, then, of course, it should not be used – the victim perhaps retreating instead.) On the whole, the availability of this kind of defense against prosecution seems well conceived to augment the public good in the long run. For in the case of self-defense, awareness by a potential aggressor that force against him is legitimate is itself a deterrent; nor could the law

---

[40] Members of the House of Lords in *Lynch* thought that the average reasonable person regards his own life as "more valuable" than that of another. See I. H. Dennis, "Duress, murder, and criminal responsibility," *Law Quarterly Review* 96 (1980), 233. The life of an aggressor may also be regarded as less valuable, since he is culpable; see Fletcher, *Rethinking the Criminal Law*, 854.

[41] Byrd, "Wrongdoing and attribution," 1331.

[42] Byrd, ibid., 1334, points out that "justified" should be construed as "legally a privilege," not "a legal right." For some interesting comments see George Fletcher, "Self-defense as a justification for punishment," *Cardozo Law Review* 12, 859–66, and D. W. Elliott, "Necessity, duress, and self-defense," *Journal of Criminal Law and Criminology* 74 (1983), 343–62.

assume that the prospect of later sanctions would stop an ordinary person from employing force in such circumstances. This
comports with the conscience-utilitarian view.

J. J. Thomson, in a recent article,[43] argues that the justi-
fiability (whether moral or legal) of killing in self-defense (or to
help someone else whose life is threatened) lies in the fact that
every (innocent) nonaggressor has a moral *right* not to be killed,
which another is violating by a threat he poses. But, she holds,
when a person is a threat to your life (intentionally or *not*),[44] his
right not to be killed by you vanishes – is forfeited. That is why
you may defend yourself by killing him. (This defense, according to her, applies to killing a fat man who unintentionally falls
on you and who is sure to kill you if his fall is not deflected – a
case in which, I suggest, an *excuse* of duress might be more
reasonable.) And the whole picture, she thinks, explains why
we may not – as we think we may not – kill others to save our
lives (such as by deflecting the path of a trolley car that is
bearing down on us by turning a switch, which will cause it to
kill others instead) when they are not about to kill us. For they
still have a moral right not to be killed by us, which has not been
extinguished by *their* violating a right of ours.[45]

Unlike the conscience-utilitarian view, which permits killing
an unlawful (or morally culpable) *aggressor* on the ground that
this right to kill is a deterrent, Thomson's view affirms but does
not explain why there is a right to kill a threatening person who
is not an *unlawful* aggressor. Thomson's answer seems to be
merely that we do have such a right and that we can see we do:

[43] "Self-defense," *Philosophy and Public Affairs* 20 (1991), 283–310, see also *The Realm of Rights* (Cambridge, Mass.: Harvard University Press, 1990), chap. 14. See Larry Alexander, "Self-defense, justification, and excuse," *Philosophy and Public Affairs* 22 (1993), 53–66.

[44] It may be questioned whether *endangering* another's life is *violating* his right to life. See Michael Otsuka, "Killing the innocent in self-defense," *Philosophy and Public Affairs* 23 (1994), 79ff.

W. D. Ross, in a rather qualified way, seems to hold that a person's failure to respect the rights of others abolishes his own corresponding rights. See *The Right and the Good*, pp. 60–1; but also see pp. 54–6.

[45] Thomson, Introduction., *The Realm of Rights*, pp. 4–5, 15–20, 32–3.

That is a necessary truth. The Model Penal Code limits the right of self-defense to protection against "unlawful force" (Section 3.04), which is explained as an "offense or actionable tort . . . except for a defense (such as the absence of intent, negligence, or mental capacity. . . .)"[46] Thomson's view, however, seems to have some support from George Fletcher, partly in deference to Continental legal theory, according to which "the innocent aggressor infringes upon the integrity and autonomy of the resister," and therefore the threat's conduct "is wrong and the resister's is right."[47]

The conscience-utilitarian explanation thus concerns only "self-defense" as a defense for using force against unlawful or morally unjustifiable attacks, and hence as falling within the scope of justification or necessity. Another question is whether there should be moral/legal permission, based on grounds of social benefit, to kill innocent parties when there is a simple choice between losing your life or theirs; it also puts in question whether a lethal defense is permitted against an attack that is unlawful but excused. The present conscience-utilitarian view may at most excuse such use of force in self-defense as action under *duress*. This view leaves open the question of whether a third party may come to one's aid if one's own self-defense is not legally justified but only excused. May I use my ray gun to disintegrate a fat man falling unintentionally on someone else?

LEGAL EXCUSES

The other part of the criminal law I suggested that may not need substantial research and rethinking – although it may well need some major reformulation – is the part dealing with conditions in which a person guilty of unlawful conduct that is not justified

---

[46] This exception seems to bring the Model Penal Code close to Thomson's view.

[47] Fletcher, *Rethinking the Criminal Law*, pp. 860–4; see L. A. Alexander, "Justification and innocent aggressors," *Wayne Law Review*, (1987), 1177–89, especially 1178–80.

is nevertheless not subject to criminal punishment. Such conduct is said to be *excused* although not justified.

Traditionally, an action was regarded as criminal only if it had two aspects: first, it was unlawful and unjustified (= actus reus), and second, it was an expression of an evil mind (= mens rea). Recently, legal thinking has attempted to merge these two elements by incorporating the mental element in the definition of the crime, so that the definition of a crime must include a requirement that the unlawful act was done purposefully, knowingly, recklessly, or negligently (except when the law specifies otherwise, as in strict liability offenses). This tendency is awkward: As Herbert Packer has pointed out,[48] it is simpler first to identify the kinds of conduct the law aims to prevent and then to list the various mental features that exempt the perpetrator from punishment. Also, Glanville Williams has noted that including mental elements in the definition of an offense causes problems about the liability of accessories.[49]

What I propose, as part of a conscience-utilitarian account, is that we employ the concept of a person's *legal/moral motivation* – what we may call the agent's "character" (explained in terms of motivational strengths)[50] – as a unifying concept that enables us

[48] Herbert Packer, *The Limits of the Criminal Sanction* (Palo Alto, Calif.: Stanford University Press, 1968), chap. 6; and Glanville Williams, "The theory of excuses," *Criminal Law Review* (1982), 734ff. I do not accept his definition of an "excuse."

[49] It is also true that to count as a culpable action at all, a mental element must be present – whatever is required for the act to be voluntary, such as not being a reflex action, or one committed while unconscious or asleep, or a result of hypnotic suggestion, but a product of "determination" of the actor. (See the Model Penal Code, Section 2.01.)

[50] Such a view seems to be defended by George Fletcher in "The individualization of excusing conditions," *Southern California Law Review* 47 (1974), 1269–1309; see also *Rethinking the Criminal Law,* pp. 193ff., 799f., and 805. Michael Bayles states: "If an act does indicate an undesirable trait, then blame is appropriate; if it does not, then blame is inappropriate" (in "Character, purpose, and criminal responsibility," *Law and Philosophy* 1 [1982], 5–20). See also J. J. Walsh, "The concept of diminished responsibility and cumulative intent," *Criminal Law Quarterly* 33 (1991), 229–46.
Some writers object to a "character theory" because they do not under-

to understand the excuses actually recognized by the law and to see why such excuses are ones that an informed, rational person would want to have embodied in the law of a society in which she expected to live – in that their general recognition, compared with alternatives, would maximize public well-being. We should note that this is not inconsistent with the distinctions the law makes between a criminal act being done purposefully, knowingly, recklessly, or negligently, since these features, in order, are indications of different degrees of lack of legal/moral motivation.[51]

To clarify this conception, we must turn to the psychological (and commonsense) theory of motivation and note that it holds that what a person does is a function of five variables: (1) his beliefs about the options open to him, (2) his beliefs about the situation he is in, (3) his beliefs about the consequences that might occur if he adopts one of these options and how likely they are, (4) the vividness of his representations of all this, and (5) his desire for and aversion to these consequences (counting as a "consequence" the fact that an action will be one of a certain sort, e.g., a lie or theft). The theory asserts that a person will perform that act the consequences of which he most wants (including the type of action as a consequence), but this want is reduced by the anticipated improbability of each given consequence if the action is performed. Some people express this by saying that an agent always acts to maximize his expected utility (see Chapter 2).

If this is correct, a person's criminal action is to be explained in terms of *desires/aversions* in addition to *expectations* about the consequences of action. The desires will include ones for the

stand "character" to refer to stable, long-term motives/aversions. This is just a misunderstanding.

For more on the role of motives in the criminal law, see Gross and von Hirsch, *Sentencing*, pp. 104–13. See also E. L. Pincoffs, "Legal responsibility and moral character"; Daniel Lyons, "Unobvious excuses in the criminal law"; and H. Gross, "Some unacceptable excuses," all in *Wayne Law Review* 19 (1973), 905–1006.

51 See E. M. Wise, "The concept of desert," *Wayne Law Review* 33 (1987), 1352ff.

consequences of which she does the act. (For example, she wants to elope with her boyfriend, for which the disappearance of her husband is necessary.) But her act is also affected by the presence or absence of aversions, say to breaking the law, injuring someone, or doing something she knows to be immoral. So, if she tampers with the brakes of her husband's car, expecting this to result in his death and her freedom to marry someone else, one main responsible mental feature is her inadequate aversion to causing her husband's death. But for this relative indifference, she would not have done what she did. (The degree of indifference corresponds partly to whether she acted purposefully, knowingly, recklessly, or negligently.) So, the essence of mens rea is motivational: mainly indifference to certain events – what we may call a defect of "moral-legal motivations."

What are the moral-legal motivations? They are primarily (1) empathic/sympathetic concern for others, including an aversion to injuring others and causing public anxiety, and to causing disasters like nuclear explosions, as well as a desire to bring about public benefit, especially to assist others in distress; (2) aversion to theft, lies, rape, and so on, learned in various ways but probably mostly because of its having been made clear that they are normally harmful to others; (3) a desire to pay attention to laws as such, partly because they are intended for the welfare of all and enacted by a democratically elected body; (4) an aversion to doing what one considers to be morally wrong; and (5) finally, motivation not to perform actions for which the law provides sanctions – because to do so risks unpleasant consequences. These features are relatively fixed and permanent, unlike the desire for food or sex (and rather like the motivation to achieve). These motives have to compete, in fixing action/intention, with other desires, such as those for food, water, sex, human company, compliments, and financial security. The moral-legal motivations may not always control conduct: Each has a certain level of strength, and in many situations this will not be enough to control behavior in the face of conflicting desires that are stronger at the time.

Now I suggest that "mens rea" be defined as deficiency in moral-legal motivations. Furthermore, what should *excuse* an action that is unlawful and unjustified is that, in the total circumstances, what was done is not *evidence* that the moral/legal aversions of the agent were *below* what the law expects, that is, below "the required social standards of care and concern."[52] If this can be shown, the agent is not culpable. The trait (?) of negligence may be a minor defect but may also show a lack of concern for others.[53]

How strong should motivations of these sorts be according to the law? They must be enough to resist contrary motivations that a person of ordinary firmness and law-abiding disposition would resist. A person is not expected to refrain from stealing a diamond if someone is holding a gun to his head. But *roughly* how much is expected is indicated by the severity of punishment for acting in a way that manifests a motivational deficiency: A person is more severely punished if she does not avoid doing something so injurious that she is expected to be highly motivated to avoid it. Evidently killing is at the top of the list, closely followed by rape, aggravated assault, and armed robbery; motivation to avoid such actions is expected to be very strong. At least this is an inference we might draw from the sentences normally prescribed for certain sorts of offense. A person's motivation is not deemed insufficient if he does one of these things when necessary to save his own life from an unlawful threat – but not if he does something unlawful to obtain property or a new spouse. A person's act is excused only if, in

---

[52] See Brenda M. Baker, "Mens rea, negligence, and criminal law reform," *Law and Philosophy* 6 (1987), 81, 85; Jeremy Horder, "Criminal culpability," *Law and Philosophy* 12 (1993), 173–215, especially 204–9.

[53] See Baker, "Mens rea," 76ff. If a person's moral/legal motivations are substandard, presumably that shows that he couldn't have done otherwise than commit the crime. If the offense is to be punished, the justification must be forward-looking, presumably utilitarian/deterrence reasoning.

Can pure negligence be viewed as a defect of character? On this, see Steven Sverdlik, "Pure negligence," *American Philosophical Quarterly* 30 (1993), 137–50.

context, his motivation is not shown by his action to be unacceptably weak. What the "acceptable" level should be is a question. On a conscience-utilitarian view, the answer will derive from reflection on how socially bad it would be if there were, in the general public, a reduced aversion to committing a certain crime – how bad it would be if people did not have a certain level of aversion, say, to killing other human beings. So, it may be best to require people to be so strongly motivated not to do certain types of things that they will hardly ever do them even if they are mentally impaired (but not legally insane), or if they have been provoked or aggressed against by their ultimate victim to an extent less than would permit the actus reus in a normal person.

It might seem that, on this view, a jury/judge is required to speculate about a person's motives in order to decide whether the person has committed a culpable crime or should be excused. (It is obvious that they do not have to sum up a person's motivations and decide whether, on the whole, she is morally good or bad!) Of course, it is true that a defect of motivation exhibited by an act is not open to direct observation. But neither do the nonmotivational facts about an action that the Model Penal Code regards as relevant to culpability: whether it was the "conscious object" of the agent to do a certain thing, whether she was "practically certain" of all the material elements of an offense, whether she took a risk that is a deviation from what "a law-abiding person would observe" in her situation, or whether her failure to be aware of the risk is a "gross deviation from the standard of care that a reasonable person would observe" in her situation. In all these cases, however, it seems that a person with a commonsense understanding of why people do what they do is in a position to make a sound judgment; and the same is true for level of motivation. The question for the jury/judge is whether, in the *total context*, the accused's act would not have occurred in the presence of satisfactory moral/legal motivation. This judgment *does* sometimes require a comparison of a relevant moral/legal motivation with the motivations leading to the crime. (For example, was the theft/publication of the protected Pentagon Papers desirable from the national point of view?) The law also takes into account any provocation an accused may have had for making an assault.[54] The question may be: Would the average person in the agent's society have done better?

The excuses normally recognized by the law fit the motivational theory reasonably well (at least, where thoughtful people agree with the judgment of the law).

Consider *accidents.* Suppose a causal process has unforeseeably gone awry: a bullet ricochets and kills a bystander, or a child darts out from between parked cars in front of a motorist and is killed. Here (provided the motorist was attentive and not speeding) no inference of a defective motivation is possible, and the law excuses. But not always: When a person is committing a felony and someone – perhaps even a police officer – kills another person, perhaps by accident, then the person committing the felony (who may not even have a weapon) can be convicted of homicide. One might explain this, following the Model Penal Code (Section 210.2 (1)(b)), as follows: There was a presumption that the death was caused "recklessly under circumstances manifesting extreme indifference to the value of human life." This explanation would fit the motivational theory of excuses; whether the factual presumption makes sense is a different question.[55]

---

[54] See Fletcher, *Rethinking the Criminal Law,* pp. 242–50.

[55] In a recent case (September 1993), a woman was charged with manslaughter (and apparently will receive a maximum sentence) when she drove a car to escape from a successful bank holdup in which a policeman was killed. (She was not in the bank when the policeman was killed.) The holdup was motivated not by any personal greed but by opponents of the Vietnam War, who wanted the proceeds to be used to oppose the war. This person, like other opponents of the war, may have been misguided (?), but she can hardly be accused of a defect of conscience. However, it might be argued that the aversion to bank robbery should have been stronger than the desire to oppose the war. This case seems a clear example of the felony-murder rule.

See Fletcher, *Rethinking Criminal Law* pp. 307ff; see also P. W. Low, J. C. Jeffries, and R. J. Bonnie, *Criminal Law* (Mineola N.Y.: Foundation Press, 1982), pp. 850ff.

Mistake of facts. Is a woman guilty of a crime if she kills her husband, shooting through a closed door, in the honest belief that she is firing at someone attempting to break into her bedroom to rape her? What would be the defect of motivation – except possibly negligence in not ascertaining the facts? The law does not condemn the willingness to use a lethal weapon to protect oneself from being raped. But one might say that the law does not countenance mistakes of fact, even reasonable ones. However, one may note that contemporary legal opinion (the Model Penal Code) appears to have moved toward substantial agreement with the motivation theory, excusing acts based on false and even unreasonable but actual beliefs, which would not have been crimes had the beliefs been true.[56]

Mistake of law. The motivational conscience-utilitarian theory implies that an action, which would not have been unlawful if the actor's (nonculpable) belief about what the law is had been correct, may show no defect of motivation and hence be excused. This view seems to contrast with the stand of the courts. For example, a native of Baghdad committed an unlawful "unnatural offense" on board an East Indian ship anchored in an English harbor. The act was possibly no crime in his native country, and he did not know it was in England; and he may not have thought the action immoral. But his conviction was upheld. "Ignorance of the law is no excuse" has been a traditional standard of judicial practice. However, an alternative view has been gaining support and is now perhaps dominant. Let me cite an opinion of the Iowa Supreme Court, which reads in part: "Respect for law, which is the most cogent force in prompting orderly conduct in a civilized community, is weakened, if men are punished for acts which according to the general consensus of opinion they were justified in believing to be morally right and in accordance with law."[57] This sentiment roughly coincides with a holding of the German Supreme Court in 1952: that "If in the commission of the act, the actor fails to

---

[56] But see Byrd, "Wrongdoing and attributions," 1327ff.
[57] *State* v. *O'Neil*, 147 Iowa 513, 126 N.W. 454 (1910).

perceive that he is doing wrong, and if he could not have avoided this mistake, the actor lacks culpability. If he could have avoided the mistake, his punishment may be mitigated in accordance with Sect. 49(1)."[58] This is not far from the formulation of the Model Penal Code (in earlier comments): "Exculpation should be made out in all cases where a law-abiding and prudent person would not have learned of the law's existence."[59] And Justice Oliver Wendell Holmes stated: "A law which punished conduct which would not be blameworthy in the average member of the community would be too severe for the community to bear."[60] It would appear that the emerging principle is that unlawful conduct is culpable only in the presence of a motivational defect.

Legal writers sometimes defend the practice of the courts in holding that ignorance of the law is no excuse on the ground that allowing the excuse would burden the courts, would encourage ignorance of the law, or in effect would make the law identical to whatever the defendant thinks it is; but such views seem without merit. If the courts followed the Iowa view, nobody would convince a jury that an accused thought an unjustified murder morally right or in accordance with law. And if a person is aware of moral disagreements about a type of action, she is put on notice that the law may forbid it and should make diligent inquiries. It is true that if the Iowa principle were followed, a defendant must be excused when she infringes some unadvertised regulation about which moral considerations give no warning. But such a practice would not undermine the law, especially if it were understood to apply only in the case of serious charges involving possible imprisonment.

Voluntary intoxication. Suppose a person has become drunk and commits an offense in circumstances such that, had he been sober, his conduct would undoubtedly have manifested a defect of motivation. The actual law says, in effect, that even if,

---

[58] Cited in Kadish et al., *Criminal Law and Its Processes*, p. 314.
[59] Ibid., p. 311. See *Lambert* v. *California*, 355 U.S. 225 (1957).
[60] Ibid., p. 309. From Holmes, *The Common Law*, 49–50.

in his state of intoxication, we cannot presume a defect of motivation, the agent is still liable to punishment (barring crimes the definition of which includes "specific intent") unless he took the alcohol involuntarily or for medical reasons. In criticism of this stance, we should point out that we must distinguish two acts: what the agent did after he was already drunk and his act of drinking a quantity of alcohol. Drinking is not a crime, and absent the view that it is immoral, it does not show a defect of motivation. However, a person's own past experience or observation of others must give him reason to think that in drinking what he does, he is running a *risk* of becoming drunk and committing an offense in that condition (e.g., in driving a car). In that case, his initial act showed some defect of motivation: indifference to taking this risk. The subsequent offense arose out of this defect only indirectly. The offense for which he is culpable, on the defect of motivation theory, is running a risk. In this, the motivation theory seems to be out of line with the law. But in this the law is inconsistent: On the one hand, it declares that an act must be voluntary (e.g., purposeful, knowing, reckless) in order to be criminal; on the other hand, it affirms that acts not so controlled may be fully liable. Actually, the courts tend to strike a compromise, applying the notion of "specific intent" fairly broadly, so that being intoxicated negates the specific intent of many acts otherwise classified as offenses. Another way of viewing this matter, embodied in German law, is to hold that by voluntarily getting drunk the agent has recklessly endangered others. The law can then elect to punish him for what he subsequently does, punishing him to some extent for murder, assault, and so on, not just as if he was not intoxicated, but still as punishment for the offense of reckless endangerment. The law in Germany, although rather harsh, seems to be along this line: "Section 330a. Whoever intentionally or negligently becomes intoxicated through the use of alcohol . . . is punishable up to five years in prison, if while in that intoxicated condition he commits a wrongful act and if by virtue of the intoxication is not responsible for that act. . . . (2) in no event may the punishment be greater than that for the wrongful act committed in the state of intoxication."[61] Here, taking the risk is the responsible act that is punished. And willingness to take that risk is a defect of motivation. The U.S. law would be more coherent if it adopted something like this stance consistently.[62]

Duress. The conscience-utilitarian motivation theory gives a clear, plausible account of why and when duress – constraint on action by coercion or threat – is an excuse.[63] It says that a crime exists only if there is a defect of motivation. But how strong must be the motivation to avoid a certain offense, or to act in a law-abiding fashion, compared with the agent suffering someone's making good a threat? It depends on the offense. For example, aversion to killing one's wife is expected to be strong enough to outweigh the threat to lose one's job otherwise. But aversion to breaking some laws is not expected to be able to compete with certain motives, such as to defend against a present threat of death or serious bodily injury to self or others close to one.[64] So, the Model Penal Code (2.09) says that a person threatened with "unlawful" force[65] "which a person of reasonable firmness in his situation" (not just the agent herself, with her particular degree of fortitude) would be unable to resist has a valid defense.[66] Indeed, it is not necessary for the force

[61] Cited by Fletcher, *Rethinking the Criminal Law,* p. 847.
[62] See Fletcher, *Rethinking the Criminal Law,* pp. 846–52. See also Baker, "Mens rea," especially 63–5.
[63] For a discussion of problems about distinguishing justification from excuse, see Greenawalt, "The perplexing borders of justification and excuse," 1197ff.
[64] George Fletcher suggests that a more serious threat is needed to excuse holding a victim down while he is stabbed compared with merely driving prospective murderers to the scene of the crime. The presumptive reason is that a person shows worse motivation in the former case, so that excuse requires a stronger threat. This view fits the motivation theory. See Fletcher, *Rethinking the Criminal Law,* p. 832f. See *Abbott v. The Queen,* 63 Crim. App. R. 241 (1776) P.C.
[65] It has been questioned whether the specification of "unlawful" (in Section 311(1)) is appropriate. See Gross, *A Theory of Criminal Justice,* pp. 289ff.
[66] See Kadish et al., *Criminal Law and Its Processes,* pp. 791–9, especially 795–6.

against which one's act is directed to be unlawful for the defense of duress to obtain. Of course, if one's act in breach of law is not serious, the choice of a breach could be *justified*, not just excused, on the ground that the action was *necessary* for the sake of a greater good. So, the excuse of duress is significant generally when the breach of law is a serious matter, such as homicide, although it has been used successfully in various other types of case. But a defense of duress is possible even in the case of homicide. Blackstone thought that it should not be available then; he said that a person "ought to die himself, [rather] than escape by the murder of the innocent."[67] But this view is not standard and is not accepted by the Model Penal Code. Rather, the level of motivation expected by current law falls short of the requirement of proving oneself a hero; it requires not acts that a saint might perform, but only ones a person of reasonable moral strength could be expected to perform.[68]

See also P. Rosenthal, "Duress in the criminal law," *Criminal Law Quarterly* 32(1990), 198–226; and H. P. Holgate, "Duress and the criminal law," *Cambridge Law Journal* 47 (1988), 61–76. For Kant's supporting view, see Fletcher *Rethinking the Criminal Law*, p. 819.

[67] Blackstone, *Commentaries on the Laws of England* (Chicago: University of Chicago Press, 1979), vol. 4, p. 30. See K. J. M. Smith, "Must heroes behave heroically?" *Journal of Criminal Law Review* (1989) 622–8; and articles on "Duress per minas" by Lord Kilbrandon, Anthony Kenny, A. E. Anton, and J. L. Mackie in M. A. Steward (ed.), *Law, Morality, and Rights* (Dordrecht: Reidel, 1983). Also see G. L. Peiris, "Duress, volition, and criminal responsibility," *Anglo-American Law Review* 17 (1988), 182–208.

[68] See I. H. Dennis, "Duress, murder, and criminal responsibility," *Law Quarterly Review* 96 (1980), 208–38. Also see J. Dressler, "Exegesis of the law of duress," reprinted in L. M. Corrado, *Justification and Excuse in the Criminal Law* (New York: Garland, 1994), especially pp. 402ff.

We should note that the criterion of "reasonable firmness" does not avoid judgments of what is a defective level of motivation. What a reasonable person would do is taken to be what a man of good character would do. It is presumed a reasonable man would not kill in response to a slap in the face. See George Fletcher, "The individualization of excusing conditions," *Southern California Law Review* 47 (1974), 1269–1309. Elsewhere, Fletcher said that determining the threshold of what a person of reasonable firmness would resist "is patently a matter of moral judgment about what we expect people to be able to resist in trying situations" (*Rethinking the Criminal Law*, p. 804).

Insanity. The Model Penal Code (Section 4.01 (1)) holds that a person "is not responsible for unlawful conuct if at the time . . . as a result of mental disease or defect he lacks substantial capacity either to appreciate the criminality [wrongfulness] of his conduct or to conform his conduct to the requirements of law." This is not very precise. What is it to "appreciate"? Is it the ability to represent the whole situation to oneself vividly? Or is it awareness of generally accepted standards for the type of behavior in question? Or is it to have a reasonably strong aversion to performing an act of that kind for reasons other than self-interest? Moreover, the Model Penal Code does not state whether responsibility is contingent on a person's believing that his act is "criminal" or "morally wrongful."

How might a motivational account of excuses state the principle the Model Penal Code formulates? It could say: "An unlawful act is nonculpable when an agent's mental/brain condition is such that his act (might have) occurred even if he otherwise possessed an acceptable level of moral/legal motivation." The Code's rule could then be construed as saying that no defect of motivation is proven in the presence of a confirmed, relevant mental disease or defect.

On this theory, how could a decision be reached on whether the exculpation applies? Presumably it is the job of the defense to support arguments in favor of such a claim and expect to succeed by a preponderance of the evidence. Here the psychiatrist will enter the picture: to testify about reasons for thinking that the accused's motivational or emotional state, defect of cognitive processing, or total breakdown of the machinery (e.g., extreme schizophrenia) was responsible for the action, or may have been, compared with a defect of legal/moral motivation. It is for the jury to decide whether her explanation, or that of a defective level of moral/legal motivation, is the best and simplest explanation of all the facts. What sort of evidence might the psychiatrist adduce? Perhaps a record of emotional instability in the past, or a record of a recent head injury of a kind often followed by bizarre behavior, or recent strange behavior, or the results of an examination. In addition, there may be evidence of character witnesses about past manifestations of a high level of moral/legal motivation (say, when there was strong self-interested motivation to do something incompatible with the law). What the jury has to do is make a commonsense reconstruction of the accused's motivation. The very absence of a motive for the crime is itself a relevant fact.

There is, of course, no clear line here that makes it easy for the jury to decide which explanation is best. One can feel some sympathy with George Will's remark, cited by Joseph E. di-Genova and Victoria Toensing:[69] "The most morally indefensible crimes are becoming the most legally defendable . . . the more odious the crime – premeditated or spontaneous – the more reasonable doubt there is about the person's sanity at the time." This objection, however, will hardly be convincing to readers who reflect on a recent case of Henriette Cornier, who asked to be allowed to take a neighbor's 19-month-old child for a walk, took the child to her room, severed its head, threw the head out of the window, and calmly waited for the police.[70] This act was morally wrong beyond a doubt, but when such an act is apparently unmotivated, which a jury cannot imagine a normal person doing in those circumstances, there *is* some presumption of some other mental problem unrelated to standing moral/legal motivations. The motivation theory here seems sound.

The severity of any problem for the plea of insanity is somewhat mitigated, however, in that the disposition of convicted criminals and those judged not guilty by reason of insanity may not be very different in a rational system of penal and mental institutions.

We must now return to the question of why an informed, rational person would support such a system of excuses embodied in the criminal law – what I have argued would count as a defense against punishment. Why should these defenses be embodied in a conscience-utilitarian defense of the criminal law?

We may recall that utilitarianism is a theory not only about

---

[69] In the *Baltimore Sun*, cited in *South Texas Law Journal* (1984), 728.
[70] Reported by Thomas Maeder, *Crime and Madness* (New York: Harper & Row, 1985), p. 42.

morality but about the whole system of social institutions, including the system of criminal law. Its thesis is that all of these should be appraised for their impact on public or social well-being. One important cause of ill-being, of course, is harmful behavior of others. Hence, one of the aims of an optimal system of institutions, according to the utilitarian, is to minimize harmful behavior where this does not disproportionately impair achievement of important goals such as freedom to plan one's own life, personal privacy, or a considerable degree of social and economic equality. The system of criminal justice is designed to reduce harmful or antisocial behavior (as are the educational system, churches, the system of medical care, and positive morality). But the criminal law must operate under some constraints to avoid intolerable intrusion or undue interference with freedom of planning. So, the system cannot give everyone psychological tests to determine whether, to maximize the general safety, certain persons should be in custody; a person must be left alone unless she actually does something contrary to law. So, a person cannot be held criminally liable unless there is an actus reus – an unjustified unlawful act.

What can the system of criminal justice do to achieve its primary function of reducing harmful behavior within these constraints?

1. It can be educational. In effect it announces, in a forceful way – a forceful censure – because accompanied by a threat, which forms of behavior society considers harmful to the extent of being intolerable. This announcement, by conditioning, will tend to increase the motivation not to do the forbidden things.

2. It can deter harmful behavior. It is true that most people have well-internalized moral standards; hence, their conduct tends to conform to the law in any case. But if there were no parking meters, even decent people would take more than their share of parking space. So, although a deterrent is unnecessary for most kinds of harmful behavior, for some kinds it is beneficial, inducing the average (or below-average) person to behave properly. Not that long prison terms are needed for the average person: A hefty

fine for running a traffic light renders one more cautious about obeying traffic signals.

3. The system of criminal justice can prevent persons from repeating their crimes. At least, when a person is imprisoned, there is no danger of further criminal behavior (at least, outside the prison). There is the further hope that imprisonment will change his ways if this experience includes certain forms of education. It would seem that the prison system should return inmates to normal life as soon as is compatible with public safety – and that means after providing such things as treatment for drug addiction, job training, assistance in finding a job on leaving prison, and so on.

With this background in mind, what justifies exempting persons from punishment altogether when they have committed a legally unjustified offense by an action that would normally not have occurred but for a defective system of legal/moral motivation but in the present instance may not manifest defective legal/moral motivation? The utilitarian will answer that such a system of excuses will maximize the public benefit. Why?

1. If a person has broken the law but not from defect of motivation, no benefit is gained from punishing him as far as his own future behavior is concerned. To allow him to circulate is no more dangerous than in the case of those who have not broken the law. So, the person (and presumably his family) would be penalized by a criminal penalty with no public benefit.[71] Of course, the standard system, which excuses on the basis of lack of intention or knowledge, or recklessness, has much the same effect, but the point of it must be that people already adequately motivated are excused – the indirect effect.
2. What is the alternative to the motivation theory or something essentially identical to it? One possibility is a system of strict liability: A person convicted of unjustifiably break-

---

[71] Suppose the person's motivation is unsatisfactory but not very much so. What then? This seems a case where judicial discretion in sentencing makes good sense.

ing the law would be given a specified sentence, depending only on the definition of the offense. Such a system
could be a nightmare. What would life be like if one had to
anticipate a year in prison, or worse, for accidentally running down a child due to no fault of one's own? Of course,
how horrendous it might be depends on the rest of the law.
In any case, strict liability is surely advocated, not for the
general run of offenses but only for some, such as mislabeling of drugs or statutory rape. In such types of cases the
application of strict liability might not be horrendous, but it
is far from clear that there would be long-range public
benefit from the use of strict liability in contrast to requiring a moral/legal fault for imposing punishment. Even in
the case of statutory rape, there is surely a question of
benefit in punishing if the accused clearly believed, without taking undue risks, that the victim was of age. Surely it
is not irrelevant to punishment if the accused can present a
convincing account of his mental processes along this line.
Or, in the case of mislabeling of drugs, it is possible that
this act could be explained – perhaps that it was a stupid
mistake but not one involving negligence. In light of this, it
would clearly not be beneficial to punish.

3. The main reason for legal punishment, according to most
    writers, is the deterrent effect of the threat of punishment
    on potential wrongdoers. Some writers think that the in-
    corporation of excuses in a system of criminal law dimin-
    ishes the deterrent effect of the system, and that therefore
    a consistent utilitarian would be opposed to a legal system
    with excuses. But as far as I know, no comparative studies
    show that excuses increase the crime rate. Which crimes
    would not be deterred by a system with excuses such as
    the motivation theory advocates? Not those committed by
    persons who do not know the law. But suppose a rational
    man knows the law and wants his wife out of the way.
    How will the system of excuses affect his planning? Can he
    manage to have his bullet ricochet? Or can he convince a
    jury that he mistook his wife for a burglar or that someone
    threatened to kill him if he didn't shoot her? I think the
    rational prospective murderer will do better to spend his

time thinking about how to commit the crime so that the jury will not be convinced that he actually did it. True, people may be encouraged to commit crimes in the knowledge that criminals are often not punished. But how many of these escape via the excuse route? I suggest there is no hard evidence that the availability and force of excuses has a detectable effect on deterrence.

So, I conclude that a rational and informed person, otherwise disposed toward a conscience-utilitarian appraisal of institutions, will want a system of criminal law that includes excuses for persons whose moral/legal motivation may be up to standard even if they have unjustifiably broken the law.

Still, it is proper to register a final general doubt about the whole system of criminal law, which I have expressed elsewhere.[72] I do not think a person should feel happy about the operation of criminal law because of the great inequalities in our society, not only economically but also in terms of intelligence, health, energy, and the type of family in which a person is reared. Many persons with high intelligence and the good fortune of being raised in a good family and given a good education are never put in a position where they are strongly motivated to disobey the law. With others the opposite is the case. Even a humane system of excuses, one that punishes a person for a crime only when her motivation is defective, does not remove the unjustified inequality in the lottery that bestows good things on some and bad things on others. What justifies the criminal law is that it is the best compromise among unhappy alternatives for the world as it now is. On the one hand, life would be intolerable if no criminal law existed and no one were deterred from doing as she pleased by the threat of punishment; on the other hand, with the system, many have to suffer who would not have had to suffer if the lottery of life had not put them where they are. There is so much truth in the contention – and only so much truth – that the fact of determinism is a

---

[72] In "A motivational theory of excuses in the criminal law" in *Morality, Utilitarianism, and Rights* (Cambridge: Cambridge University Press, 1992; first published in *Nomos* in 1985).

general excuse for antisocial behavior, but not one that the criminal law should respect. So, the criminal law has to remain an uneasy compromise, attempting to accommodate both the need to protect society from harm and the obligation to avoid imposing unnecessary suffering on those who have broken the law. A system that exempts from punishment offenders who are not at fault – that is, defective in moral/legal motivation – is an advance toward humanity without significant loss in protection of society.

Chapter 10
Is being moral rational?

Since at least as early as the time of Socrates, philosophers have wondered, and debated on, whether a person is not foolish or irrational, in some important sense, if he does what (he thinks) is morally right when it is also true that (he thinks) so doing conflicts with his own good. This controversy has continued, seemingly unabated, down to the modern period. For instance, Henry Sidgwick, with a hedonist twist, spoke of the "wide acceptance of the principle that it is reasonable for a man to act in the manner most conducive to his own happiness."[1] (But Sidgwick also thought it self-evident that a person ought to aim at promoting the good of others.) Earlier, Bishop Joseph Butler described (possibly assented to) this same thesis when he wrote: "Let it be allowed, though virtue or moral rectitude does indeed consist in affection to and pursuit of what is right and good as such; yet, that when we sit down in a cool hour, we can neither justify to ourselves this or any other pursuit, till we are convinced that it will be for our happiness, or at least not contrary to it."[2] The controversy has persisted in the present century, as attested to by numerous discussions in periodicals and in

---

[1] *The Methods of Ethics* (London: Macmillan, 1922), p. 119.
[2] *Sermon* XI of 15 preached at the Chapel of Rolls, first published in 1726, reprinted in *The Analogy of Religion* with other essays (London: Henry G. Bohn, 1860), p. 497.

influential recent books such as Derek Parfit's *Reasons and Persons*.[3]

Suppose we assume that a person has been convinced, by the reasoning presented in Chapter 5, that a certain kind of utilitarian moral system is the optimal morality *for her society*. But suppose it is questioned whether it follows that for a given person to embody such a moral system – to have the optimal aversions (etc.) in herself – is necessarily a *good thing* for the person's self-interest. What if a person comes to doubt whether it is? Then two questions may arise. First, if she has children and loves them, she might hesitate to do her part in instituting moral motivations in them if she thinks it is not for their own good. Moreover, if she thinks the answer is negative, that might, over time, undermine her enthusiasm for having the optimal aversions and behaving morally herself, as we shall see. In any case, some theoretical questions remain: Will it necessarily be (1) for a person's own good or self-interest to incorporate in herself the optimal moral system so strongly that she will act accordingly, or (2) will it be at least *rational* (in some appropriate sense, possible senses to be explained later) for a person to incorporate the optimal moral system when, or so far as, so doing would conflict with her own good?

THE CONCEPT OF SELF-INTEREST

We should note that it is one thing for something to be intrinsically good or desirable from the point of view of a given person, as explained in Chapter 2, and another for something to be in his self-interest or for his own good. We have seen that the well-being of a second person can be intrinsically good from the point of view of an agent, but it may not be at all to the agent's own self-interest or good or life going well for him. It is the latter concept we want to explore.

Let us begin by surveying several well-known conceptions.

---

[3] Oxford: Clarendon Press, 1984. Hereafter referred to as RP.

1. The first is a hedonist theory: that a person's life goes well for him if and so far as, on the whole, he has introspectible experiences that he likes (= are pleasant) and that an *act* is self-interested insofar as it is *designed* to bring this about for the agent. Presumably we must include not only sensory pleasures but also the joys of satisfied desires and pleasant recollections of all of these. The opposite of pleasant experiences is unpleasant ones. One set of experiences counts *more* heavily to making life go well (to a person's self-interest) if the person likes it more than another set (= is more pleasant). To maximize the contribution to one's well-being is to maximize the net balance of all pleasant experiences versus unpleasant ones, taking both duration and intensity into account.

2. One might, however, take a less atomic view of "happiness" than this, not identifying the degree of happiness of a more extended segment of one's life as the sum (balance) of pleasantness over unpleasantness of experiences in it but taking it as the degree of *present informed satisfaction* with ("satisfaction" being construed as implying a *preference* for – or wanting – it that way) that segment of one's life (not necessarily just *experiences*, but including them) on reflection.[4] A person's satisfaction with her *whole* life, in this sense, *need* not correlate with a *summing* of the pleasantness of experiences in her whole life.[5] For instance, I may be better satisfied with my life if I know I have

---

[4] John Harsanyi states the view this way: "a person's *informed-satisfaction level*" is "the degree to which his subjective experiences and the objective conditions of his life, as they are now and as they can be reasonably expected to be at various future times, given his own likely behavior at various contingencies, satisfy his *present* informed preferences." This notion of "informed satisfaction with" has been developed by Harsanyi in "Utilities, preferences, and substantive goods" in a paper (unpublished in 1992) for a volume in honor of A. K. Sen.

[5] This sort of view is similar to one use of "happiness" as briefly discussed by Ed Diener, "Subjective well-being," *Psychological Bulletin* 95 (1984), 542–75. See also Angus Campbell, *The Sense of Well-Being in America* (New York: McGraw-Hill, 1991) and *Subjective Well-Being*, ed. F. Straak, M. Argyle, and N. Schwartz (Oxford: Pergamon, 1991). Also see a critique by Alvin Goldman, "Ethics and cognitive science," *Ethics* 103 (1993), especially 345–50.

achieved something, or that other people admire me for some good reason, or that I have influence in some wanted direction, or if other people enjoy my company or even love me. I may be better satisfied with my life if I know (or believe) that these things are true of me or even that they *will* be true. (People can admire or respect *me* even after my death.) We should bear this in mind as a possible, or at least partial, conception of "self-interest" or "my own good," since it is *my life*, or a segment of it the preferability of which is being weighed.

3. A very different proposal about well-being is that one's desires are satisfied, in the sense of the *occurrence* of any event the person *wanted*, at *any time*, for itself.

This theory may take the form of affirming that one event contributes to well-being *more* than another (1) if and only if it is what was more strongly wanted at the time of action (or at the time of decision/deliberation) or (2) if and only if it is more wanted for itself, on average, from birth to death, weighing all past desires (but these could be skipped in view of the fact that most of us think that what we wanted in the past is pretty irrelevant to what it is rational to do now[6]) along with expectable future desires, the average being computed by summing the products of a certain strength of desire by the length of time it obtained. Parfit usually seems to take the desire-satisfaction theory in this second way.[7] According to this general conception, a person's lifetime desire satisfaction (well-being) can be enhanced by events after his death and independently of any subjective pleasure he takes in the occurrences. Parfit also lists another form of this proposal; call it (3) the "success theory." Here the satisfactions are limited to those that concern the person's own life, although it is not clear what this comes to, since

---

[6] This can be questioned. All his life, a person might have wanted no priest to be called when he is dying, but, when he is actually on his death bed, he requests that a priest be called. Is the record of his past firm desires irrelevant to what it is best to do now? This example is due (I think) to Parfit's remarks in a seminar.

[7] RP 128, 149.

a desire for the benefit of a loved child whose good future one had earnestly tried to promote is counted (as relevant to one's well-being), although a desire that a stranger met on a train should fare well in life is not counted. (Presumably this distinction needs to be made because the satisfaction of the one kind of desire has more impact on the gratifications of the agent.) Parfit also thinks the desire theories are more plausible if the desires are "global," in the sense that they are about "some part of one's life considered as a whole, or . . . about one's whole life."[8]

If one construes the theory, as Parfit (with James Griffin) does, with "satisfaction" meaning only the *occurrence* of the event once (etc.) wanted, irrespective of whether the person even knows that it has happened, much less whether she is excited, pleased, or bored with the event, it seems a bit less plausible. Why should it add to the well-being of a person to have her wants "satisfied" only in this sense? What we need to add is a concept of something being desired only in view of its favorable impact on one's own life. But just how shall we explain this?

Mark Overvold, in a series of papers, attempted to sharpen this notion of a self-interested desire.[9] Suppose I wish some friend well and would be *sorry* to see him forced to drop his philosophical education. Shall we count this desire as involving my own good or self-interest? Overvold denies this and says that a project is one to the agent's self-interest or good only if the desire for that state of affairs is rational (would exist in the presence of vivid awareness of any facts that might change it) and if the description of the state of affairs entails that *the agent is alive at that time.* This seems to me to be not quite right. For

---

[8] RP, 497. What he seems to mean by a "global" desire may be illustrated as follows: A desire for a "high" from a shot of cocaine now is nonglobal, but a desire to live a whole life including the shot of cocaine with its total later impact is global.

[9] "The concepts of self-sacrifice," *Canadian Journal of Philosophy* 10 (1980), 105–18, "Self-interest and getting what you want" in H. B. Miller and W. H. Williams (eds.), *The Limits of Utilitarianism* (Minneapolis: University of Minnesota Press, 1982), pp. 186–94; and "Morality, self-interest, and reasons for being moral," *Philosophy and Phenomenological Research* 43 (1984), 493–506.

instance, if, suffering from delusions of grandeur, I want a career of philosophy because I think future history books will list me along with Aristotle and Kant, I would say that we would regard this as a self-interested consideration, even though (among other things) I may not be alive at the time. (And there does remain a question, moreover, of whether a desire for such posthumous recognition is rational!) We might, however, accept a weakened form of Overvold's requirement, so that, for an act to be for one's own good, a description of its consequences must at least include some ineliminable reference to the agent; this requirement is met by our example, which includes posthumous recognition of *my* philosophical work.

But in view of Overvold's definition, what shall we say about a person who *desires* to *be* and act like a morally good person and to act only in morally right ways? Overvold's view was that since this desire can be satisfied only if the agent is alive at the time – she can't be morally good or act in a morally good way unless she is alive – satisfying this desire is to her self-interest. Contrariwise, I think we would *normally suppose* that a person who does what she considers to be the moral thing when doing something else is decidedly unfavorable to her own good (like informing a friend of the date at which a fellowship application is due, with the expected effect that she and not the agent will receive the award) is *not* acting so as to augment her own good or in her own self-interest.

Should we specify, in addition to the wanted event's necessarily being one that can be described only by some phrase relating it to oneself, but, along the lines of the "informed satisfaction" theory, that it is something that would please him, *moral considerations aside*, and indeed independently of any concern for the well-being of *other* persons? Suppose a person wants, as Overvold speculates one might, to be and to act as a moral person, or wants to be helpful to others just because he cares about the well-being of other persons. Is he augmenting his own good (or self-interest) if he behaves accordingly? My tentative guess is that the concept of "self-interest" or "own well-being" is in fact so used as to *exclude* such actions.

My conclusion about self-interest or one's own good is that it can be comprised either of one's own pleasure or (roughly), in contrast with an atomic view, of some self-related state that one wants, given full information – but independently of moral desires/aversions or indeed of any concern for the well-being of others.

WHAT IS IT TO ACT MORALLY?

In Chapter 3, I claimed that what it is for a person to have a morality is for her to have intrinsic (not self-interested) aversions to her acting in certain types of way, to have a disposition to feel guilty if she knows she has acted contrariwise and to disapprove of others if she thinks they have; and to think all these attitudes are justified in an appropriate way. We may use this conception as a basis for an explanation of "acting morally"; as doing what one is motivated to do by one's moral aversions. But we might well add something to our definition of "acting morally": that a person not only acts in accordance with her aversions about actions that she *thinks* are justified, but also in accordance with aversions that really *are* justified.

At least for our present eventual aim, to determine whether it is *rational* to act morally when it conflicts with the agent's own good or self-interest, I suggest we should employ the more restricted notion. If a person's own moral code tells him to do something that we can see is morally objectionable, why should we want to know whether it is rational so to act, in conflict with his self-interest? It makes sense to consider only the best-justified examples of morality – so to consider the case of a conscience the "rules" of which are backed by long-range considerations of social benefit, as explained in Chapter 5. This is our central question. (This conception, of course, leads us to the conception of an optimal morality developed earlier: that, roughly, the motivations of an optimal morality are ones the teaching and prevalence of which, among all persons [except problem cases: see earlier] in the society, would, all costs and benefits considered, maximize social benefit.)

Now what a person actually does, we know (Chapter 2), is to perform the act for which she has the strongest action tendency at the time – the act supported by the greatest vector sum of desires/aversions (of any sort) for its consequences, each reduced by the (subjective) improbability (on the agent's evidence) of the consequence occurring if the act is performed, the real world being as it is. So, the person *will* perform the moral act if and only if her desire to perform that type of action (or aversion to the alternatives) is stronger than the vector (adjusted for probabilities) sum of the motivations to perform some alternative action. If a person fails to perform the truly moral act because of a (at least, a significant) moral defect (deviation from the socially optimal code) in her motivation to perform that act, she is morally blameworthy; but, on the other hand, if she fails to perform what she thinks will be the most *socially beneficial* act, but does so because her already *optimal* moral motivation (moral motivation, especially in view of the costs of teaching, can be optimal even when it does not bring a person to make a socially most beneficial sacrifice) falls short of moving the agent to perform that act, she is not blameworthy; she has done all that an optimal morality requires. Of course, failure to do the socially most beneficial act may occur perhaps because of some purely intellectual error like being mistaken about the kind of act it is, or because of lack of skill or ability or inadvertence, in which cases again the agent is not morally derelict. So, our basic question is whether it is *rational* for a person's *motivation* to perform the morally optimal (= conscience-utilitarian) types of action to be strong enough to get her to do the corresponding morally optimal thing when it conflicts with self-interest of a certain level. (I am assuming that a person's moral aversions are a relatively enduring feature of her, not just episodic, although with a caveat to come.)

This realistic way of putting matters is somewhat different from just raising the question of whether it is rational to perform a certain specific action in the face of a serious cost to self-interest. The question is not whether it is morally required to do something specific like use a machine gun to cover the retreat of one's comrades when so doing is very likely to result in one's death. (I assume that using the machine gun may be a requirement of optimal morality when one is the only available competent person and the lives of one's comrades are at stake, and perhaps one is ordered so to do.) The basic question is whether it is rational for a person's (justified) *standing* moral motivations to be strong enough so that, when a particular situation arises when acting morally would be costly to self-interest, he will do the morally required thing in the face of that cost to self-interest. So, the question is not about some particular instances; it is a long-term question about how strong it is rational for one's several moral aversions/motivations to be in view of the *risk* of serious clashes with self-interest. This means that our question may be answered by long-term considerations.

THE RATIONALITY OF MORAL MOTIVATION WHERE IT CONFLICTS WITH SELF-INTEREST

Let us begin with the case of a person who already has moral motivations/aversions (etc.) with a direction and strength the same as those of an optimal moral code for his society. This is a relatively stable fact about him; if some situation now poses a conflict between morality and some large personal good, he will follow his moral motivations. But he might have reflections that, over time, could change this: He might, for instance, notice the roles of identification, parental punishment, and modeling by admired persons in acquiring his aversions (etc.) and he might not think much of these processes, regarding them as modes of intimidation. Or he might notice how often people get away with nonoptimal behavior. These reflections might reduce the strength of his moral motivations by some kind of conditioning. But, more relevant to our present interest, he might also reflect on morality's long-term possible costs to him in enjoyment, serious injury, or failure to satisfy important desires. He might convince himself that his moral code is not *good for him*, possibly with a resulting diminished strength of demanding motivations of his code, also by conditioning.

Let us assume he cannot find good reasons to change his conception of the optimal moral code *for his society*. Nevertheless these reflections might lead to a somewhat similar effect: They might so alter his actual moral motivations so that they are no longer in accord with the optimal code. But to do that on the ground that morality is not good *for him*, his reflections will have to meet various arguments philosophers have offered that tend in a contrary direction. Let us look at some of these arguments.

1. Philosophers have often argued that if one lives by the moral code optimal for one's society, one will be happier in the long run, even with occasional short-term bumps – that there is no real conflict between moral requirements and the agent's self-interest. There are many reasons for this. One is that *most* persons will probably have independently, possibly native, empathic/sympathetic attitudes constraining them not to do what is hurtful to other people and will be very uncomfortable if they do. Again, it is important to people to have the *esteem of others*, which will (in the morally optimal society) be lost if others believe that one has behaved immorally. Of course, this will happen only if others notice what has happened and are moved to disapproval by the fact, so if one behaves immorally without others identifying the fact, one will not have this loss. But in the real world this may or may not be easy to manage: To be seriously immoral without seeming to behave immorally requires a good deal of thought,[10] perhaps not if one fails merely to give appropriately to charity. Many believe that the easiest way to have the reputation of being moral is not to *be* obviously immoral and to act morally. If so, and if high repute among others is an important goal for a person (this taken along with the *material advantages* of others respecting one, like recommendations), there may be little conflict between being moral and self-interest. (But the disadvantages of acting immorally may not be very severe; a lot depends on one's situation. If one lives in South Africa and one's associations are primarily with the Afrikaner, one's failure to live by the optimal moral code will do no damage to one's reputation, and one will be warmly treated by

---

[10] This sort of thought has been emphasized by Philippa Foot, "Moral beliefs," *Proceedings of the Aristotelian Society*, (1958–9), 103.

all those with whom one has close contact and about whose respect one cares. And the same holds if one has close associations with certain classes in the United States, perhaps conservative politicians,[11] or indeed with any who are rather tight-fisted.) Then there is the matter of the size of the risk. Should a person who loves her children encourage them to have a morality that might cost them their lives? One might think not in principle, but a parent might reasonably suppose that the chances are very small that such a situation will arise. The same is true for one's own moral motivations: The *risk* that these will lead to catastrophic personal loss is normally rather small (perhaps not for cases like opportunities to acquire wealth). According to these arguments, then, with some exceptions, there is much to be said for optimal motivation to act morally from the point of view of self-interest. So, perhaps the answer to our question of whether it is to one's self-interest to *retain* a disposition to act morally is *normally* affirmative, at least for the long run. And one's moral motivations are thus justified to self-interest, even when they may lead to action involving serious sacrifice on occasion. What one will do in a situation of great stress is what one's long-term motivations will bring one to do. So, if one can justify to oneself having these long-term motivations, one has already answered the question of what to do when optimal morality requires severe sacrifice.

But we may have oversimplified matters. In the machine gun case, if one fails, one's cowardice is at once identified and despised by one's comrades. But if the choice is between meeting the needs of the starving and keeping one's money, matters may be less clear. We know that we should help the starving and may not hesitate to give CARE $100 or $500, but if there is a request for $10,000 (which one actually could afford and would prevent many from starving), we may indulge in rationalizing, finding long-term pressing personal or family circumstances, and thus discovering that one's moral aversion to allowing people to starve does not prevail when the cost to self-interest is

---

[11] See Kai Nielsen, *Why Be Moral?* (Buffalo: Prometheus Books, 1989), chap. 14.

great. So, although one might think of oneself as having a strong moral commitment to helping the seriously needy, this is not quite as clear-cut as one might have thought. (And normally others will not know how generously one has given.) It could be that I am misrepresenting moral motivations in viewing them as being continuing, firm dispositions for abstractly describable types of cases (like the aversion to committing murder) that *normally* will not conflict with self-interest. How far might this possibility undermine my argument?

It would, however, be extremely unrealistic to affirm that the previously suggested possible coincidence between acting morally and augmenting one's own good, or self-interest, holds for *everyone*. Suppose you are a person seriously deficient in native empathy/sympathy. Suppose you have been brought up in a ghetto, where your reputation depends mostly on your skill and resolution in ignoring the law, making money, say, from drug dealing, having your way with women, and refusing to tolerate disrespectful behavior. Your well-being will not depend on the regard in which you are held by moral people; you do not live enough in the mainstream of moral society to suffer from lack of respect from moral people, lack of recommendations, and so on. You will certainly not feel guilty about failing to report your income for federal taxation if it is clear the IRS will never know. You have never had the benefit of any moral education; it has never occurred to you that both law and the optimal kind of mainstream morality are devices that serve the public good (and your own), although you might well concede that you enjoy some personal benefits from the existence of a social moral system if they were pointed out to you. You might have aaversions to deceiving, or stealing from, or hurting your friends. But will not the balance between the framework of optimal morality and self-interest look very different to you from the way it looks to more advantaged persons? For such nonadvantaged persons, a disposition to conform to optimal morality hardly pays in terms of self-interest. Would it not be rational for such persons to have diminished motivation to act morally – at least in the most familiar sense of the "instrumentally rational" – maximizing expectable net personal benefit?

For such persons, the instrumental rationality of being moral would appear to be, at best, a vision of the future. If they are to be convinced of the rationality of acting morally, they need to be given a helping hand, their status so improved that they will benefit from job recommendations and find it to their advantage that moral people think well of them. They need to have some moral education, have it pointed out to them that certain actions are injurious to people, and that both law and morality make life better for everyone, including themselves. Can we even count on their having native empathy/sympathy? At least there will be some people for whom they care and whom they do not wish to injure. With that as a starter, their empathy/sympathy might be nourished. So it could be that, with luck and time, their position might approximate that of those already considered, who have a morality in them very similar to the optimal moral code. But at present, it would be difficult to argue that there is not often a straight clash between a disposition to conform to what is in fact an optimal social morality and one's own good or self-interest.

So, the argument that strong motivation to act morally in the long run is compatible with self-interest seems not necessarily to be true for everyone. I suggest we must just accept that fact. What is true for you or me, in our situations, may not be true for everyone. And even for the advantaged majority of us, we must remember there remains a *risk* that acting morally will lead to a serious disaster or loss of benefit.

2. Another line of reasoning, pursued for instance by Kurt Baier, is that acting morally is acting in conformity with rules, the observance of which by everybody is beneficial to everyone, including the agent. As he puts it, we must compare two worlds, "one in which moral reasons are always treated by everyone as superior to reasons of self-interest and one in which the reverse is the practice. And we can see that the first world is the better world, because we can see that the second world would be the sort which Hobbes describes as the state of nature. . . . We should be moral because being moral is following rules designed to overrule self-interest whenever it is in the

interest of everyone alike that everyone should set aside his interest. . . . It is not possible that everyone should do better for himself by following enlightened self-interest rather than morality. The best possible life for everyone is attainable only by everyone's following the rules of morality, that is, rules which quite frequently may require individuals to make genuine sacrifices."[12]

The question Baier seems to answer, however, is the question of whether it is best for there to be an *institution* of morality. And he is surely right that it would normally be better for everyone for there to be a world in which morality reigned supreme than one in which everyone followed self-interest. But this reflection does not seem to answer the question of whether a given individual – say, a member of the impoverished underclass – should, out of self-interest, cultivate motivation in herself to conform to an optimal morality for situations in which acting morally appears certain to cost her in personal interest, or why a given individual should not prefer, to either of those worlds described by Baier, a world in which everyone else is disposed to act morally but she is disposed to follow self-interest.[13]

There are some other arguments that equally fall short. Frankena, for instance, thought that being morally good is a kind of excellence, like athletic ability or artistic creation, and that the realization of moral excellence in life makes it intrinsically a better life.[14] It seems to me, however, that this kind of excellence does not have the self-interested payoff of either athletic or artistic excellence, and therefore this will not be a comparable recommendation of living morally. (Frankena, incidentally, did not say that the goodness of moral excellence suffices to close the gap between moral obligation and self-interest.) Rather similar to Frankena's view is one espoused by Bertrand Russell, who wrote: "The sort of life that most of us admire is

[12] Kurt Baier, *The Moral Point of View* (New York: Cornell University Press, 1958), pp. 310, 314f.

[13] See J. C. Thornton, "Can the moral point of view be justified?" *Australasian Journal of Philosophy* 42 (1964).

[14] W. K. Frankena, *Ethics* (Englewood Cliffs, N.J.: Prentice-Hall, 1973), p. 91f.

one which is guided by large, impersonal desires. . . . Our desires are, in fact, more general and less purely selfish than many moralists imagine."[15] It is true that we do *admire* such desires, but more argument is needed to show that it makes sense to give them priority in our own case if there is a conflict with self-interest.

3. A person may argue not that it is likely to *pay* to have a disposition to act morally, but that it is *rational (in some sense different* from the familiar instrumental sense of a promise or likelihood to contribute to self-interest) to give priority to moral considerations over those of self-interest when there is a conflict. This may very well be; but first, we have to clarify what we mean by "being rational" in that new sense. Derek Parfit has a great deal to say about what is rational in *Reasons and Persons*, but he never (I think) explains exactly (but see later) what he means by this term. John Rawls does. He advises us to consider all the desires we already have or know we shall have, with their actual intensities, and then consider plans to satisfy these and compare them on the basis of how well they will do. A desire is said to be "rational" if it is included in the plan that will bring most satisfaction of the majority of these desires.[16] But this conception will not give helpful guidance to a person who has a restricted set of desires or who has senseless intrinsic desires, such as to have a slim figure above all else; nor does it seem helpful in deciding whether an overriding desire to do the moral thing is rational unless the "morality pays" arguments work.

Another possible view of the meaning of "rational," put forth by Allan Gibbard,[17] is that "It is rational for J [standing on the ledge of a burning building, below which firemen are holding a

---

[15] Bertrand Russell, *Religion and Science* (New York: Henry Holt, 1935), pp. 252–4.

[16] John Rawls, *A Theory of Justice* (Cambridge, Mass.: Harvard University Press, 1971), pp. 409, 417–18.

[17] Allan Gibbard, "A noncognitivistic analysis of rationality in action," *Social Theory and Practice* 9 (1983), 199–222, especially 209 ff. See also *Wise Choices, Apt Feelings* (Cambridge, Mass.: Harvard University Press, 1990), passim.

net] to jump" expresses "If I am in J's circumstances, with his state of mind, memories, and present experience – but with no information about how things will turn out – then let me jump!" This is a noncognitivist account. But then we need an explanation of why we should adopt any set of such "norms" for behavior, especially moral ones.

A further possible view of how to construe a "rational" choice is described by Parfit as the "deliberative theory," which holds that a rational choice is one the agent would make if he were vividly aware of all nonmoral facts the vivid representation of which to himself might tend to change his aversions or dispositions to act. (This proposal is intended not just for judgments of intrinsic value but for all practical judgments.) This was the view espoused by the present writer in a volume a few years ago.[18] Parfit rejected it partly because he thought it was not obvious where such deliberations would lead and partly because it may not eliminate or endorse the right things. In its place he favors the "critical present aim theory" of rationality, but in my opinion his examples (such as that "critical" desires be transitive or that one not prefer agony on a Tuesday to a mild pain on a Wednesday), although well taken, do not explain fully what this concept might involve for choices that are realistically difficult or complex.

I propose to construe "rational choice," in the present context, in terms of the deliberative theory.

If we do this, we may get some guidance about what facts vividly to represent to ourselves by noting an earlier statement of Frankena's about what is required for resolution of the problems of metaethics: "clarity and decision about the nature and functions of morality, of moral discourse, and of moral theory, and this requires not only small scale analytic inquiries [like using 'open question' arguments] but also studies in the history of ethics and morality, in the relation of morality to society and of society to the individual, as well as in epistemology and in

---

[18] R. B. Brandt, *A Theory of the Good and the Right* (Oxford: Clarendon Press, 1979).

the psychology of human motivation."[19] That is, of course, a tall order.

What, then, are some of the things a person who wants to meet this requirement should bear vividly in mind? (1) I have repeatedly explained what morality is, and we need not discuss this further. (2) As to the functions of morality, we can construe a question about these as a question about what good moralities do in general. Here one must bear in mind their utility not only in enabling society to avoid being in a "state of nature," but also in enabling the beneficial ability to predict behavior, at least of many people in a society. But we might limit ourselves not just to morality in general – many moralities being very objectionable – but to *optimal* moralities, of the conscience-rule type, moralities that, all costs and benefits taken into account, are ones the teaching and prevalence of which will maximize utility in a society. (We need not affirm that everyone will agree on just what an optimal morality will require.) (3) As to clarity about "moral discourse," I note only that moral discussion is obviously important in the social functioning of a moral system. One function of moral theory is to clarify moral discourse: show what it is, what justifies a moral stance. (4) It is clear enough what different moralities (or at least these in conjunction with beliefs about facts that went with them) have done to societies: Nazism, Stalin-type communism, the morality of Islam on the status of women in Iran, Saudi Arabia, Turkey, and India. It is also clear how much the morality of individuals, including Abraham Lincoln, Franklin and Eleanor Roosevelt, and Gandhi, had on the social programs and well-being of various communities. (5) In earlier chapters I have reviewed the psychology of desire development and moral development in individuals, including the various strands, evolution, and conditioning/modeling, in the sources of altruistic desires. (6) Finally, as for epistemology, I have argued that it is proper to disavow claims to intuitive knowledge of moral principles; a defense or criticism of morality can make do with an ordinary sciencelike

---

[19] W. K. Frankena, "Obligation and motivation," in A. I. Melden (ed.), *Essays in Moral Philosophy* (Seattle: University of Washington Press, 1958), p. 80.

procedure for determining truth. In particular, a crucial question for moral truth is what kind of moral system we would, if fully informed, want for a society in which we expected we and our children would live a lifetime. This – and I have argued that this system would be a form of conscience-utilitarian morality – would be the kind of morality about which a person should ask himself whether it would be rational for him to share it and act on it. Doubtless both additions and deletions are called for in this list of requirements.

Now suppose an individual, already with an optimal morality, has all this clearly in mind as fully as possible. Let us call her "fully informed" or "rational" in the new (noninstrumental) sense. As part of this "full information," she will see her own moral motivation as part of this whole picture; the same holds for her nonmoral, self-interested desires. She will see her own commitment to morality as a contribution to a good society and as a part of the moral community in which she would like her children to spend their lives – something that will give her satisfaction. She will understand her own native empathic caring for other people as a (possibly) necessary part of herself and her altruism as rational (if its degree does not fall afoul of the problems described in Chapter 2), and she will see the particular moral aversions in her conscience as a consequence of awareness of how certain forms of behavior are harmful to others. She will see that morality does not require a commitment to unintelligible intuitive knowledge of moral/value principles unrelated to human well-being. But it is also true that she will see that and understand why her morality requires her to do some things that she would prefer not to do, from the point of view of her personal welfare – for example, make a contribution to charity possibly (see earlier) comparable to what she pays as income tax. The question then is: Given all this information *in mind,* as vividly as possible, might many of her moral aversions tend to become so weak, that self-interest would *more often* win out over her moral aversions where there is conflict, so that acting morally when there is a conflict with self-interest is not even *rational,* in this new sense, for her? To my mind, when we weigh all these considerations, the answer to this question is unclear but very possibly negative. For I suggest that these reflections will tend to provide some positive reinforcement for one's moral motivations by their appeal to various facts strongly moving to one, such as her contributing to a moral community or her ideal for herself as being a caring person and one whose thinking is independent of irrational confusions about self-evidence. (This would need to be worked out in detail; perhaps all of this depends on what kind of person one is – in part, how informed and clear-headed one is.) But my suggestion is that if a person bears these facts in mind, she will tend to feel comfortable with being morally motivated as she now is. So, on this wide view of "rationality," her morality may so far be rational for her.

This sort of inquiry is the best way I know to inquire whether a rational person would or would not give priority to self-interest over his justified moral motivations.[20] In some cases, he may be unable to come to a decision.

How will the typical reader of this book, with all this in mind, answer our question of whether it is rational for him to have moral motivations stronger than those of self-interest in the cases in which an *optimal* morality demands this? It is not an easy question, for the requirement of "vivid, full information" is pretty staggering.

Suppose that the reader of this book is either a professor or a student or has some comparable status. Then, I speculate, on reflection (based on personal observations) on the likely experience of such persons, there is probably not much the prospective reader can do, which is morally very bad, at least among the things he might be tempted by self-interest to do. He is unlikely to have the option of fleecing people out of millions of dollars, although he might make modest profits by minor types of dishonesty. (He might, however, make a reputation for him-

---

[20] One would like to know how some "saints," such as Albert Schweitzer or Mother Teresa, would answer this question and what they would say in defense of their answer. Possibly some people just care more about others and their suffering than do the rest of us, so that living a life of hardship in that cause is something they prefer, at least in the context of the thought that it is morally good, although not required. Admirable, but not required?

self by plagiarizing the ideas of others.) Moreover, he will almost certainly have all, or almost all, of the advantages that the truly deprived have not: He will stand to gain from the respect of other moral persons, have the advantage of knowing the benefits of a morality in a society, and so on. Moral demands will probably enter into his life *mostly* in regard to what many would think relatively unimportant matters: in the requirement to be fair and honest in his relations with persons of the opposite sex, to render careful evaluations of the work of others when it is requested or required by his position (do his job); to give thoughtful advice to students and investors, and to make appropriate – possibly substantial – gifts to charity. He will, of course, reaffirm his existing motivation not to steal, injure others seriously, be harmfully deceitful, avoid paying his full income tax and so on for the other obvious things among those he has a real opportunity to do; but surely few, if any, of the readers of this book will be tempted to do these things. A large question for him may be how much a person in his circumstances ought – on the basis of an optimal morality – to contribute to charity or to help needy relatives or friends. If he was clear about this, *maybe* he would want to do that much. So, such a personal morality seems not to make *severe* demands on him.

Then is there a significant disparity between what he will think an optimal morality requires of him and what he will really want for himself and his children as a matter of self-interest – or at least would want if he fulfilled the requirement of having full information? Or at least, is there enough difference so that, were he in a condition of full information, he would feel comfortable about infringing some of his major moral (or legal) obligations? I think the most plausible answer is apt to be no: He will not want the strength of his moral motivations to be reduced. Given such full information, I suggest we (the fortunate ones) would not want to be different from the way we are, would not want to be bereft of the "socializing" moral attitudes, despite the risks this carries for possible, albeit unlikely, situations. This seems to me probably the correct answer to the traditional question about the *rationality* of living morally in the revised form I have given it. Recall, however, the caveat noted earlier about the possibility that even normal people, faced with a situation of conflict between self-interest and what they ordinarily think of as their moral principles, will rationalize in finding extenuating circumstances, without feeling they have compromised their moral principles. Even aside from this possibility, one may not be sure what a fully informed person would be motivated to do. Would a reader of this book be willing to give as much to charity as he thinks the optimal morality requires, even if he thought others might find out and think less of him if they knew, even if he were vividly aware of the considerations I have mentioned? Also, recall that I have not said that the same reflections will work for *everyone*, as distinct from students and professors. For an account of the rationality of living according to an optimal morality, for fully informed persons who are neither professors nor students nor potential readers of this book, a survey of much wider sweep would be in order.

In some cases, the traditional problem of conflict between self-interest and morality to some extent remains, and even the problem of what it is rational to do about such cases. The most I can say on behalf of the preceding reflections is that they may show just how close it is possible to come to a resolution.

Index

Index

Damasio, Antonio, 93n58
Damasio, Hanna, 93n58
decisions: deliberation on, 60; wants and, 14–21
declining marginal utility of money, 11, 206–8, 209, 210, 211, 221
defense of necessity, 260–1, 263
delay of gratification, 19
deliberative theory, 38, 50–1, 297
deprivation, 53–4
deprivation time, 27, 29
desensitization, 56
desirable (the), 1, 11; see also good (the)
desire/belief theory about action, 14–21
desire development, psychology of, 298
desire satisfaction, 35–49, 137
desire satisfaction theory, 37–8, 284–6
desire theory(ies), 36, 38–40, 43–4; choice between happiness theory and, 45–9; criticism of, 44
desires, 9, 10, 12, 18; acquisition of, 59; appraisal of, 36–7, 49–60; and criminal action, 265–6; criticized, 49, 59–60; cultural variation in, 33–5; foreseeable future, 52–3; large, impersonal, 296; and motivation, 265; pleasure/displeasure primary reinforcer of, 193–4; problem of change of, 45–6, 47, 51, 52, 56n76; rational, 296; self-interested, 286–7; sources of, 21–33, 42–3, 50, 54, 57, 58; transitivity of, 49–50; variations in strength of, 53–4
desires/aversions: antecedent, 124; sources of, 10
desires/likings: requirements for, 60
desires/preferences: and what a person does, 14–16, 25
desires of other people, 134

determinism, 280–1
deterrence, 240, 242, 245, 248, 249, 256; through punishment, 279–80; through sentencing, 257–8
developing countries: helping poor people in, 224, 228–9, 230, 231–2, 235
Devlin, Sir Patrick, 243–5
diGenova, Joseph E., 276
direct utilitarianism, 142–5, 148
disapproval, 67, 69, 70, 238; psychology of, 181
disapproval by others, 183
disapproval of others, 94, 103, 240; costs in, 128
discriminations, 56–7, 58; preventing, 205
disorder, aversion to, 27
disposition to act morally, 292, 296
disposition to be indignant with others, 156
disposition to disapprove of others, 67, 124, 126, 288
disposition to feel guilty, 126, 156, 288
disposition to feel remorseful, 67, 71, 124
disposition to help others of same ethnic group, 92n57
distribution: of happiness, 135; laws/regulations governing, 202–4
distributive justice, 2, 9, 163; concept of, 199–200; theory of, 49; utilitarianism and, 199–221; worldwide, 235
dopamine, 24
drunkenness, 137–8, 271–3
duels, 64, 65, 80
Duncker, Karl, 15, 39n57, 80–1, 83
duress, 69, 71, 128, 262, 263, 273–4
duty: to give to charity, 222–3; imperative of, 106n11; perfect/imperfect, 226n4; term, 7
Dworkin, Ronald, 12n1, 44, 118–19

Index

with, 290–302; in social moralities, 130, 131
self-transcending interests, 131–2
Sen, A. K., 203
sense data; moral, 173
sensibility theories, 165n1
sentences/sentencing, 267; severity of, 256, 257–9
sexual attractiveness, 31–2
sexual freedom, 109, 163
sexual practices, 82, 137, 196, 255
shame, 69, 83
shame culture(s), 68–9n8
shame/disdain, 78
Sidgwick, Henry, 19, 36, 64n2, 65n3, 102, 135, 282
Smart, J. J. C., 8, 36
Smith, Adam, 93, 251–2
social benefit: in punishment of crime, 241, 244, 245; motivations of optimal morality maximizing, 288, 289–90; rules of conscience and, 288
social desirability, 111, 126
social history: neonaturalism based on, 189–98
social institutions, 196, 277; and moral code, 153
social learning theory, 85
social morality(ies), 7, 9, 10; rule about charitable giving in, 226–7; rules of conscience in, 226; variations in, 141
social nonmoral constraints on behavior, 61–6, 72
social norms, 11, 62–6; moral norms differ from, 68–9
social rationality, 195–6, 197
social subgroups: and moral codes, 146; moralities for, 124, 125
social system(s): moral aversions in, 104; reasonable objections to, 160–2
socialism, 219
society(ies): differences in mor-

al/value standards, 188–9; general structure of optimal moral code for, 123–42, 290–2; moralities in, 298; "ways of life," 75n19
sociobiology: information on sources of morality in, 72–83
Socrates, 245, 282
Southern Journal of Philosophy, 164
spontaneous beliefs, 173, 174–5, 176, 178, 179
standard of living, 227–8
states of affairs: intrinsically desirable, 1, 13; vividness of presentation of, 19, 25; wanted by people, 124, 130; wanted by a person who was fully factually informed, 9, 10, 14–15, 20–1, 35–49
states of mind: change of, 60; corresponding to ethical beliefs/judgments, 8–9; desires based on misleading, 59
statutes: crime and punishment, 247–59
Stevenson, C. L., 8, 104, 164
stimulus generalization, 54–5, 56, 57, 58, 59; and moral norms, 81, 83
strict liability, 278–9
Sturgeon, Nicholas, 5, 165, 167, 170, 173–4, 179, 180, 181, 182, 187
substantive good theories, 44
success theory, 285–6
suicide, 80, 94, 109, 187, 246, 253, 255; principle forbidding, 138
supervenient value property(ies), 168
supererogatory acts, 72, 154, 238
Supreme Court, 252
survival of the fittest, 30, 32, 54, 73
survival value: of desires/aversions, 31, 32
sympathetic/benevolent motivation, 41
sympathetic distress, 30
sympathy; *see* empathy/sympathy